GOOD
CLEAN
FUN

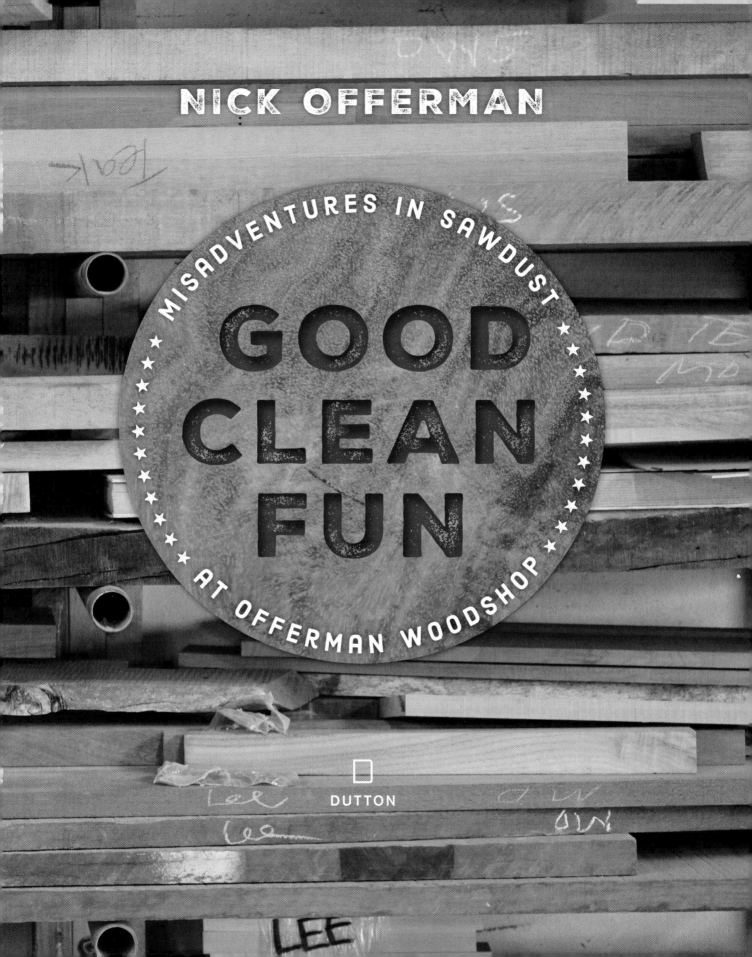

NICK OFFERMAN

MISADVENTURES IN SAWDUST

GOOD CLEAN FUN

AT OFFERMAN WOODSHOP

DUTTON

Dutton
An imprint of Penguin Random House LLC
375 Hudson Street
New York, New York 10014

DUTTON is a registered trademark and the D colophon is a trademark of Penguin Random House LLC
OWS on-site photographs © 2016 by Christine Fuqua and Josh Salsbury
OWS on-site photograph art direction by Jane Parrott
Collages © 2016 by Pat Riot
Floor plan and border sketches © 2016 by Ian Phillips
Technical illustrations © 2016 by Ethan Nicolle
OWS logo and spread © 2016 by Andrew Leman
Illustration on p. 10 by Shozo Sato
"A Quiz About Wood" © 2016 by Ric Offerman
"Essay on Wood" © 2014 by James Richardson, *The New Yorker*, June 9 and 16, 2014
Woodshop Chapter Credits:
*Laura Zahn: pp. 86 and 87 courtesy of David Welter; p. 89 courtesy of Molly Mahar; all others courtesy of Laura Zahn
*Jimmy DiResta: all photographs courtesy of Jimmy DiResta
*Mira Nakashima: all photographs courtesy of George Nakashima Woodworker, S.A., New Hope, PA, www.nakashimawoodworker.com: p. 131, 132 (Butterfly Gate), 135, 136–137 (original design by George Nakashima, executed by Mira Nakashima in 2015) by Christian Ginelli; p. 132 (Concordia Chair) by Bob Hunsicker
*Christian Becksvoort: all photographs courtesy of Dennis Griggs
*Bear Mountain Boats: p. 180 courtesy of Bill Lockington; all others courtesy of Ted Moores
*Laura Mays: all photographs courtesy of Laura Mays
*Peter Galbert/North Bennet Street School: pp. 239, 240, and 243 courtesy of Dana Duke; pp. 242 and 245 (drawing) courtesy of Peter Galbert
*Garry Knox Bennett: all photographs courtesy of M. Lee Fatherree

LIBRARY OF CONGRESS CATALOGING-IN-PUBLICATION DATA has been applied for.

ISBN 978-1-101-98465-9 (hardcover)
978-1-101-98598-4 (e-book)

Printed in the United States of America
10 9 8 7 6 5 4 3 2 1

BOOK DESIGN BY SHUBHANI SARKAR

To **SHOZO SATO**, my sensei

To **LEE**, my hero

To **MEGAN**, my lignum vitae

CONTENTS

INTRODUCTION

HOWDY, NEIGHBOR. Here comes a good-looking book chock-full of woodworking mirth and knowledge. In this brawny tome from the fine folks at Dutton books, you will be treated to:

1. Many words from me, as well as some phrases, with maybe even a diatribe or two, on the topic of woodworking, plus a buttload of punctuation.

2. A dozen or so "how-to" project chapters, featuring each member of Offerman Woodshop, including my dad (handsome, sure, but he also features the wisdom of his age); my brother, Matt; and myself.

3. Tomfoolery (a.k.a. grab-ass). As in any good shop or shop book, we also take the occasional break for some ribaldry, which means irreverent behavior, which means fun.

You will see a lot of really beautiful photography, so I encourage you to pace yourself, and maybe have a pot of coffee ready to hand before digging in so that you don't swoon too easily at the woodworking prowess of our Michele and our Lee and the rest of the tribe here at Offerman Woodshop. Whether you have cut a thousand dovetails or have never wielded so much as a hammer, we have projects for all levels of skill contained within this text. There's a lot of ground to cover, so let's roll up our sleeves and get to work.

You seem pretty sharp, so you probably gleaned from the front cover that my name is Nick Offerman, and I am the author of this quality piece of bookery as well as the proprietor of Offerman Woodshop in Los Angeles, California, where most of the book's action will be set. I also often work as an actor on stage, screen, and television and am perhaps best known for my role as Ron Swanson on NBC's *Parks and Recreation*, a fine comedy program that I can recommend for your downtime from the shop—that is, if you have run out of books to read. Ron had a large moustache and complicated relationships with his two ex-wives, both named Tammy, and the audience seemed to respond to him in a generally favorable fashion, to my great relief. What's more, I tour as a humorist, and I have a comedy special on the channels and whatnot entitled

American Ham. They probably put some of this on the book cover, but if you'll excuse me, I'll cover my own fanny here, because you never can tell about what exactly these bookselling types think they should use to market a book in this bleak modern landscape of electronic tablets and delivery by drone and what-have-you (if you're reading this on a tablet—fine, but please do not hold me accountable for the deleterious effects of sawdust and linseed oil upon your newfangled gewgaw).

Why am I writing this book now? you may ask. Because woodworking is one of the great passions in my life. The others are, of course, my wife, my family, my friends, our dogs, music, cheese curds, the great outdoors, bacon, eggs, my bride, the Chicago Cubs, puzzles, Beef Wellington, the theater, my canoe, my wife, Wilco, and single-malt Scotch whisky. Some of those topics may be touched upon briefly in the following pages, but we'll mainly be focusing upon woodworking. Welcome.

It occurs to me to lay out a quick synopsis of my own history with tools by way of illustrating the point that there are many wonderful things that can be done with wood and tools that don't require the moniker of "fine" woodworking. We all start with building a tree house of some sort, and then some of us are happy to just call it a day and hang out up there (a noble pursuit, no question), while others of us continue to work on building a better tree house. We don't rest until we have hung sash windows in our tree houses, which then causes us to be labeled as "troubled." That is, until it begins to rain and we can close the windows and keep our comic books from getting wet, at which point we are then considered "gifted." Tool skills have certainly helped me earn a living over the years, but much more importantly, they have opened me up to a *way* of living, often in collaboration with other tool users (a.k.a. "artists"), that has never stopped paying me dividends.

My education began at a traditional American institution: an old farmhouse out on Bell Road in the southeastern corner of Kendall County, Illinois. And my teachers were no less than local superheroes: Mom and Dad. On our three-acre plot, they were legendary for their ability to pull fresh turnips out of black garden soil, steaming loaves of bread from previously empty ovens, hand-sewn garments out of thin air, gravel from barked-up knees, and even smiles from tear-strewn faces. Mind you, they performed these feats of excellence whilst juggling two daughters, one regular son, and one exceptional son—one of the most exceptional smartasses, that is, that the tri-county area had ever known. One of my absolute favorite series of novels was the Little House books of Laura Ingalls Wilder, in no small part because they reminded me so much of my own parents' resourcefulness. When these Bell Road superfriends found the household wanting some necessary implement or accessory, they taught my siblings and me that there was a quicker and cheaper way to acquire things than shopping for them: One could make things.

"Dad, where'd that grape arbor come from?"

"I built it."

"Get outta here."

"Okay, son. But I did."

"Sweet Peter, Paul, and Mary . . . can I do that?!"

Tinkle
Box

My dad was always building something, it seemed to me, when he wasn't planting garlic or skunking us in a game of H.O.R.S.E., so it would have stood to reason that he grew up amongst carpenters of yore, raising barns before lunch and then installing staircases after. In fact, I later learned that he taught himself to build furniture by simply doing. For example, when my mother wanted a new bookshelf to hold reference books and photo albums, he just copied an antique oak china closet that was in a corner of the dining room. My mom has pointed out, though, that the first thing he built was born from a parenting need: I was the first son; therefore I was the first initiate in the household who needed training in the field of, technically speaking, "peeing standing up." I had the inclination right, and my jaunty stance was satisfactory, not to mention my acumen for judging the wind trajectory, but still, faced with the modern lavatories of the early 1970s, there was the serious obstacle that I was too damn short. Undaunted, my dad built me a little wooden step from which I could show off my skills to any spectator interested in the fine arts of arc and stream.

I grew up learning the use of tools from him, mainly, as well as from my uncles and grandfathers, but I want to come clean here and point out that I wasn't very good at it. They were generous and patient teachers, and so they would watch me attempt to swallow the digestible effects of their tutelage until they were satisfied I could merely use the given tool without injuring myself or the object I was "fixing." For so many years, I would whack a nail with all my might, only for them to admonish me with a shouted "Hit it!" Then they would stand, hands on hips, and wait for goodness knows what, as though I were about to be able to magically hit the nail harder because of the clarity of their instruction. "Oh, *hit* it? Okay—I didn't realize when I was hitting it just now that I was supposed to *hit* it." The thing is, however, I don't think young people are *supposed* to be all that good at work. Sure, there are some exceptions to the rule (egg-suckers, brownnosers, and the like), but most of us kids were too busy thinking about fishing or baseball or Paula Abdul. Or huffing glue and WD-40, for the future gourmands.

The important thing was that they stuck by me in their teaching, despite our apparent differences in interpretation of the verb *to hit*. From their fidelity I eventually gained a work ethic, by which I understood that if I kept trying to succeed at changing that truck tire, or mending those fence boards, or *hitting* that son-of-a-biscuit nail, I eventually would succeed, and then, with further effort, I would succeed even more better than I had the last time. I would sink a nail with one easy hammer swing, finally, but by then they would not praise me—they would have resumed their own work, because I no longer needed chiding; I could now be trusted to drive a nail without supervision, which was better than any compliment.

By the time I started theater school at age eighteen, I had become pretty darn medium with a hammer. I'd give my swing a 7 out of 10, maybe an 8 right after breakfast. I had worked a summer framing houses and also had done a lot of carpentry around our place with my dad, so I could hammer a nail with a decent confidence that I wouldn't leave more than one or two elephant tracks. But I was still young, a couple of years away from filling out to my full strength, so I was a bit cautious when asked to hammer together some two-by-fours in theater shop class. When I successfully, albeit slowly, buried some sixteen-penny sinkers into a floor platform's frame, I noticed the other kids in my class just staring at me with abject wonder. "How can you do that?" one ventured. Huh. Interesting. On the framing crew, I was a kid laborer who was learning to swing his "persuader" like a grown-up, but in this classroom I guess I was a veritable Thor.

I ended up working in that estimable scenery shop for wages during my tenure of study at the University of Illinois, and my lifelong love of the woodshop was born. The man in charge, Ken Egan, ran a very tight ship, and among his lessons was the importance of keeping one's shop clean, organized, and tidy. They were producing a rolling repertory schedule of scenery for the three theaters in the building, so efficiency had reign supreme. It was my first run-in with shop safety as well, learning the proper equipment and techniques to use around the massive milling machines and the treacherous table saw.

Kenny Egan's training, as well as that of his crew, proved invaluable when I arrived in Chicago to make my own way in the world of professional theater. The skills I took away from his shop qualified me to be immediately hired as a professional scenic carpenter at a few different theaters, where my education continued. This time, I was to learn how to achieve the construction of ambitious set designs without the benefit of a healthy college budget—or a healthy shop facility, for that matter. I recall one shop in the basement of an apartment building in Wicker Park (it's probably a Coffee Bean & Tea Leaf now, or an artisanal butter outlet) that had no ventilation other than the door, which worked okay unless it was ten degrees below in a blizzard or simply sleeting to beat the band, one of Chicago's favorite weather conditions. The table saw didn't have enough infeed space to mount an eight-foot sheet of plywood flat, so one had to hold the sheet up at head height and curve it into the blade to start the cut, until a couple of feet had passed through and the plywood could be dropped to horizontal. Cowboy carpentry.

Of course, adversity and necessity can be the cruel mothers of invention, so my fellow woodchucks and I learned tricky ways to achieve every task required of us, just maybe without utilizing the safest of methods. I would ask you not to mention it to the administration of the Wisdom Bridge Theater, but that venerable institution has long since folded, so the truth of our malfeasance can now be told. Hey, we made it

pretty by opening night—that's the point, right? We'll look into being a stubborn idiot in a little more detail later in the text.

The main tools required of the scenic shop are (ideally) a table saw with a big outfeed table (a *lot* of sheet goods pass through that saw), a "chop" or miter saw, some cordless drills, and an air compressor with a couple of pneumatic brad/staple nailers. Eventually, a router becomes necessary, or at least right handy, for milling trim and doing edge work on floor platforms and such. Once I had collected this kit—some new, but mostly a hodgepodge of old, used items—I was able to open my own little scenic concern in the very North Avenue warehouse where I was also hanging my hat. Running my own shop allowed me to work on scenery jobs for various little theaters as well as build outside commissions like trade show sets and minor pieces for people's homes, like built-ins. The problem with paying a scenic carpenter to do lasting work in your home is that he/she is perhaps not so good at building it *well* but is instead very good at imbuing the work with the *facade* of quality through any number of aesthetic tricks, usually involving toothpaste. So my work was pretty spotty at this point, but at least I was cheap. My clientele were mainly friends from the theater, so they were very understanding participants in my wood-based education.

Around this time, age twenty-five or so, something very important happened to me in regard to my journey with tools. My very good friend Rob Ek was an actor and fight choreographer who also paid the bills with roofing and light carpentry. While the framing skills of my youth didn't really translate smoothly to the scenery shop, his own youthful family-training in roofing and carpentry had stuck with him in adulthood. Rob hired me to help him do some work at a recording studio, which included hanging a new door. As we prepared to install the knob-and-lock set, he pulled out a chisel and deftly mortised the doorjamb for the deadbolt and strike plate, and I was gob-smacked. "How did you do that?" He showed me how sharp his chisel was and patiently explained how to use the flat side and the beveled side. I was slowly trying to shed my boyhood practice for a man's habits, and the example Rob set (one I already recognized as worthy of emulating—he cooked a week's worth of stew and baked cornbread to stretch his paycheck, while we all blew ours on burritos, beer, and pizza) had changed me. I knew that if I could get my hands on one of those sharp chisels and a bunch more of his brand of know-how, then I too could perform work upon wood that would last longer than the run of a play.

In the late 1990s I moved to Los Angeles and made a good deal of my living building decks and cabins for houses in the hills (when I wasn't lucky enough to be working in films and TV). My bosom pal Martin McClendon and I took a lot of pride in the transition from building scenery (he is a top-drawer scenic designer) to building rugged structures, out in the elements, no less, that would last. As we were both new to Southern California, we were quite edified to discover the architecture and furniture work of Charles and Henry Greene, commonly known as Greene and Greene. As a couple of the shining stars of the Arts and Crafts movement at the start of the twentieth century, Greene and Greene elevated the exposed joinery

of post-and-beam construction to a pinnacle of elegance and artistry.

Marty and I immediately began to infuse our work with nods to their style as well as that of their superstar contemporary Frank Lloyd Wright. Their inspiration put us immediately on the scent of more complex and attractive joinery, a hunt that continues to this day. Before we knew it, while building a charmingly wacky timber-frame "yoga hutch" in a friend's yard, we had become obsessed with woodworking. I acquired Jim Tolpin's essential book *Table Saw Magic*, and we were completely blowing our labor budget by experimenting with sleds and jigs on our crappy contractor's saw because—by crikey—we were hooked. We had become woodworkers.

This transition can be identified by a couple of different chalks—and of course, it's different for every girl and boy—but one way to confirm that the bug has been soundly caught is this: Your tolerance becomes laughably small. Let me take a moment to explain: When using a tape measure, the amount of acceptable deviation from the exact "correct" measurement is known as the "tolerance." So, when framing a house, for example, the tolerance was a quarter inch, or $1/4"$. I could cut you a dozen studs, and if they were within $1/4"$ too long or short, it was acceptable, although frowned upon. In theater scenery, the tolerance was more like $1/8"$, depending on the application, and that seemed pretty small and persnickety at the time. Imagine my surprise, then, when I learned that the tape measure actually had regularly marked increments smaller than $1/8"$. Twice as small, in fact. In the woodworking shop, though, even those $1/16"$ notations were still too large a tolerance.

When it comes to fitting joinery, a deviation of even $\frac{1}{64}$" can render a piece unacceptable. Hilarious, right?

Over the next several years, I had the good fortune to create my own woodshop, which I creatively dubbed Offerman Woodshop, where I continued to build furniture commissions and explore the limits of my own clumsiness. Inspired by the likes of Garry Knox Bennett and George Nakashima, I began collecting slabs of trees from Northern California from which to construct trestle tables. I met Ted Moores of Bear Mountain Boats and built a few small watercraft. Eventually, as my clowning career began to pick up momentum in a healthy way, I realized that I would need some help at the shop if I wanted to keep the tools running, and so I began to seek out

the members of our collective, which has evolved over the years into the current team of stalwarts, who I am proud to say have found marks on their fine Starrett measuring devices denoting $\frac{1}{128}$". I have to take their word for it.

Whether you choose to pursue that level of precision or not, let's see if we can't get you making sawdust or shavings at some level in the following pages.

I want to briefly point out that I am not a "Master Woodworker." I only say this because I have often been erroneously called as much by well-meaning members of the press corps, so let's clear up that misapprehension right here at the get-go. In my opinion, a master of any particular craft is a person who spends a good deal of her or his life devoted to the perfection of said craft, whether it's baking bread or raising livestock or building furniture. Within these very pages, in fact, besides learning about woodworking and my woodshop, we will also examine the lives and workshops of some contemporary heroes of mine, some women and men who have committed themselves to just such a mastery of discipline.

I, in all likelihood, will never have the simple pleasure of such a life's devotion, as I too greatly enjoy my main pursuit of entertaining the folks who will have me. As long as I continue to be tolerated upon the stages or screens or bookshelves of the world, then woodworking will remain only one of my jobs. That's not to say that I won't apply myself to a constant pursuit of betterment with every project—I most certainly will, as that's the whole point; just please don't mistake me for a master. The point of this book is that working with wood can be fun and productive on every level, not just the most refined. As long as the working status of my hands remains intact, please let me remain a pupil.

Which brings me to one of the most important adages of my life's philosophy: Always maintain the attitude of a student. I was taught this in college by my Kabuki theater sensei, Shozo Sato, and it has stuck with me tenaciously. (You can see some of his art on page 10.) Whenever I perform as a humorist, I encourage the audience to find something to make with their hands. It really doesn't matter what you make so long as you're solving problems with both your brain and your hand skills. There is a special part of the brain that becomes engaged when you need to apply intelligence as well as coordination to your hands as they manipulate tools and materials. As

Wendell Berry tells us in his essay "Poetry and Marriage": *"It may be . . . that when we no longer know which way to go we have come to our real journey. The mind that is not baffled is not employed. The impeded stream is the one that sings."* When we work in the woodshop, we crave nothing more than new problems to solve. Exercising that part of the intellect and skill set, such as they are, provides a tangible thrill of satisfaction, which is a state to which I hope this book can bring you as well.

Now, I am of the opinion that my childhood in rural Illinois played a very important part in my successful development as a practical adult. Left to our own devices, my cousin Ryan and I, along with my neighbor Steve, were free to undertake great adventures in the county's creeks, fields, and forests. This meant riding bicycles and skippering go-carts and building tree houses, complete with armaments with which to protect our fortresses (we made effective slingshots, spears, and swords, but my specialty was the PVC-pipe blowgun with poisonous darts of tape and trim nail—evildoers [sisters], beware!).

We had to learn mechanical engineering to keep the bikes running and structural architecture to establish our strongholds. We chose the biggest-limbed tree down by the creek, scrutinized our pile of wood scraps, and then, with some nails and a hammer, discerned how to apply the wood to the tree in a fashion that would see us comfortably seated at a height over the creek from which we could actually fish. We were problem solving for fun back then, but developing a habit that would become a means to very productive lives. Ryan is now a successful farmer and paramedic, and Steve is a successful contractor, and I am a dancing jackass with very nice chisels. You see? Do the math.

By the way, I don't think I've ever picked up a tool and used it successfully on the first try or often even the twentieth try. But on that twenty-first go-around, when I manage to correctly make a shaving cut with a drawknife—well, I feel the very eldritch magic coursing through my musculature and my nifty opposable thumb digits that have allowed us to leave our simian ancestors in the developmental dust.

If you are new to woodworking, it's important to understand that you will make mistakes, but that the mistake making, in a weird way, is the fun part. Pretty much all the woodworkers I know, when talking about this addictive craft, aver their affection for problem solving: "How can I take these five rough-sawn maple planks, this bench, and these tools and craft a performance that is part puzzle, part dance, part sculpture, part punching the wall, and part common sense so that the end result looks an awful lot like a Shaker dining table?" There are many routes to victory and, of course, some paths that will lead to defeat, but I think that with patience and know-how, your winning percentage can always remain quite high.

How does woodworking seem to cast a spell over so many initiates? What is woodworking's deal? I think a lot of its allure has to do with the first half of its name: wood. For many millennia, humankind has been "getting its craft on" with wood. As a structural/sculptural medium, it has no equal in nature. Stone is amazing and wonderful and pretty, but have you ever tried to chop a mortise in it? Stuff is hard as a rock. I'm also a big fan of steel and bronze and brass and aluminum . . . the so-called metals, but the use of metals as a medium in fabrication just feels cold to me when compared with wood (although when I think about what toolmakers like Lie-Nielsen Toolworks make *with* metals for me to use *upon* wood, I warm right up).

Wood, which is found on the inside of trees, has an incredible charisma on many levels. It's strong enough to form the hull of a gigantic sailing ship of the line, like Lord Horatio Nelson's HMS *Victory*, for example, his British navy flagship in the 1805 Battle of Trafalgar. Constructed almost entirely of white oak, this heroic tub weighed in at 3,500 *tons*. If my math is sound, that's 7,000,000 pounds. (Because the nations of earth cannot seem to decide upon one regulated system of measurement, I drew this calculation based upon the weight of *American*, or "short" tons. If indeed the weight corresponds to the ship's country of origin, Great Britain, then we need to tabulate 3,500 *Imperial*, or "long" tons, for a jaw-dropping total of 7,840,000 pounds. Sigh.) Either way, that's some wood with gumption, guv. Meanwhile, its tensile strength is such that you can steam-bend it into knots, allowing one to form a bow back for a Windsor chair or the thin, curved sides of a guitar. You can build a wooden lamp and then shave wood thin enough that it can be used as a translucent lampshade as well. It's incredibly versatile and forgiving. We strive for perfection in our work, but when we fall down, wood allows us to cover our tracks with either charm or imperceptibility. There will be plenty more in the coming chapters concerning the correction of errors.

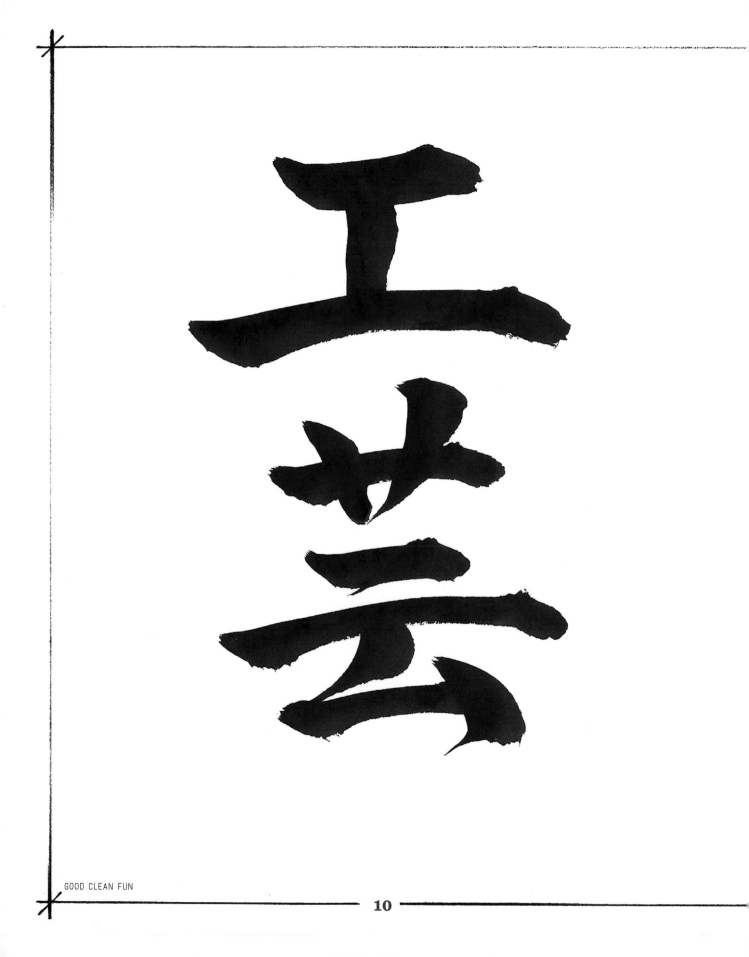

If you have read either of my previous books, you may recall some words of gratitude and celebration in describing my relationship with my sensei, or teacher, Shozo Sato. His lessons to me—the discipline of the Zen arts—have perpetually blossomed in my life and will continue to do so as long as I keep my eyes open, as I suppose that the curating of a life is the ultimate creation in Zen art. Among his many instructions is the notion that every choice one makes can be made artistically, and this consideration can color one's life with beauty and enjoyment. Why shamble down the hallway at work when you can sashay? Why order a thin, watery lager when there is dark, bread-like stout to quaff your dry throat?

In my woodshop hang two scrolls of Japanese calligraphy painted as gifts for me by my sensei, in this same style, known as Shodo. One scroll translates: "The teacher and the student walk the same path," which moves me deeply. I can see him far ahead of me on the path, and he has also left me a trail of whimsical breadcrumbs that delight and nourish me.

The other scroll means: "The Way of Art is the Way of the Buddha." I digest this devoutly as a constant reminder that whenever I am creating art of any stripe, my honest labor is an endeavor that should be assayed with reverence and devotion.

This artwork to your left simply contains the characters meaning *craft* and *art*. Not only is it beautiful taken as a whole rendering, but it represents one of the questions woodworkers often face: Is what we do an art or a craft? For my money, I think the two are inescapably intertwined, as there is as much craft required to achieve our art as there is art pulsing through our craft. It's easy to imagine myself saying, "Hey, you guys have got to get a load of this meal. Matty has crafted a red sauce that is an exquisite work of art."

As long as my table or my canoe pleases your eye when you look upon it, and your other senses as you enjoy its employment, then you may call me whatever you please. As for Shozo, I will call him sensei and count myself among the many very lucky initiates to trace his footsteps upon the path of a life blessed with moments of art and craft and also beer. Look again upon his brushwork—you may discern a trailhead of your own.

WABI-SABI

I would be remiss to craft this book without a nod to this venerated touchstone of traditional Japanese aesthetics. Sato sensei describes the two words thusly:

Wabi: "Humble by choice, not by necessity. Desolation, forlorn, abandoned with humility, the hint of sadness in recognition of perfection in any human achievement springs from the knowledge that with the bloom of time comes the first embrace of oblivion."

Sabi: "The patina of age that produces richness. It is a state of perfection that has to do with ripening, maturing, and acquiring a patina that can come only with time."

Scholars have a hard time pinning down a precise definition of this elusive style note, but I know it when I see it, and our OWS style leans naturally toward it. When we make a beautifully simple maple drawer front and then use a small root burl as the pull, that is wabi-sabi. When we create a slab walnut table that is flat and level but features the natural edges of the tree's outline, that too is wabi-sabi.

Wood as a sculptural material will always communicate the message of its natural wisdom and inclination to the maker, and if we can get out of our own way and let that information inhabit our projects, then we are on the path to wabi-sabi. *Domo arigato gozaimashita.*

The secret to working with wood is to simply understand and love the personality of the wood. Here is the heart of every joinery problem you will encounter: Wood is an organic material, and it will inexorably expand and contract with the humidity in the air, no matter how forcibly you try to keep it from doing so. Trust me, I have learned that particular lesson the very hard way. A great many of the techniques in this book will give you an understanding of how wooden members can be joined together in a sturdy fashion while still allowing for that inevitable movement. That's what makes it like a puzzle, and as we all know, puzzles are the best!

I want to encourage you to find the place in your own life where woodworking might fit. That place might be a sweet shop space, or a corner of your apartment, your barn, or even out in the woods. I'll talk about different ways to set up a shop in your life, and also in your mind—for once you begin to enjoy these different projects you'll

find that an obstinate tinkerer has taken up residence in your body's attic, eyeballing every aspect of your life to see where improvements might be made through the crafting of raw materials.

You will find that making things with your hands brings you solace (when you're not cussing out a visible glue seam) and better hand-eye coordination, improving your internal health in general, but you can also feel good about the external effect you will have on your world. In the immediate sense, you will be crafting items for your home and/or loved ones, and you'll be occupying your time fruitfully, which is pleasing to both yourself and your parents/spouse. If you're enjoying time in your shop, then you're not out getting into trouble/eating fast food/drinking too much beer (or so I've read—ahem). It's simply an organic good time, which my gut tells me has to be healthier than any factory-made diversion. Robert Penn puts it so well in his delectable book

The Man Who Made Things Out of Trees: "The pleasure we take from things made from natural materials is an extension of the pleasure we take from nature itself."

A community or neighborhood containing citizens who make their own goods is clearly a stronger community, relying upon themselves and one another to thrive instead of sending their wealth outside the area, which serves to buttress instead the strength of foreign producers. Naturally, the same can be said of a nation, and so by woodworking you will be doing your part to serve your country as well as your local fellowship. Furthermore, you will be helping our society to do battle against the forces of consumerism that have turned furniture (and every other manufactured item) into disposable products of fashion. The recent movement of stores like IKEA, for example, has a very slight DIY quality in that their furniture requires the purchaser to assemble the units with an Allen wrench, but don't be fooled: The inferiority of the materials combined with the proliferation of packaging waste makes their transgressions as severe as any cute catalogue-furniture factory. It all takes up the same space in our overflowing landfills. Given our dwindling natural resources, it seems only decent that we make everything we have the time and means for and imbue our objects with a timeless quality that can serve generations to come.

As one good work begets another, so does handcrafting foster its own community of support and education. When you get involved with makers, you invariably begin to rub elbows with the kind of women and men who show up with an unsolicited jar of jam or some leftover meatloaf. Bartering reenters your daily economy, which also strengthens a neighborhood. Further, I never cease to be amazed at the availability and generosity of makers in clubs and forums, especially since the advent of the Internet, answering the most specialized questions about the most meticulous topics you can imagine.

I couldn't run my shop without the fulsome support of the Offerman Woodshop crew. We love to get our heads together on any question, whether it concerns woodworking or animal husbandry or romance (a redundancy in some regions). The shop operates as a co-op so that each craftsperson sets her or his own production schedule whilst juggling the custom commissions that come in on a regular basis. My invaluable shop manager and our fearless leader, Lee, runs the outfit with pluck, talent, and aplomb, and she is sincerely the first of many heroes you'll hear about in these pages. We love to solve problems together, all of us, and we love to make one another laugh as well, which happens quite a bit when we get together on a Friday afternoon for a potluck cookout. You'll be invited in to witness all these facets of our lives here, especially since I couldn't have done this book without my teammates in sawdust. That's why each of our contributing woodworkers—who you'll meet through my words, their words, and artist Pat Riot's encrypted collages—has a chapter in the book, instructing us how to build everything from Matty's kazoo to my dad's birdhouses to Lee's kick-ass headboard and bed frame. Let's get started.

SETTING UP YOUR SHOP

THIS IS ONE OF the most titillating steps in a woodworking practice, not to mention one of the easiest to accomplish. Easy, that is, if you just execute it in your imagination.

Why, I have set up many *amazing* shops in this way without breaking a sweat or spending a dime. For that matter, I also find it very satisfying to strategize about how I'm going to fit my imaginary vintage automobiles, boats, and TARDIS collection into my imaginary vehicle barn/fort/hobbit-hole on my nonexistent Fun Ranch (it's gonna be so dope!), but that's neither here nor there. Using one's imagination, a scale rule, and a sketch pad is a great way to start planning what tools and machines to put where, in whatever space you may have available for your shop. (It occurs to me to mention here two books by Jan Adkins that I love for their brilliant simplicity and artistic presentation: *Line: Tying It Up, Tying It Down* and *Moving Heavy Things*—these volumes have been invaluable in helping me remember the old-fashioned ways people have historically moved things like blocks for the pyramids or a massive planer.)

People often ask me what kind of woodworking they can get up to in a small/clean place like a big-city apartment or the bedroom of a house, and my suggestion to them is that the less electricity they can use, the friendlier their

craft will be to that restricted environment. I generally find that the more electricity I use, the likelier I am to produce sawdust pollution, unless I have a *really* good dust collection system, which is, in turn, usually very *loud*. If you can set up a sturdy table or bench, there are a lot of projects to be achieved using only hand tools, like small boxes, picture frames, toys, puzzles (!), and chairs and stools. You could make your own Japanese–style hand planes, perfecting your work until other woodworkers are paying handsomely for your creations, and then you can use that revenue to rent a shop space.

If I had only a small bench/vise in the corner of a city living room, I might get myself some good clamps; a few good bench chisels in sizes like $1/4$", $1/2$", and $3/4$"; a block plane; and a coping saw. A good cordless drill is always handy as well, or to keep it old-school get a bit and brace or a sweet eggbeater-style drill. With this small collection I would make small lidded boxes for things like jewelry, fishing tackle, or tea . . . or maybe gold coins (if you're burying your gold, I suggest a rot-resistant wood like teak or lignum vitae).

To some I also suggest a small lathe in this circumstance of limited space. Wood turning is incredibly fun, and there are a great many projects that can be created on the lathe. Again, use your cleverness to improve your situation. For example, turn an inventory of blackjack-like cudgels on your small lathe, then sell them to the weaker children at your school so that they can wield them to ward off the bullies on the playground. Use your earnings to improve your shop. You'll be making a buck and performing a valuable public service. Now, if you happen to be a bully yourself, you obviously won't want to be arming your victims against you, so I would instead recommend you learn to turn some cool wooden pens and stop being a jerk. Nobody likes a bully, pal. A lathe makes more of a mess, so you'll want to protect your mother's afghans with proper dust collection and screening.

If I should be lucky enough to have some real space and the inclination to be setting up a shop of my own, there are some things to consider before I begin to spend my wife's earnings on the latest monster band saw from Laguna Tools.

First of all, I think of my neighbors. Will my shop be the sort that makes what my mother calls "an unholy racket" (a good deal of very loud noise)? Will I be able to contain my dust output so that it doesn't seem like a light beige snow has blanketed the surrounding properties every time I fire up my palm sander? When I lived in the Silver Lake house known as Rancho Relaxo, my only shop space was two sawhorses and a tabletop that I would set up in the narrow street of our cul-de-sac. I did my best to limit my power tool use to the hours of public decency: eight A.M. to six P.M. After each day's work I would sweep

my dust assiduously and hope that my neighbors would be kind enough to tolerate me again the next day, but it was far from ideal.

If you do have a situation in which you are upsetting your neighbors, try to make them some kind of tribute or gift that they will like very much. This makes them complicit in your transgressions, and if you have chosen the gift correctly, then the next time they think to complain at your sanding noise, they might instead look at the LA Dodgers cutting board you made them and think better of their bellyaching.

When looking for a space to set up your board-shortening operation, be sure to investigate all potential areas in your sphere. Chances are you might find a neighbor, or building super, or handyman/-woman who knows an available spot for projects in the parking structure, on the roof, or in the steam tunnels. I have found that if one exhibits an interest in back-scratching by, say, helping a groundskeeper to rake leaves, then you might find yourself with access to some tools, a workbench, or even a bit of teaching. The worst thing you'll have made is a new friend. (If, on the other hand, the person looks at you strangely whilst wielding some rope in a "snaring" motion, then best not follow her to the steam tunnels.)

Garage, basement, attic, or shed space can be nifty for small projects. Depending upon your personal constitution and local climate, even an awning, carport, or tarp can provide a haven for your habit. If you hope, however, to be producing medium to large woodworking projects on a consistent basis, then you'll want a dedicated shop space that is dry, level, and as spacious as possible, since the more freedom you have to operate with care, the safer you will remain.

No matter what you're looking to produce, unsavory people do like to steal tools, so having a lockable space that you can heat or cool is the realistic ideal.

From this book and our website, you can get the general idea of the sorts of pieces we like to make at Offerman Woodshop. We really love live-edge slab tables, for example, of all shapes and sizes. Using the massive tree slabs necessary for this furniture style requires some hardy table space and equipment. If we were making only kazoos and coasters, we could get away with much less space.

I have been extremely spoiled in setting up my own shop over the years. My dear friend and fellow woodworker Martin McClendon and I first began making our own push sticks and featherboards and other assorted wonderfully geeky accessories for the shop machines around fifteen years ago. (I have done a great deal of work here on my own, which has its advantages, but from that experience I can attest that anytime you can involve two heads on a project, it is vastly superior to one.) We laid out the workstations to our liking, but I would recommend always maintaining a malleability to your machine stations, since your needs can change. You don't want to bolt a whole bench area to the wall, only to later discover it's in the way of your planer's outfeed, etc.

I'll run you through the tools that I love, and give you an idea of what they can do. Of course, every shop is as different as every woodworker, so start small and engage in some trial and error before you take out a second mortgage. I always recommend spending as much time as possible with an experienced hand, to see and feel the methods by which we make our shops work.

SAFETY FIRST

No matter what you're getting into, tool-wise, woodworking involves very sharp metal blades, not to mention spinning motors and pinky-crushing clamps. There are more ways to hurt yourself in a woodshop than there are whiskers on my chin, and I am very hirsute:

You generally want to wear eye protection at all times, and ear protection as well when the machinery gets fired up. Any operation that creates dust should see you reaching for your dust mask, and if you are using a finish that creates fumes, then you want to strap on an appropriate respirator. They even make a couple of different models of breathing protection if you happen to prefer a healthy beard, like myself. All of this headgear will go a long way toward protecting your precious sense organs and lungs, but it can become cumbersome, which is another argument in favor of working with hand tools. Treat your shop area with extreme reverence so that not only will you remain vigilant about safety, but any visitors to the shop will understand that tools must be respected as well.

Another important factor in shop safety is your wardrobe. I prefer sturdy britches like jeans or Carhartts, and a T-shirt or flannel that can take a beating. If you wear long sleeves, be sure to keep them rolled up so a spinning blade or chuck doesn't catch them and ruin your mood (not to mention your hand). The same goes for long hair, hoodie strings, and jewelry. Anything dangling can be caught in a motor-driven tool and cause severe injuries. I always wear work boots (White's Boots—Spokane, Washington) myself, but any shoes that provide you with stable footing should do. I avoid sandals or anything open-toed, in case I drop my awl.

Speaking of ghastly puncture wounds, make sure you have a complete first-aid kit standing by and that everybody knows how to use it. A good set of tweezers and Band-Aids have been our most popular items at OWS so far, knock on wood. While we're at it, be sure to keep your fire extinguisher up to date and ready to hand. We haven't needed ours yet, thankfully, but there are some items in the shop that can spontaneously combust if not properly addressed (see *dust collection, oily rags,* and *Nick's fly dance moves*).

Finally, I can't stress enough the importance of keeping your shop clean and tidy. Sweeping regularly will lower your risk of slipping/tripping over wood detritus (which can get very slick), and it also promotes a sense of well-being. I find that if I want to sweep correctly, then I need to first brush off the tables, benches, and machine surfaces, and so in order to do that, I need to put away the tools and clamps and whatnot, so proper sweeping actually creates the impetus to keep everything in its proper place. Common sense also dictates that, by taking proper care of your tools, you're more likely to maintain sharp edges without dinging up your chisels, and so forth. In addition, I can't tell you how many hours I've wasted working in messy shops, just looking through the messy piles of gear to find a particular socket or countersink bit. Keeping your tools put away will greatly increase your efficiency as well as your safety.

MACHINES

Before I get into individual tools and their attributes, I will just opine here for a moment, and it's just one man's opinion, so please don't get your knickers in a twist. I believe that you get what you pay for. Cheaply made tools, as a rule, will not have the accuracy and finish in their construction that more expensive tools have, so they won't work as well, engendering a lot more cussing on your part. This is a generalization, of course, but I have learned this lesson the hard way, many times more than once. Reading tool reviews is a great way to find out which toolmakers deliver the highest quality, or at least the best bang for your buck. With all tool purchases, be sure to look up as many reviews as you can find, because your fellow woodworkers may point out advantages or flaws particular to your own needs.

Another OWS rule of thumb: the older, the better. Again, this is very subjective, but the hand tools and machines that treat me and my maple the best are from a seemingly bygone era when tools and machines were built to last. The fact that so many woodworking machinery companies have moved their production to Asia does not bespeak an increase in quality, and so when I need a planer or jointer, I comb the state of California for a vintage beast, made in the USA or Germany, because they are virtually indestructible. Like any rule, there are exceptions, like the hand tools of Lie-Nielsen and Veritas, two companies that emulate the quality of vintage items. No matter from where or what era your tools arrive, take the time to tune them up and dial in all their adjustable parts before using to ensure their accuracy and also add a degree of comfort in your handling.

One minor upshot of the tragic dearth of respect for the trades in our country is that a great many hand tools and machines are gathering dust in basements and garages in every town, waiting for you to find them. Ask around—you may be surprised at how generous people can be when they want to see their grandfather's tools get put back to use. Estate sales can also be a gold mine for old tools and clamps.

Since renting my warehouse shop in 2000, I have had very good luck with acting jobs, in that they have afforded me all the shop toys I could desire. That said, one thing I love about woodworking is that you don't need to land an NBC sitcom in order to afford some good clean fun. Here follows a compendium of the machinery in my shop, which is only lacking a wide-belt finishing sander, as I can't bring myself to spend the money or the real estate (they are huge!) to get one. If only there had been a Ron Swanson spin-off...

TABLE SAW: I've seen compelling arguments citing the table saw as the backbone of any woodworking shop, though I could make a solid case for the band saw as well. But why argue? Why not get one of each, or get the one that suits your needs best? The table saw is a very powerful tool for many foundational operations in the shop. Primarily, it is ideal for accurately ripping and crosscutting lumber to size, but it can also be used to hog out dado troughs and rabbets and, using the appropriate jigs and fixtures, cut joinery with great repeatable precision. Box joints, tenons, and even dovetails are a cinch when you have all the parts of your table saw system dialed in.

If you're aiming to use accessories like a dado stack, then it makes sense to get the most horsepower your local grid situation can handle. I also recommend spending a little more cash on a large cast-iron table surface. Trusting your table saw to remain flat and square to your fence is an imperative cornerstone in the shop. A beefy fence that can accommodate lots of different functions whilst remaining accurate is a must.

Using those two channels in the tabletop to either side of the blade, known as the miter slots, can really tickle you. We have a crosscut sled, with runners that ride in those slots, that is perfectly dialed in to cut off the end of a workpiece at an exact 90-degree angle. Using an adjustable miter gauge that also utilizes one of the slots, we can cut off any angle as well on the end of a piece. These accessories, combined with the tilting blade feature of the saw, allow us to achieve compound angles as well as tapered pieces, like a table leg.

"Kickback" is the second greatest peril awaiting you on the table saw. This exciting feature occurs when the wood traveling past the blade is tweaked out of parallel to the blade so that the spinning blade teeth catch the workpiece and hurl it back at the user with all the force of a Johnny Karate face-punch. I have caught just such a piece of walnut right above my pubic bone that left me on my fanny on the floor, doubled in half, thanking the wood nymphs that I wasn't about six inches taller. Preventing kickback must command a great deal of your focus whenever you use the table saw. A riving knife or splitter behind the blade will help a lot.

In the Marvel Universe, the demigod Galactus is known as the "Eater of Planets," but in the woodshop it is the mighty table saw that reigns as the most fearsome of creatures, or the "Eater of Fingers." This invaluable tool is by far the one that must command the greatest respect in use, but I cannot speak on this topic without trumpeting a recent innovation that has changed the game drastically when it comes to reducing membership in the nine-fingered woodworkers club: I am speaking, of course, of the SawStop (see next page).

Nearly as important as the saw itself is a sturdy and spacious outfeed table. Mine is massive, custom made by our charismatic neighbor Daniel Wheeler, with a beefy tube-steel frame, industrial leveling feet, and a replaceable layer of $1/4$" Masonite on top of a 1" Europly top. The adjustable feet allow me to dial it in perfectly level just a hair below the table saw surface for smooth sliding. This table was essential in a scenery shop when we were processing sheet goods (plywood, lauan, Masonite, etc.) by the truckload. Some pro shops opt for a massive European table saw with a nifty built-in crosscut sled/sliding table, but I have never felt the need to step up to that luxury. Perhaps with age it will become a more attractive option, hopefully by the time my knees begin to complain.

(I would be remiss if I did not include a few words about Daniel Wheeler—a museum-level sculptor and maker who can seemingly fabricate anything you like out of impossible materials. If there's one thing that will help any shop [or homestead] survive, it's a benevolent neighbor or two, and this Wheeler fellow is that in spades. He is a generous collaborator, and we readily borrow tools and machine time from each other, although I think we at OWS get the better end of the deal.

SAWSTOP

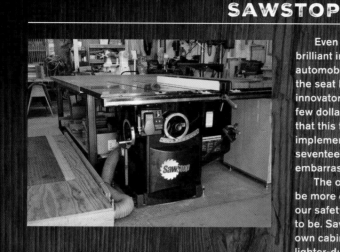

In 2004 inventor Stephen Gass released his new SawStop table saw, which houses flesh-sensing technology that has effectively changed the face (or phalanges) of woodworking. Upon contact with human flesh (or a hot dog, as YouTube will attest), the mechanism shuts down the spinning blade in a microsecond and retracts it below the table, leaving the user's finger very lightly scratched but still attached and wiggling with relief instead of tossed in a baggie of ice as it's rushed to the ER.

Despite the 1999 emergence of his invention, the power tool industry has astonishingly failed to get on board with it, due to a morass of liability concerns and Gass's own demands for royalties that some consider excessive (he's a patent lawyer by day). I guess I shouldn't be astonished that yet another undeniable advance in workplace safety that would prevent thousands of injuries a year hasn't been implemented (according to the National Electronic Injury Surveillance System [NEISS], Americans logged an average of 36,400 table saw injuries *per year* from 2001 to 2008), but I am. It's hard to take sides in the convoluted battle, but I would like to expect more character from American tool companies. I suppose I am naïve that way. We afford our corporations the rights of human individuals, and then we're surprised when they don't exhibit human traits like conscience or remorse. Silly rabbit.

Even if Mr. Gass is trying to get paid for his brilliant invention, so what? How would we feel if automobile manufacturers refused to implement the seat belt or the airbag because the innovators of those safety measures wanted a few dollars more? To my way of thinking, the fact that this technology has been available but not implemented across the board for as long as our seventeen-year-old intern has been alive is just embarrassing.

The opposing parties in this argument may be more concerned with their profit margins than our safety, but the good news is: you don't have to be. SawStop developed and released their own cabinet saw in 2004, as well as subsequent lighter-duty contractor's models for the jobsite. Gass is SawStop's innovator, but he's also a woodworker, and so he has engineered his dream tool that is every bit as deluxe as the best domestic saws on the market; plus, his can't take off your fingers. In his glowing *Fine Woodworking* review of the PCS175 Cabinet Saw, Roland Johnson avers: "Overall, the SawStop PCS175 is excellent. Throw in its safety device, and it's tremendous."

If you have other people in your shop making use of your saw, and you can remotely afford it, then there is no excuse to refrain from upgrading to this tool. I have had macho acquaintances scoff at me on the topic, claiming that they "know what they're doing," and I tell them that three of the people I know who have lost or nearly lost fingers are also three of the best woodworkers I know—it's often comfort with the machines that can breed the momentary lapse of attention that allows such an accident to occur. People also cite the slightly higher price as a dissuasive factor, to which I would simply ask, When your employee loses three fingers in a table saw mishap and you lose your house and shop paying for it, will you be okay telling him or her that you were just trying to save $800?

Let the business worry about itself, and you worry about you and your shop mates. If you're looking for a table saw, look long and hard at the SawStop and ask yourself, "How much are my fingers worth?"

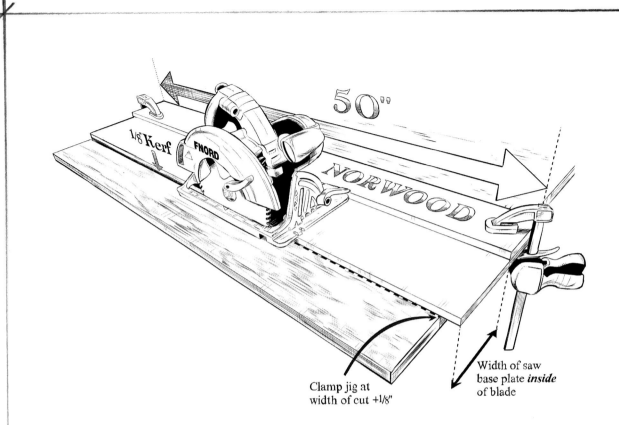

1/8 Kerf

FNORD

50"

NORWOOD

Clamp jig at
width of cut +1/8"

Width of saw
base plate *inside*
of blade

He's what I've heard some of my East Coast friends call a "mensch," and we are grateful.)

If you don't have the space or means for a table saw, I always did pretty decently with a couple of sawhorses, a chalk line, and a circular saw, but nowadays you can get these newfangled hand saws in a guide track that are pretty spot-on for slicing up sheets of plywood. You can also make your own jig out of plywood, which we always called a "Norwood," obviously named after Richy Norwood, the inventor of the rolling paper.

BAND SAW: Whoa, Nellie, and good night, Irene, because you are in for a treat. This tool is so much fun it's hard to believe it's legal. Of course you can cut out all kinds of curves on it, and sculpt chair parts Sam Maloof–style, but the first time I resawed a board into two "book-matched" pieces, I

just about had a conniption fit. I have a Laguna 24 from 2003 that I am crazy about. It can resaw up to about 17", which allows me to make really nifty matching panels, as well as make my own veneer, which is terrifically valuable aesthetically and also saves some dollars on materials.

If you have room for only a band saw, you can also use it to do all of your ripping. It won't leave a glue-ready edge like the table saw, but you can rip close to your dimension and then clean up the edge with a plane or on the jointer, and the action is exponentially safer than on the table saw, especially with rough stock (no kickback). I also love the versatility the band saw affords me. I can cut out joints of many different types, but specifically the big tenons I love to use on my trestle tables. Many companies make respectable small band saws with roll-away kits so you can

HOW TO COIL A BAND SAW BLADE

METHOD ONE: Two Hands

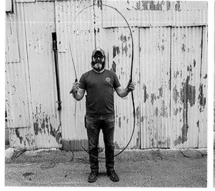

1. Teeth face away from you. Grip (with gloves) like a hammer in each hand.

2. Rotate right hand forward and left hand back.

3. Hang on . . . dang it.

METHOD TWO: One Hand

1. Teeth face away from you. Palm up, foot down.

2. Flip top hand over so thumb points at right hip pocket.

3. Finish with ease.

4. Beware envious peers.

5. Vow to coil blade in privacy henceforth.

tuck them into the corner when they're not making you giggle with delight. Be sure to do good research on this machine, though, as you want a cast-iron table, with quality guide block/rollers, rubber on the tires, and a decent resaw capacity.

The band saw requires constant vigilance for optimal use. Blades can dull quickly, so we change blades pretty frequently at our shop. With every blade change comes the opportunity to check the fit of the guide blocks, which are ceramic on our Laguna tool. Keeping all the details finely tuned makes for a much more pleasant experience and gives you the best chance of accurate work on this saw. Neglecting your guide blocks or your fence alignment can lead quickly to a drifting blade, which can really spoil your day. Also, this is another machine that can lop off a finger in the blink of an eye, so please be very respectful of it.

SLIDING COMPOUND MITER SAW: Here is another invaluable soldier in the board-shortening department. I always try to have at least eight feet of square fence on either side of this saw so we can handle long lengths of lumber. This tool will really earn its keep when you have many multiples to cut at a specific length. The fact that you can set up a stop block at the correct length, against which you rest your piece and then neatly cut it to length, is invaluable. This tool is also extremely handy for cutting compound angles on a board.

You can imagine that in order to make pieces that are perfectly square, one needs this tool to cut materials at a perfect 90-degree angle. The slight "run-out" of the blade on most models makes it extremely difficult to keep this saw turning out perfect corners, so we used to turn the table saw when we needed accuracy. Then we got the Kapex by Festool, and it seems to be earning consistent high marks.

PLANER: When I discovered that I could mill my own wood to whatever dimension I desired, rather than depending upon the only sizes available from the home improvement store, I felt like I had just been equipped with an incredible superpower. Once you find a source of rough-sawn lumber, you can mill the timbers down to whatever size you please! It's a gas!

I have a big old 18" planer made by Powermatic back in 1983, when they were still building their tools in Tennessee. It will also accommodate timber up to 6" thick, which covers pretty much anything we want to put through it short of table slabs. We never buy presurfaced lumber, so we put a heck of a lot of board feet through our planer every month. That is why I located it as close as possible to the dust collection system. It's a workhorse and we love it. Make sure you leave enough room to clear your board's infeed and outfeed egress.

If you are looking for a smaller or more portable arrangement, there are some really hardy 13" planers on the market that have knocked my socks off. DeWalt makes one of the better ones, and I can state that with enthusiasm, as I ran thousands of linear feet of old reclaimed Douglas fir through one of their portable planers without a lick of complaint. The knives are also very easy to change out—if you treat your planer right, it will give you many years of pleasure, by way of smooth and clean wood faces.

JOINTER: The planer's indispensable sibling. Again, we have a vintage beast from 1963, made in Minnesota by Northfield. It will handle a tree slice up to 12" wide, and we keep it tuned up just right. Properly milling your wood from jointer to planer to table saw (we'll get to milling later in the book!) can make all the difference, helping your project to go smoothly rather than causing you to slowly yank out your hair by the handful. Think about it—if your jointer is setting your board edges at 89 degrees instead of 90 degrees, then you have that errant one degree showing up in all of your joinery, which will have to be fixed in one way or another, most often with a sledgehammer. This is also especially key when creating square edges to glue up planks into a larger panel.

A big jointer takes up a good amount of room as well, since the boards need a proper runway for both landing and subsequent takeoff. My dad has a little 6" jointer that works like a charm, and I can't say enough about how easy your life can become when you properly flatten your material on the jointer and then square up the edges. These machines are all designed to make your projects as idiot-proof as possible, which is a constant necessity when your well-meaning author happens to be involved.

ROUTER TABLE: I'd love to shake the hand of whoever came up with this one, as it is indispensably versatile, and so much safer than attempting similar operations with handheld routers. We're talking about a small table underneath of which a router is housed so that the bit extends up through a central hole, rendering the table itself as the operative router base, which greatly increases the stability of the work. Add a fence and some featherboards and you've got yourself a picture frame and trim milling machine. This is another good spot for attentive dust collection because a lot of wood is being removed. Always take your sweet time with setting up a router and determining the right direction of cut for the orientation of your bit. Once you're good to go, employ light passes to sneak up on your full depth of cut rather than trying to bite it all off in one go.

Handheld routers are also very valued players in the woodshop. This freestanding motor that spins a very sharp profiled bit that one then applies to the material of his/her affection can do incredibly accurate work. Employing jigs and templates allows the user to repeat that accuracy again and again in multiple pieces. I eventually find a lot of use for a small trim router, a medium-duty router for light edge work and thin stock, and finally a beefy router for the muscular chores, like surfacing a slab or hogging out dado troughs.

BISCUIT AND DOMINO JOINTERS: The biscuit jointer was pretty revolutionary when it showed up a few decades ago, allowing woodworkers a fast way to secure rails to stiles, as well as align a flush joint between the boards of a tabletop or other panel glue-ups.

I have used a great many biscuits in my day, but I haven't reached for that jointer too often at all since the arrival of Festool's Domino fastener system. For us old folks, the Domino feels like something out of a sci-fi movie—it's basically a specialized router that works like a biscuit jointer, except it routs out a mortise to receive an engineered floating tenon, with the long grain transversing the joint. Because of this, it's exponentially stronger than a biscuit, without losing any of the accuracy or alignment. Lee even thinks the accuracy is improved, or perhaps that means that there's even less chance for operator error, which I guess amounts to about the same thing. I have learned to pay close attention to the things she says.

DRILL PRESS: As anyone who has ever tried to drill a Forstner hole freehand into an oak trestle leg will tell you, a drill press is a damn good idea. A good drill press will allow you an unlimited set of choices when it comes to positioning and securing your work in order to drill the most awkward of holes with surgical precision. We have a charismatic 1943 Delta machine named Bill (thank you, Scott King) that has all the bells and whistles we could ask for and has never required a lick of maintenance in the eighteen years we've been together. They just don't make them like this anymore, and he's awfully good-looking to boot. Our drilling workload is heavy enough that we picked up another big drill press from General Tools for production work, particularly on the pencil holders.

Not only can you use the drill press for countless normal drilling operations, but you also can manipulate your slabs in several ways so as to drill out most of the waste in big mortises, which is a huge time-saver. We also have an assortment of small sanding drums that chuck into the drill press for some terrifically handy sanding tasks that are hard to get at with other sanding tools.

HOLLOW CHISEL MORTISER: This is a real luxury item, saving a great deal of time when it comes to chopping out numerous mortises in furniture pieces. It looks like a drill press, and actually works like one, except the specialized drill bits are housed within a very sharp, four-sided square chisel. The adjustable clamping table allows you to fine-tune the alignment of your piece, and then work your way along your mortise if it requires more than one square dimension. For example, three side-by-side holes with the $1/2$" bit will yield a mortise $1/2$" × $1\,1/2$". The table on mine is on a 2-axis (x, y) roller system that allows you to adjust the entire assembly front, back, right, or left rather than releasing the workpiece every time you need to reposition (not included on cheaper models). The action is achieved by a long lever arm, with which a lot of power is generated by the extra leverage. As you bear down on the arm, the drill bit removes most of the waste as the square chisel surrounding it removes the rest of the side waste, resulting in a perfectly square hole. It is, in a word, pretty dang neato.

LATHE: This is a fantastic and ancient tool that is easier to use than it looks. I have seen woodworkers with foot-treadle lathes turn out work more beautiful than anything I have ever laid hands to. Like so many shop techniques employing simple machines and sharp steel, turning wood depends upon a few simple fundamentals to succeed, allowing an endless variety of round items to be crafted, from knobs and finials to baseball bats and salad bowls.

You can opt for a smaller or "midi" lathe, which is right handy when it comes to producing small items like pens or chess pieces. For chair parts or baluster spindles, you'll want to move up to a medium or large machine. We have a Oneway 2436, a terribly nice and beefy tool that we are still working our way up to deserving. I have enjoyed terrifying videos of turners chucking up massive oak stumps onto monster lathes, to turn expansive, gorgeous vessels from a two-hundred-pound trunk section. I do not think this is a challenge to which I aspire, myself. However, the nice thing about a lathe is that it's very safe, relatively speaking, since you are holding the cutting steel to the wood, as opposed to applying the wood to the cutting steel, as in most other woodworking machinery. This means that a lathe mishap will usually just leave a piece of wood briefly spinning off its mounting and clattering to the floor. On the other hand, the large amount of real estate spinning at high speeds can grab your cuff or bracelet and really spoil your day, not to mention your radius and ulna.

SANDING MACHINES: Another great luxury. We have three machines that are really convenient for a lot of operations.

Oscillating Spindle Sander: This table has a cylinder covered in sandpaper that both spins and thrusts straight up and down (oscillation!) from a hole in the table's center. The combination of sanding directions prevents the grit from leaving visible gouges and scratches, which is a really handy feature. With a variety of cylinder diameters to choose from, this machine is priceless when I need to quickly sand away the band saw marks from curved furniture parts.

12" Disc Sander: This is the sibling to our 1943 drill press, also by Delta. It has a small table set at 90 degrees to the disc surface, although the tilt of the table is adjustable for beveled work. We keep an aggressive grit on this one and utilize it mainly when we need to quickly shape an item, as it will accurately and brutally remove a corner from your chair seat (or your index finger).

Horizontal Belt Sander: This bad boy (or girl—gender unclear) wields a 6" × 89" belt that runs horizontally along a 90-degree table. The entire belt mechanism also oscillates up and down. This machine takes care of many small cleanup jobs that would often be achieved with a block plane on a one-off, but when we get to making multiples, it is a convenient station at which to plow through a box full of Pop Tops or pencil holders.

COMPRESSOR: We have a very sturdy Ciasons twenty-gallon compressor that has been serving our needs admirably for fourteen years now. A compressor is very valuable for the number of pneumatic tools it can power. Brad, staple, and nail guns are extremely useful in the shop, and if you have the horsepower, die grinders are also commonly used for carving applications. The main feature of this tool upon which we rely, however, is simply the compressed air itself. No matter what you are working on—routing a dado, drilling out peg holes for shelves, or carving the recessed details on a canoe paddle—nothing clears the view or removes the dust like a blast from the compressor. Wives and husbands also appreciate the compressor, as it allows us to blow our raiments relatively clean of sawdust before walking in the front door.

DUST COLLECTION: I cannot describe how much nicer your shop will feel once you have installed a proper system for the collection of dust. Well, actually I guess I can: Before you get a dust collector, your shop is choked with sawdust and every surface is covered in a layer of the stuff, not to mention every nook and cranny housing piles of dirty powdered wood. For much of my early career, it was just a way of life—being covered in sawdust, both outside and inside, like in my ears and nose and lungs.

Portable collectors are very handy and they have become quite advanced in their effectiveness. For years I had such a unit, which I would attach to my table saw and planer, mainly, which made a really big difference right off the bat, since those are two of the biggest transgressors when it comes to producing sawdust.

Eventually I installed a complete network of ducting powered by a system by Oneida, the leaders in shop vacuum systems. The only thing wrong with my dust collector is that I wasn't able to locate it outside, so it's quite loud—if I had the room, I'd build some sort of soundproof closet for it. Other than that, it does a masterful job of clearing away the dust from my chop saw, table saw, planer, jointer, band saw, router table, and sanding machines.

The only major dust-producing system in the shop that isn't covered by the collection network is our copious use of hand sanders. There are neat designs for sanding tables—perforated with holes—that will suck away your sanding dust, but I have not gotten around to making one. Instead, we are blessed with a few sanders and companion vacuums from Festool, and I'll tell you what: They cost a bit more, but their engineering leaves

such an absence of dust that I am tempted to eat off the clean wood surfaces left behind, and often do (until Lee catches me and hits me—not soft hitting, either). I can't say enough what a difference it makes to suck up your dust at the source—meaning a vacuum hose on all your sanders. Yes, it's cumbersome, but I just sling the hose over my shoulder and get used to it. Your sandpaper will also enjoy the benefits of a much longer life once the dust is out of the way.

SANDING: While we're at it, let's talk about sanders. Famously, woodworkers hate sanding more than any other activity in the shop, but I often love this process, apparently because I am dumb. Sure, it can get super monotonous, at which time it's important to be good at meditating or at least whistling, but it's during the sanding that a project often goes from good-looking to gorgeous. Especially when you're close to done and you wet the wood to raise the grain before final sanding—you have removed all the machining and tool marks, and you get to see the saturated color and figure for the first time—it's one of the most magical moments in working with wood.

A belt sander is great for aggressive work, like knocking the hills down on a slab you're trying to flatten, or relying on the flat plate, or platen, of the sander to sand all the parts on the face of a chest of drawers flush. Many consider this sacrilegious, but if it works, then I say it's fair game. Besides, I learned that trick from a Christian Becksvoort article; so if it's good enough for the modern master of the Shaker style, it's plenty fine for me.

Finish sanders have become very effective in my lifetime, with the advent of the random orbit sander. By working your way up through the grits from coarse to fine, a really nice finish can be achieved in a comparably short time. If you think sanding is boring today, imagine how tedious it must have been forty years ago, when sanders just vibrated! The hook-and-loop sanding disc system has also made changing grits a breeze, saving a lot of the fuss that using sanding sheets used to require.

STEREO: It's no secret that one of my favorite reasons for being in the shop is that I get to listen to my favorite music as loud as I please, because my name is on the sign! (Of course, I don't get too loud, so the neighbors don't run me out of town.)

Our stereo is a most prized tool—it hooks into any number of sources like iPods and tablets and laptops, and the volume can be controlled separately in the shop side and in the finishing/slab storage room. In proper shop parlance—it's pretty bitchin'.

HAND TOOLS

If I were starting a woodworking practice from scratch today, I like to think I would start small and quiet, like Vic Tesolin suggests in his nifty book *The Minimalist Woodworker*; but knowing me, I would not resist the siren song of the machines for too long. Like my heroic pal Jimmy DiResta, I am too enamored of the ability to make anything I want, usually by more than one method. I have had just as much fun shaping parts with a band saw as with a drawknife, and usually I just determine which method or tool sequence will give me the best result in a fashion that my budget would consider "timely." Building

for a client places different needs and pressures upon your practice than building for pleasure, and the secret to my own happiness is ensuring that even when working on commissions, the pleasure is retained.

It's easy to drop a king's ransom on finely crafted hand tools, but you can also find some great deals on secondhand implements, especially if you pay attention to local garage sales and thrift stores. There are also a great many books to educate you about the hand tools I will list here, but if you can, get to Lie-Nielsen Toolworks in Maine and see if Deneb is available to tell you about their wares in person. I have gone in there looking just for a dial caliper but walked out with a couple of spokeshaves and a sharpening jig. He's a very enthusiastic user of their handsome tool line, enabling him to sincerely lionize the integrity of each item, sure, but it's watching his dinner-plate hands handle a plane blade that really seals the deal. Damn, now I want to go back. Lie-Nielsen and Lee Valley/Veritas have generally been considered the finest purveyors of high-quality hand tools in my years of experience, and with good reason; but I'm delighted that now there are many smaller artisanal operations springing up all over the globe, as traditional woodworking reestablishes its hold on our psyches.

CHISELS: When friends come to visit my shop, I show them a Japanese bench chisel—tipped by its razor-sharp wedge of steel—then I proceed to explain how every operation with every tool in the shop is basically employing some version of that chisel. A table saw utilizes a few dozen little chisels on a spinning wheel; a plane or spokeshave is really just a wide chisel in a clever rigid frame for specialized cutting and shaving; even sandpaper is made of thousands of tiny chisel-edged grains that are shaving away minuscule amounts of wood. It's all about the chisel and how to apply its edge to wood to achieve your desired purpose.

If you can afford only one really nice chisel, shell out for a $1/2$" or a $3/4$" bench chisel and learn to properly sharpen it. Once you have experienced the power that a sharp chisel affords the woodworker—kid, you will be hooked. Whether you're paring a fine shaving from a tenon's cheek (bevel up) or gouging out a large waste area on a canoe paddle (bevel down), the chisel is your best buddy, good buddy.

You will frequently require a means by which to "persuade" your chisel through the wood fibers with some force, a chore which traditionally falls to the mallet. My favorite is one I turned from lignum vitae, which

Bevel Up

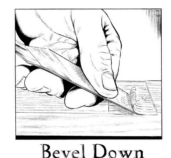

Bevel Down

serves me well from the lighter tapping up through the more fulsome whapping. When chopping large mortises in timber framing or some of my more massive trestle-table bases, I will use a big framing chisel with an actual steel hammer.

PLANES: Planes are a gas. A plane is basically a blade held securely at an angle in a sled of some sort. It is adjustable, which allows the user to take a very controlled shaving. The first time I saw the magic of a plane in use, I had just arrived in Los Angeles and I was renting space in my pal Christopher Kelly's shop. I was working away on some custom drawer units for a client's closet while Chris was finishing up a long, low shelf unit commission in oak for a tony Silver Lake living room. He grunted as he noticed a few faint tool marks in the front edge of the top shelf, whipped a strange apparatus out of his apron, and much to my surprise, zipped a

Mallets and chisels   Assorted planes

continuous $1/64$" shaving squarely off the front of the board.

"Whoa," said I, "that was scary."

He held up the tool and the curled shaving. "Block plane."

"Got it," I replied, turning my head quickly to conceal my tears of terror and relief.

The more skilled we slowly become at Offerman Woodshop, the more we seem to revert to the use of planes. They come in all shapes and sizes, to remove wood from your material in a variety of profiles and finishes. I most regularly reach for my shoulder planes, my block plane, and a #4 smoothing plane. The engineering in these sweethearts goes back centuries and has changed very little, which makes them fascinating and powerful to me. In Japan, woodworkers are considered masters once they can shave an entire timber with a large plane, producing an unbroken shaving that is no thicker than the meniscus inside a hard-boiled egg. YouTube It: It's crazy. You can skip the woodworking and make an entire career of collecting planes, tuning them up and mastering their use, and I wouldn't blame you.

SPOKESHAVE: The spokeshave was created by the wheelwright, who needed a specialized version of a plane with which to *shave* the wooden *spokes* of wagon wheels. It has a blade much like a plane, protruding through a much shorter sole, which allows it to operate well on curved pieces, assisted by two handles attached to the right and left sides of the apparatus. You can push or pull this tool, and it comes in a few assorted sole shapes to accommodate concave surfaces and also small-radius curves like the shaft of a canoe paddle.

Spokeshaves

With a well-tuned shave, I have felt the most like a sculptor as I have used it to shape a canoe yoke or thick stool leg with organic curves. This freedom has caused my choice of projects in recent years to lean more toward sexy curves and away from the comforting solidity of rectilinear shapes, although combining the two can also be quite satisfying.

DRAWKNIFE: The axe, hatchet, and splitting maul are specialized wedges of steel—we're pretty familiar with how they operate. The chisel is a refined version of the wedge, and the plane and spokeshave are basically wide chisels in specialized housings. The drawknife, then, is a really, really wide chisel, with a flat back and a bevel on the top, but instead of one handle straight above the blade, this tool has a handle bent off each end, so the long blade is most effective when pulled toward the user. It's used for the rapacious removal of material, as it can lop off whole chunks at a slice, but wielded with skill, it can also perform delicate tasks of exquisite carving. I'll tell you more about this wicked shaver in the chapter on Peter Galbert, as the drawknife was more like a butter knife in my hands until he awoke the force within me and it.

CARD SCRAPER: Now, I want you to listen to me here. I'm trying to avoid strong opinions in this text, as I am personally always turned off by purists who insist that one method of woodworking is better than another. It is my hope to present the information that I possess, much of it won by repeated clumsiness, so that you might choose your own adventure in the shop.

Having said that, here I go with a strong opinion: Get yourself a card scraper and learn to use it. I heard this from others, and I kind of rolled my eyes and thought, "Okay, Tage Frid, then why are random orbit sanders so popular?" I believe the answer to that question would be that the sanding tool companies have had a much healthier advertising budget than the folks hawking card scrapers. After all, a scraper is merely a small scrap of thin steel. You can easily make one from junk. Or buy one. They're cheap.

Now that I can effectively use this godsend, I can't tell you how many surface flaws I have resolved, which in the past I would have literally dug out with the edge of a sander, leaving an amateurish crater of one sort or another. Good planing technique followed by the card scraper will give your sanders a lot more shelf time, and when it comes to smoothing difficult grain like the godforsaken red eucalyptus in my three-legged stool chapter, there is simply no alternative to the scraper.

DRILLING: I spent many years drilling utility holes with conventional bits and spade bits before I discovered the wonders of better versions, like brad point and Forstner bits, and then finally the good old-fashioned brace and bit. In my scenery work, I was usually just drilling bolt holes or pilot holes for lags, neither of which required any particular neatness. Once I got into woodworking, however, the frayed edges of the holes produced by my dull, old bits were not going to cut it (by the way, spade bits and regular "split-point" bits can work just fine as long as they're sharp). Drilling holes for dowel joinery or neatly hogging out mortises with a drill bit is intensely satisfying for the accuracy one can achieve. Using a bit and brace is also really fun in the amount of bang you get for your buck, utilizing that good old dependable elbow grease.

MEASURING: It should be clear by now that accurate measuring is just about the most important part of woodworking. The surgical precision (or lack thereof) in one's ability to lay out lines appropriately square, straight, and legible will directly affect the success of every subsequent step. I use a tape measure for most run-of-the-mill rough operations, but when it comes time for me to absolutely nail my measurements for cutting furniture parts, joinery, hardware placement, or persnickety projects like inlay, I turn to my team of experts: a high-end woodworker's square (like a 16" × 24" framing square but more dependably accurate) for larger distances, then I dial in the details with a combination square from Starrett. The 6" and 12" versions of this tool are among the most valuable players in any shop. Their steel rules are also very handy for guiding a pencil or marking knife without fail. I also depend upon a dial caliper pretty heavily, for finding the exact thickness of my material, or the perfect width or depth of a mortise or rabbet.

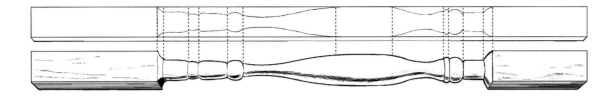

Another handy method altogether for repeated accuracy is to be found in what is known as the story stick. If you're building chairs, for example, you can take just a nice length of lath and mark off the length of each disparate chair part along its length: the front legs, the back legs, the seat rails, the back rails, etc. Then you can just mark off each part using the stick, needing never concern yourself with those pesky $1/64$" bits on your tape measure. I like to use a story stick on the lathe, demarcating each detail in my spindle turning, as above.

These methods are all well and good, but don't forget your eyes and fingers. Viewing the light under a straight edge held against your work or the way your fingers perceive friction or resistance in fitting a joint are the final bars by which to measure perfection.

MARKING: Measuring's inseparable twin, marking your work is just as imperative when it comes to getting things done right. After all, what good is meticulous measuring if you can't then correctly mark your distances?

I always keep a length of chalk or lumber crayon handy for the first step of coarsely marking out the projected dissection of my timbers when they arrive from the lumberyard. Contrasting colors work well, as well as bright hues of orange and yellow, to allow my notations to stand boldly out from the wood's rough surface texture.

Once you set to working with your milled pieces, the main standby of the carpenter is, of course, the pencil. They come in a few shapes and sizes, but the sharpness of the point is all that really matters. If you're marking out fine details or trying to execute rigorously precise operations, then you want as tight of a pencil line as you can muster.

However, you can take things even a step further by utilizing a marking knife. These gorgeous scribers are built like a chisel, with one beveled edge, except they come to a point. The general idea is to achieve your line by pressing the flat back of the knife tight to your straight edge, with the bevel facing out, and instead of scratching the wood, you're ideally *slicing* the wood fibers as you scribe. Not only does this method create a razor-thin mark of exactitude, it also creates an ideal divot in which to place your chisel, or along which to steer your plane, preventing the fibers from tearing out and leaving instead a very crisp edge.

CLAMPS: They say a woodworker can never have enough clamps. By gum, I believe I am the one to have beaten the idiom. If I don't have enough clamps then I am in some deep trouble, because it means I must have a job coming up that will require more than the seven thousand I seem to have acquired. The point is: *I Love Clamps!* Clamps, properly used, will be your very best friends in woodworking. They are another item upon which I recommend spending the dough for the good stuff. Bar clamps in the style of Bessey's K Body are a solid investment, considering the accuracy with which they apply force while maintaining a square corner. The better understanding you have of clamping pressure, clamping cauls, and wedge tricks, the less money you can spend on fancy clamps and still get away with solid glue-ups. Trigger-style clamps like Quick Grips are a constant fanny-saver, so you'll want at least a couple pairs of those to act as an extra set of hands, but for real results you want clamps that are contracted by the force of a screw action. Nothing beats the muscle of an all-steel C-clamp when you can bring its limited throat depth to bear upon your project, and the double-handed wooden hand screw is also a great heavy hitter. Different clamps have different strengths and weaknesses, which is how you can so quickly amass so many of them in all varieties of shapes and sizes. Start collecting now, and maybe one day you'll catch up with a screwball like me. (Word to the wise—take care to keep your bar clamps free of glue, as dried glue really gums up the sliding action of the clamp head upon the shaft.)

BENCH: This is the real backbone of any hand-woodworking practice. A solid bench with a vise or two and some holes for bench dogs and hold-downs and doe's feet and other simple,

clever ideas will provide all the support you need to achieve any piece of traditional furniture, from a candle holder to a chest of drawers. I have learned my own woodworking in a somewhat backward fashion, first mastering scenery construction, which is all sheet goods and 1" × 4" assembled with drywall screws and air fasteners. Eventually I was able to make the leap from the table saw and compressor to the bench, armed with chisels, planes, and scrapers. Now whenever I plan a project, I try to place as many of the steps as I can on the bench, because my hand tools are flatly more enjoyable to use in every way, plus I can still hear the Wilco jams on the shop stereo. There is one bench accessory that you will also find indispensable—the bench hook, which is a simple board with a cleat to catch the bench edge, and a second cleat against which to hold a workpiece:

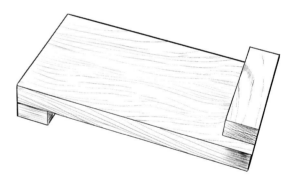

SHARPENING

To most of the woodworkers at Offerman Woodshop I would give an A or at least a B-plus in sharpening, but for my own evaluation: I would be *lucky* to squeak by with a C-minus. It would probably require the instructor to hold me in special favor. Like any small domestic step that is lazily ignored by human nature (putting the cap back on the milk, taking out the garbage, feeding the children), sharpening is terribly easy to procrastinate. When you have already gone to all the trouble of designing your piece, selecting lumber, and laying out your cut list, the last thing you want to do is go all the way over to the sharpening station and maintain your steel blade edges. Ugh. It's like when you commit to the toil of running around and playing ghost-in-the-graveyard like a mad goblin until you're stumbling tired and ready to crash right into sleep, but you have to get up and brush your teeth before you do. It'll take only a minute, and it's unquestionably the right thing to do, but it just seems like the worst possible punishment in the moment.

Quite simply, sharpening your tools properly is the foundation of good woodworking. Your chisels, your plane and shave blades, your scrapers and slicks—none of them will do anything but frustrate you if you have not learned to put a fine edge on them. There are many ways to do so, some of which I'll briefly touch upon here, but I highly recommend you do some more homework before you start spending money on equipment. We are very fond of *The Perfect Edge* by Ron Hock but have also benefitted from the tutelage of Thomas Lie-Nielsen and Leonard Lee in their respective sharpening tomes.

On the lower end of the dollar spectrum, you can slap some sandpaper on a piece of glass or flattened granite and go to town, working your way up through the grits to emulate coarse to fine sharpening stones. Stones are the tried-and-true standby that most of us at OWS use. I have never seen an oilstone, as we utilize water stones, but both are very effective at maintaining your sharp edges. There are also some very nice sharpening machines on the market, which all have names that sound suspiciously like spaceships. To wit, I have had positive experiences on the Tormek Water-Cooled Sharpening System, the Work Sharp 3000, and the Veritas Mk.II, whilst traveling through the Dagobah system in my *Millennium Falcon*.

When my work was more scenery/home-construction based, laziness and ignorance also played a huge role in my jobsite negligence when it came to sharpening the power saw blades on table saws, chop saws, and circular saws. Many companies make "disposable" blades that are slightly cheaper than higher-quality blades (like the Forrest and Amana blades we prefer), but that supposed "savings" just encourages more waste headed for the landfill, when you could instead be saving money for real by buying the better blades with carbide teeth and getting them re-sharpened on a regular basis. The same holds true for router bits.

Keeping your cutting edges as keen as possible affords you the best opportunity to do accurate work. Why go to all the trouble of meticulously milling material, designing and laying out intricate joinery, only to have a dull chisel veer off the mark and spoil your joint? On top of that, sharp tools make everything work more smoothly, whether we're talking about your wrists and shoulders or the motor on your table saw, and smoother work is safer work. The extra attention paid to sharpening will pay great dividends in tight joinery, happy machines, and happier woodworkers.

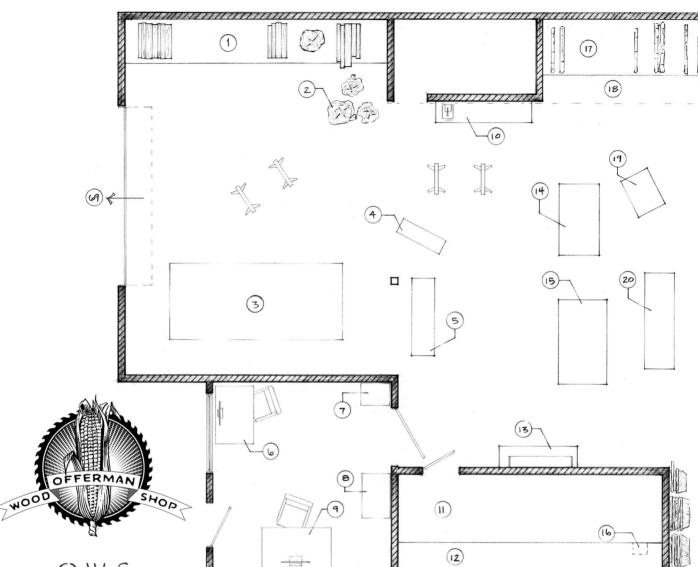

O.W.S.

1. RECLAIMED LUMBER
2. STUMP PILE
3. SLAB DRYING AREA
4. FINISHING SUPPLIES
5. FLAMMABLES CABINET
6. INTERNET DESK
7. CABINET
8. TABLE
9. INTERNET DESK
10. WOOD BURNING & BRANDING
11. FOXY'S HIDEY HOLE
12. SHIPPING SUPPLIES
13. WRAPPING PAPER
14. FINISHING TABLE

15. FINISHING TABLE
16. PORTAL TO THE SHIRE
17. BURL SLABS
18. LOFT ABOVE
19. FINISHING TABLE
20. WORKBENCH
21. BIG OL' SLABS
22. SURFACED SMALL SLABS
23. TURNING BLOCKS
24. CLAMPS
25. SAFETY TACKLE
26. STICKY STUFF & GLUES
27. HARDWARE
28. HARDWARE

29. POWER TOOLS
30. SHARPENING STATION
31. LATHE
32. WORKBENCH
33. WEE WORKBENCH
34. MORTISING MACHINE
35. FESTOOL MFT
36. WORKBENCH
37. HAND TOOLS
38. DRILL PRESS
39. HAND TOOLS
40. DRILL PRESS
41. BANDSAW
42. HARDWARE

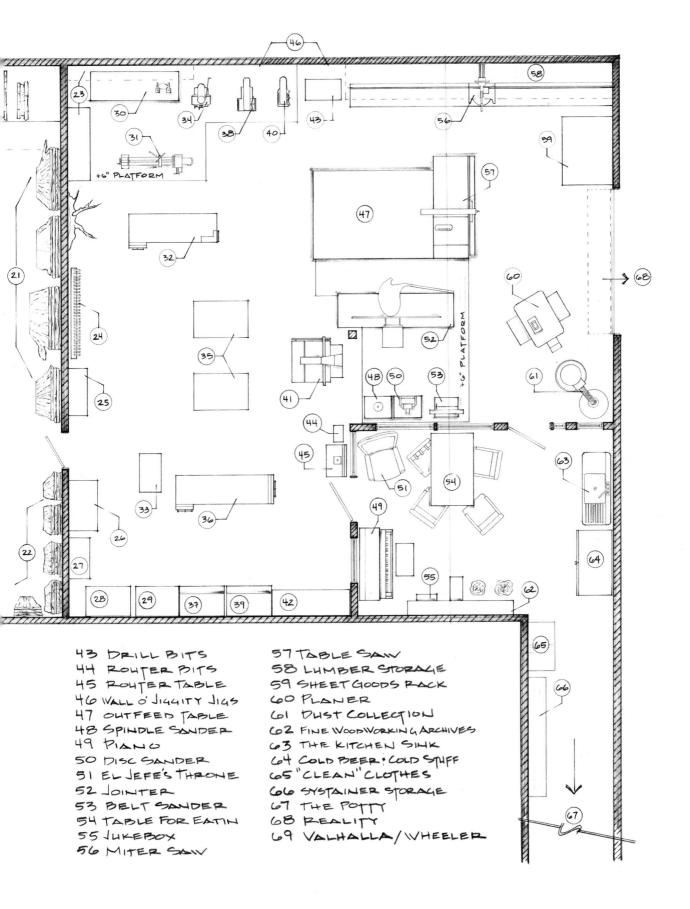

43 DRILL BITS
44 ROUTER BITS
45 ROUTER TABLE
46 WALL O' JIGGITY JIGS
47 OUTFEED TABLE
48 SPINDLE SANDER
49 PIANO
50 DISC SANDER
51 EL JEFE'S THRONE
52 JOINTER
53 BELT SANDER
54 TABLE FOR EATIN'
55 JUKEBOX
56 MITER SAW

57 TABLE SAW
58 LUMBER STORAGE
59 SHEET GOODS RACK
60 PLANER
61 DUST COLLECTION
62 FINE WOODWORKING ARCHIVES
63 THE KITCHEN SINK
64 COLD BEER & COLD STUFF
65 "CLEAN" CLOTHES
66 SYSTAINER STORAGE
67 THE POTTY
68 REALITY
69 VALHALLA/WHEELER

Cthulhu LIVES!™

THE H.P. LOVECRAFT HISTORICAL SOCIETY

A PARALLEL UNIVERSE
SINCE 1984

OFFERMAN WOOD SHOP

This is to Certify

Our auspicious **SHOP LOGO** was created by my dear friend of twenty-five years or so, Andrew Leman, who happens to be one of the most terrifically talented people I have ever known, and I know Amy Poehler. He is an actor, writer, producer, sculptor, artist, and typographer with whom I attended theater school in the previous century. He runs an astonishing company called The H. P. Lovecraft Historical Society (with his bud Sean Branney) that specializes in the production of entertainment and goodies based upon the works of the famed father of modern horror fiction, H. P. Lovecraft. From fully realized feature films; to books, music albums, and radio plays of the highest quality; to assorted props and accessories and delightful swag, their company is a veritable (and darkly comic) wonderland of all things Lovecraft. Everything that comes out of their collaborative efforts is either scary or hilarious or both, with extremely high production values. It has been my extreme pleasure to play with these fellow miscreants over the years, particularly in the live-action role-playing versions of

Lovecraftian adventures we enacted during our college years, and then again when they built sets and miniatures for their first film, The Call of Cthulhu, in the half of my shop that is now our slab storage and finishing area. Many years ago, when I realized that my shop might actually become a legitimate furniture operation, I asked him for help with my logo. I simply suggested a saw blade with an ear of corn in the middle, representing my upbringing amidst the charismatic cornfields of Illinois. Ever the generous neighbor, Andrew turned in this beautiful design and then refused payment, the selfless bastard. For that reason, I implore you to visit my vengeance upon him by apprehending his company's website and availing yourself of the many wonders that await you there: a Cthulhu ski mask, books, films, props, you name it. You can even purchase your own Certificate of Insanity!

Andrew H Leman

(Even these two pages have been designed by Andrew, including some of his fonts. He must pay for this insolence.)

Issued by
HPLHS INC.
WORLDWIDE HEADQUARTERS
1839 DANA ST. GLENDALE, CA 91201
WWW.CTHULHULIVES.ORG

Ludo Fore Putavimus

OWS YEARBOOK

Ronnie Aveling
Handy Jack of All

Sally Browder
Shop Bookkeeper

Michele Diener

Gus

RH Lee

Matty Micucci

Matt Offerman

Nick Offerman

Ric Offerman

Jane Parrott

Josh Salsbury

Krys Shelley

Thomas Wilhoit

Bill

PAT RIOT

When Pat Riot breached his mother's hidey-hole, all the mincing tooth-polish makers ran screaming for the hills. Tipper Gore shivered on her scaredy-porch, wrapped her pashmina tight around her shoulders, and shambled back inside her censor-pod. As a kid (boy or goat? You decide), Mr. Riot loved to muck up the governmental brain channels with his esoteric "hollow-grams": cartoony cloud/Dobbshead images worthy of Tex Avery, farted subversively into the public purview via his "talent." He has been heard asserting, well past the witching hour, that he is a Komodo dragon, a moray eel, yea, a killer whale bereft of its pup. Pat Riot will never cease *nor* desist from pumping our municipal Kool-Aid supplies of thirst-quencher full of pure, unadulterated Slack. If you put your ear very close to the fracking vent you will apprehend his whispered anthem: "O my dodie eye."

JOHN HARTMAN

John's life story is a rich example of the many vocational twists and turns that can be ultimately required to arrive at a place of contentment. He started with a Fine Arts education and an interest in this type of illustration, but a combination of impatience and a rebellious streak led him to pursue a Fine Arts career in Brooklyn. His journey as an artist began to veer from "fine" to "starving," so he combined his technical acumen with a love of music and began rebuilding pianos, which turned into a prosperous business. The *Piano Technicians Journal* hired him to do some illustrations. He became so good at it, developing his own style employing both hand and digital skills, that he quit working on pianos and became a highly successful illustrator, with a woodshop for his beloved hobby. Fantastic. His beautiful illustrations speak for themselves and can be seen regularly in *Fine Woodworking*, *Woodcraft Magazine*, *Fine Homebuilding,* and more.

ETHAN NICOLLE

I first became aware of Ethan Nicolle when I was handed his hilarious and original comic book series *Axe Cop*. His talent for drawing stories is superseded perhaps only by his ability to render humor with or without words. His uncanny knack for capturing emotional situations with a delicate rendering of facial expressions and gestures makes me relish his work more than that of most pencil jockeys—a breed of entertainers I already adore. We became friends thanks to the benevolent meddling of my sometime writing partner and bud Martin Garner, and the result was an animated series of *Axe Cop* for the Fox Broadcasting Company that has been called "the finest cartoon ever done shat" by several members of our families. Ethan masterfully drew portraits of the twenty-one heroes in my second book, *Gumption,* and I am gratefully privileged to tax his skills once more all over this funhouse of a textbook.

You can go to AxeCop.com to feast upon all things *Axe Cop*, as well as Ethan's other titles, the chuckle-riffic *Chumble Spuzz* and the hilariously terrifying *Bearmageddon*.

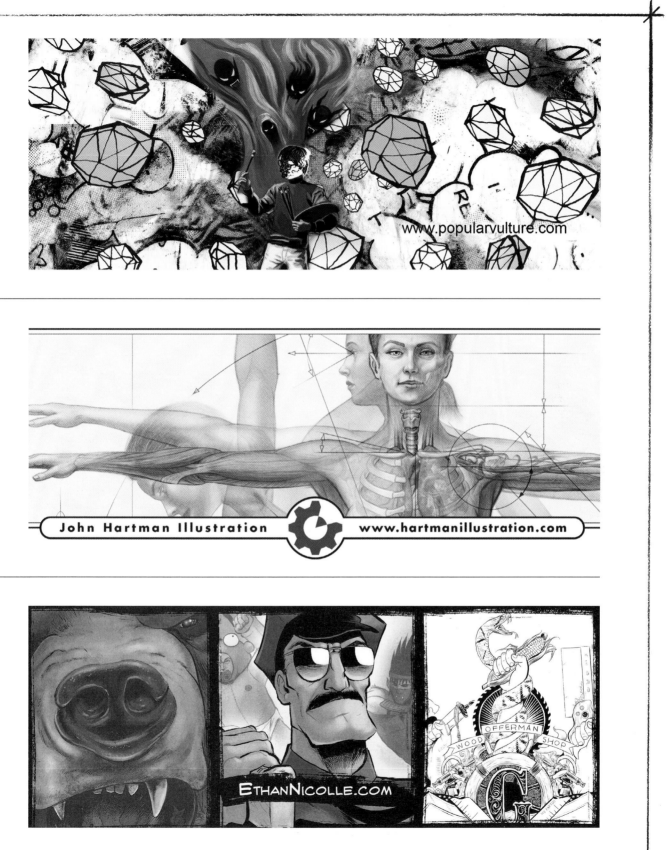

www.popularvulture.com

John Hartman Illustration   www.hartmanillustration.com

EthanNicolle.com

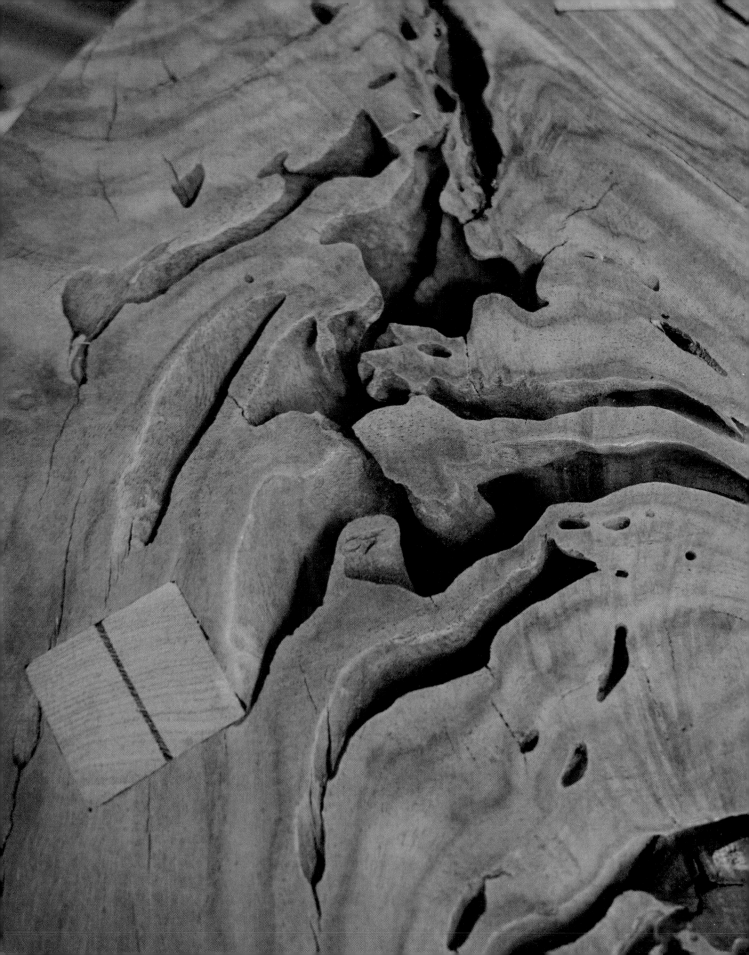

ON WOOD

I'M NO WOOD SCIENTIST, but I thought I would take a moment to talk about this bewitching material itself. After all, it's the very reason we're all here on this page today.

Since the first time that we humanoids lashed a rock to a stick to protect ourselves from our vicious sisters, wood has played an imperative part in our lives as civilized mammals. Across the globe, the number of ways in which wood has been positively employed in the service of mankind is almost too great to tally. I mean . . . baseball bats. Three-masted ships. Clarinets. Tree houses. Toothpicks. Everything.

So many useful objects manufactured by human hands have also been prototyped in wood, even if they end up being produced in metal or glass or plastic. Whenever we people have a great idea for an exciting innovation, like the automobile or the airplane, we commence to tinkering, cobbling initial parts together out of wood. The reason for this choice is because wood is so damn friendly. You can break off a big piece by accident and glue it back on so strongly that the break is undetectable. Wood nobly retains a great deal of mass and strength while succumbing politely to the application of sharpened steel tools. The resilience in wood timbers allows well-designed items like chairs

and boats to have spring and flexibility, which lends them comfort and longevity.

If you're at all like me (an ardent reader of Tolkien), then you have felt a certain sentience from trees when standing in their quiet, majestic presence. When sliced portions of those noble structures then occupy your bench, there is a natural wisdom retained in the organic cells. Although the tree itself is no longer living, the cells never stop breathing, as it were, in their perpetual tendency to expand and contract with the relative humidity in the air around them. Each piece of wood has a personality, even boards harvested from different parts of the same tree, and in its particular attributes and behavior, the wood will speak to you ("I like to lie straight!" "I like to get all curly!" "Ha! I refuse to cooperate, foolish human.").

Woodworking has everything to do with learning to listen to your material and then doing your best to cooperate with its requirements (shucks, that's actually pretty good marriage advice as well—if you sweeten it up a bit). The more acquainted you can become with your tools and materials, the more clever wood will make you. It's exciting to achieve early success with a chisel or a tenon saw, but you'll arrive at another level of triumph altogether when the tool becomes part of your arm, and you and the steel and the wood operate in concert to make something beautiful, artistic, and practical.

In general, wood has great tensile strength in more than one direction, which means that when you dig your spade into the ground and pull back on the handle with all your weight, it's not going to break. It means you can sling a bunch of timbers together up over a gulley in a structure they call a "bridge" and roll freight trains loaded with pig iron across it. You can also hang yards upon yards of sail on a pole of eastern white pine, call it a mast, and sail across the sea. The earliest wagon wheels were slabs of solid wood, but it didn't take the wheelwright long, relatively speaking, to discover the benefits of a lighter-weight spoked wheel made up of several pieces, which was stronger, more consistently round, and easier to fix. Heck, there are still *cars* being produced in England with frames constructed of ash, by the chaps and ladies at the Morgan Motor Company. The reason that all these applications call for wood over any other material is also the reason why wood makes the best axe handles and floor joists and bench seats and catapults: It bends without breaking. You can twist it and pull it and smush the living heck out of it. Wood cells and the fibers they form can take a great deal of punishment without failing, much like many teachers and parents I terrified in my youth.

For our purposes in woodworking, there are some key attributes to this dependable material that I would like to elucidate here. Wood can wear different hats when called upon to serve us, and so I want to split the conversation into a couple of categories: hardwood and softwood. If you're looking for a species that will provide structural strength but is easy to handle and not too heavy, like for wall studs and rafters, then you want a softwood, also known as a *conifer.* For more of a heavy-duty durability and overall toughness, as required by furniture parts and croquet balls, then you're in the market for a hardwood, or a *deciduous* species.

I apologize for getting a little boring here, but I'll promise to keep the science brief. Conifers are also known as *gymnosperms,* which means "naked seeds," because their seeds fall unprotected to the soil every year. Generally, conifers are evergreens, a derivation that includes spruce, fir, pine, and cedar varieties, among others. As you probably know, these trees grow fast and tall, which makes them perfect for use as the supportive skeletons of building structures. Some pine flavors are hard enough to use for tables and cabinets, but softwoods are generally not going to take the punishment that hardwoods will withstand. That said, it all depends upon your locality and the quality of softwood species available. I have worked with old-growth yellow pine and Douglas fir that was perfectly hard enough to pleasantly machine and craft into furniture, so be sure to look around for wood sources and then experiment with the available options to discern what wood will best suit your project.

One invaluable use for a conifer's timber is in the hull of a canoe. The cedars, especially western red cedar and Alaskan yellow cedar, have been widely recognized as ideal for small watercraft because of their combination of high tensile strength and very light weight. I have made three boats, all cedar, and that ancient, pleasing shape manifested from this decidedly workable (and fragrant) material, in the sweet silence of hand-tool work no less, is indeed a consummation devoutly to be wished. (More on this delectable topic can be found in the chapter on Bear Mountain Boats.) Members of the spruce and cedar families are also highly prized as soundboards, or "tops," of stringed instruments, like violins and guitars. Their impressive stiffness compared to their light weight makes these species ideal as the lid of the resonation chamber that is a stringed instrument's body. While the guitar wants a top membrane that will vibrate like the skin of a drum, the rest of the structure needs to be much more densely solid and rigid to effectively hold the string apparatus in place (and in tune) without any give.

Which brings us to hardwoods! Luthiers use a lot of maple and mahogany in their instruments, as well as a whole panoply of choices for a guitar's body and accessories—from African ebony to Hawaiian koa to the "Cadillac" of guitar species: Brazilian rosewood. These applications, however, are merely a drop in the bucket. Hardwoods are used for so much more than musical instruments; they could truly be considered the rock stars of the woodshop themselves. Sorry, pine, but I'll line up around the block for the species commonly known as the cabinet woods. Cherry, walnut, oak, maple, and mahogany are the starting five, but nearby on (and in) the bench you'll find beech, birch, ash, hickory, chestnut, and butternut, and in

California we have some local beauties like black acacia, madrone, and eucalyptus (frequently a bad seed, but tragically beautiful, as is so often the case with troublemakers).

These deciduous trees, known as *angiosperms* ("covered seeds"), produce a flower every year, followed by a wrapped or jacketed seed, like in an apple or an acorn (my science book says they're wrapped in an "ovary," but I don't want to get into politics—this is a book about woodworking). These are the trees that grow leaves and then shed them in the fall, by and large. Unlike softwoods, these trees have pores through which the tree's metabolism is able to transport nutrition and water from the roots all the way up and out to the leaves. So . . . botany. Not to brag.

The nature of this woodsy digestion system creates a wood flesh that is very dense, which makes it a joy to shape with properly sharpened tools. The hardness also ultimately protects the wood from dings and scratches, which is why these varieties have come to be preferred for furniture items that see a lot of activity, like tables, chairs, and "case goods" (cabinets and chests of drawers).

Not only are the hardwoods hardy, but their colors and grains can be exceptionally beautiful. No matter how schmancy my work ever gets (I dream of the ball-and-claw foot—someday, grasshopper), the most savory moment of any project is when I have successfully constructed my piece, scraped and sanded it to a finish-ready level, and I wipe on the first coat of oil. It is at this moment that the voice of Gandalf resounds in my head—a reverberating "Well done, Master Offerman." It's worth noting that he's not actually complimenting my tool skills, but rather my ever-burgeoning understanding that there is nothing I can do in the shop that will be more impressive and artistic than what Mother Nature has wrought within the wood itself. A successful design (I think) is one that gets out of the way of her magic, because the natural beauty of the wood will always earn more "oohs" and "oh mys" than my band saw feats, however nimble they may be.

A note on trees: People often express to me the misapprehension that woodworkers must be responsible for the murder of a lot of trees. This notion would be false. Most of the woodworkers I know are mellow souls who love to experience the woods and the outdoors in general, as our lives tend to pursue a rhythm somewhat in step with that of nature. For this reason, we *love* the forest, and are loath to ever cut down an august tree for any reason, including turning it into furniture.

Half of the wood we use at Offerman Woodshop comes from local California sources, mainly small woodcutters who are called when trees come down in storms or need to be removed because of construction or disease. The other half comes from our local dealer, Bohnhoff Lumber, which responsibly acquires their wood products from Forest Stewardship Council–approved sources around the globe. If sustainably maintained, a stand of hardwood trees actually benefits from careful thinning, known in England as maintaining a coppice. If you know where to look, there is available wood in every nook and cranny of civilization. Farms often have old piles of timber secreted away in that disused corncrib, and in the city, one simply needs to comb the alleyways, basements, construction sites, and junkyards. I fell in league with a couple of contractors who let me bring in a crew to salvage the framing timbers from a couple of old houses they were tearing down, yielding truckloads of old-growth Douglas fir. Anytime we can utilize recycled lumber, we do, as it is usually of a higher quality and/or it has

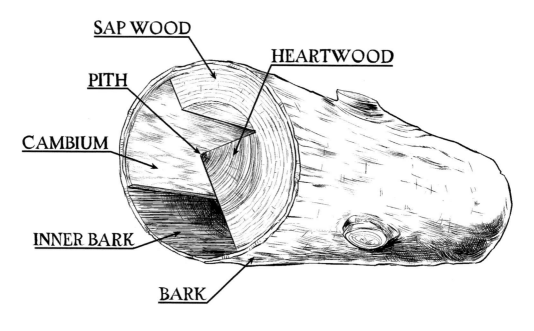

SAP WOOD

HEARTWOOD

PITH

CAMBIUM

INNER BARK

BARK

desirable "character" like nail holes or handsome wear and tear. Most importantly, working with salvaged timber means we're doing our part to keep the forests from being completely denuded.

TREE JAZZ

Ideally, the sawyer (the person at the sawmill turning trees into lumber) is looking for a gorgeous *boule*—a straight section of trunk, from the top of the roots until it splits into limbs, preferably with no branches. This straight section of growth holds the best possibility for straight grain with no knots, bends, or other defects that can make cutting more difficult. As you may know, the layers of wood accumulate in concentric rings, with each ring representing a year of growth. Therefore, if you cut the tree off in cross section, it looks like the first drawing.

It stands to reason, then, that depending upon how you orient those rings as they are passed through a mill saw, the resultant ring lines, or grain, will determine the stability and the aesthetic qualities of the cut board.

Examine the cut end of a board, seeing what we call the end grain: If it runs more horizontally across the board, that is known as flat-sawn timber, which is more prone to cupping and twisting, but can yield beautiful patterns known as cathedrals.

Conversely, if the grain runs perpendicular to the face of the board, this is known as quarter-sawn material, which is considered the most structurally stable. The grain will appear as tight parallel lines, which is quite handsome in its own right. Quarter-sawn material is so called because the log is cut into quarters before being sliced into boards.

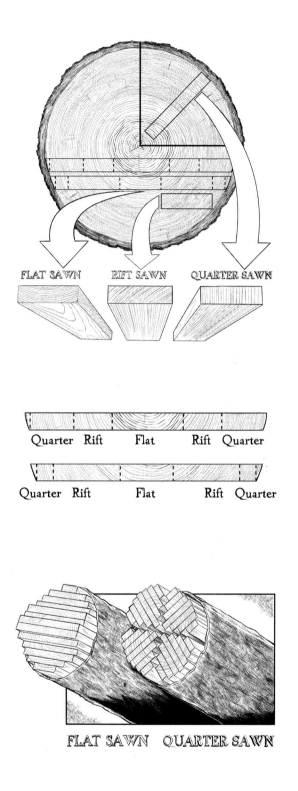

FLAT SAWN   RIFT SAWN   QUARTER SAWN

Quarter   Rift   Flat   Rift   Quarter

Quarter   Rift   Flat   Rift   Quarter

FLAT SAWN   QUARTER SAWN

Splitting the difference are rift-sawn sticks, in which the grain falls across the end of the board at around 45 degrees. This grain is ideal for squared-off furniture parts like table and chair legs, as it combines stability with the attractiveness of equal grain striping down all four sides.

Now let's take a look at this "personality" that wood can exhibit. First of all, attention must always be paid to wood's obdurate tendency to expand and contract with the changing humidity. Simply put, wood is made up of organic fibers that run up and down the tree like drinking straws. I always encourage people to imagine a handful of uncooked spaghetti. If you imagine that spaghetti soaked with water, you know that it won't increase in length nearly as much as it will increase in width—or, put another way, the strands get much fatter than they grow longer. Thus, when the humidity increases, wood fibers drink in water from the air and expand. When the humidity drops, the wood expels water and consequently contracts. This is why the doors and windows in your home might stick shut during humid seasons whilst they swing freely when it's dry outside.

This phenomenon must absolutely be respected at all times, because you cannot defeat this force. The Jedi Knights have nothing on wood movement. To give you an idea of the strength of this ebb and flow, since the time of ancient civilizations like Greece and Egypt, one way to split out massive blocks of granite has been with wood movement. One need only drill strategically located deep holes, pound in a wooden dowel, then soak its end grain with water until the force of the swelling wood fibers actually splits the granite. Amazing.

Therefore, throughout the ages of our education in working with wood, it has been with great respect that men and women have come up with some very clever ways to build furniture that will dependably perform its desired function while allowing the wood to expand and contract according to its wont.

The other critical factor when it comes to inflicting tools upon wood is the grain direction. Unless you're riving green wood with a froe (see Peter Galbert), chances are your grain is not perfectly parallel to your board length. If the grain is even slightly squirrely, it might well run on and off the edge of the board.

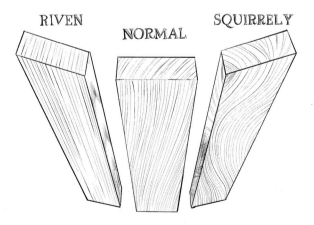

SEASONAL MOVEMENT

Humid — Dry

RIVEN — NORMAL — SQUIRRELY

Let's switch our wood-grain metaphor from a handful of spaghetti to a cat. Cats are nice, right? Sometimes. As you may or may not know, if you pet a cat's fur from head to tail, the hair lies down naturally and the cat likes it. If you rub your hand from tail to head, however, it's unnatural and awkward, the hair fibers stand up uncomfortably, and the cat does *not* like it, at least most of the cats I have known. They call that ill-advised petting rubbing the cat "against the grain." This is because "they" have read my chapter, this very one you're delighting in right now. (I have heard tell of cats that actually enjoy this petting "against nature," and they are actually legally prohibited from using litter boxes in some southern states, but perhaps that will be covered in the next book.)

Similarly, if you take a sharp chisel and shave it along a board in the direction the grain is lying, then it will shave nicely, and if you're very quiet you might even hear the board purr. But if you go "against the grain," then the chisel will catch and tear out the wood or split the board, or hurt your feelings in any number of unfortunate ways.

With this in mind, you should always understand the grain direction in your material and how, then, your tool will address that grain. It's especially crucial when using a planer, jointer, or router, not to mention a chisel, plane, or spokeshave. After you have been brought to tears often enough, it will become a matter of course for you to discern the grain direction every time you're about to lay steel to wood or wood to steel. There are multiple ways to discern the grain direction visually, but the ultimate test is to let the tool tell you if you're right or wrong. If you are indeed in the wrong, then simply flip your piece and address the grain in the opposite direction.

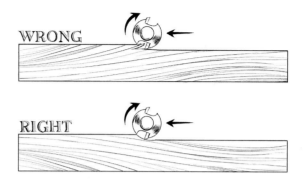

FINISHING

This is the step that occurs after you have given up on hiding any more of your mistakes. There are a multitude of finishes and methods of application: varnishes, polyurethanes, oils, lacquers, shellacs, etc. I have multiple books about it that I really like by Bob Flexner and Michael Dresdner, but our needs are very specific at Offerman Woodshop. If we need to do something outside of our wheelhouse, like spray lacquer onto a massive oak slab table, we job it out to a professional finisher—well worth the cabbage.

In-house, we try to never alter the natural color of the wood—the idea being that there is nothing we can do to improve on what Mother Nature has already done so richly. I also prefer that my wooden creations feel like wood and not like plastic, which is how some of the heavier protective finishes feel to me. For these reasons we usually employ some blend of oil (linseed or tung), varnish, and sometimes beeswax. It's not the fastest way to the finish line, but hand-rubbing an oil finish creates a glowing sheen that is like the glaze on a piece of pecan pie—delicious. It also allows one to triple-check for any missed indiscretions in the sanding/scraping department. The caveat is that an oil finish doesn't provide a level of protection as durable as a urethane or straight spar varnish. If we're making a dining table for a family with kids, or, say, a horde of orcs, then we go ahead and sheath the top in an armored coating of polyurethane, but otherwise we just try to educate our clients in the loving maintenance of beautiful, natural oiled wood.

In Los Angeles, there is a very healthy amount of commerce conducted by interior designers. These individuals can have great taste and be a gas to work with, or they can be total duds. The one thing almost all of them have in common, though, is a learned ambivalence for wood's natural beauty. Don't get me wrong. They are in the business of aesthetics, so they love the look of natural wood as much as the next cusser; they just don't care how it's achieved or whether an ash slab is its natural blonde color or dyed bright orange. I'm not making a judgment, per se; it's just that our shop is not so into the orange ash. Designers like any of it just fine, so long as it serves their palette, but they don't think twice about asking us to discolor wood with stain or dye, or what's worse, bleach it. Bleach the wood. So that it fits the palette. We do it, but we're not smiling as we see the luscious pigment disappear from the wood's surface.

Over the years, we've developed the habit of making up a set of finish samples for a client so that we can all agree on the final appearance before burning through a considerable amount of material and person-hours only to discover that "they didn't think it would be so caramel." We experiment with different recipes to offer our customers a choice of differing levels of sheen and saturation. Designers are dealing with a lot of elements, and they need the furniture to work in an ensemble. I get that, and I mean them no disrespect whatsoever. It's a great talent to be able to design whole rooms so that they look like works of art. I am probably so attracted to unaltered wood tones partially because I have no eye for design myself. My wife, Megan, did our entire house, soup to nuts, and it looks so incredibly good I would think someone much handsomer would live there. Please don't give her any ideas. Of course, our favorite professional designers are the ones who create their palette around *our* work, because those are the rooms in which our furniture gets to be the leading lady.

Whatever finish you choose, don't forget to educate your client about its proper care and maintenance. We always encourage the folks to run their hands over the surfaces, to sensate the handwork that we have lovingly inflicted upon their commissions; to get down and look underneath the table at the subtle details, which they can point out to their guests to indicate that this object has been made by a craftsperson, with her or his own two hands, with love and probably a little mirth.

MILLING

WHEN YOU THINK OF "LUMBER," what does it look like? Where do you picture it? If you depend on a home center or a big, commercial lumberyard for your wood supply, chances are you're paying a premium price for sticks (boards) that have already been surfaced to specific dimensions.

That means you're paying *extra* for a wood surface that's probably less than mediocre at best, on lumber cut to dimensions you didn't get to weigh in on! When I first learned to mill my own material, I felt such a powerful sense of liberation from the corporate overlords of BIG TIMBER. Using their inferior products in the past, I could design furniture that could be made only from one-by and two-by lumber dimensions (or 4 × 4s, if I was feeling beefy). If you have the wherewithal to mill your own lumber, by which I mean the space, the means, and the inclination, your creative opportunities explode into myriad choices exponentially greater than anything a home center can offer.

The first thing you need to find is a source of *rough-sawn lumber.* This term means that the wood has come direct to you from the sawyer, whether he or she is a lumber-mill operator or your great-aunt or -uncle with a chainsaw, cutting trees out behind the corncrib. Your wood

needs to be dried until it's cured and stable, by the rule of one year per inch of thickness. So, if your great-aunt Myrtle slices up a walnut tree into four-inch slabs, those beauties must sit and acclimate for four years before they can be relatively trustworthy to become furniture without warping into a shape resembling a potato chip.

The alternative to air-drying is to use a kiln, which speeds up the process considerably and kills any bugs lurking in your wood. The downside is that using a kiln can cause some color loss.

There is a great lumberyard southeast of Downtown LA called Bohnhoff Lumber, and that's where we go for what is called our dimensional lumber. Instead of the miserly world of the two-by-four (which is actually a mere $1\frac{1}{2}$" by $3\frac{1}{2}$"), dimensional lumber comes in thicknesses listed by the quarter inch—so 6/4 (six-quarter) would be an inch and a half thick, 8/4 (eight-quarter) is two inches, and so forth. The most common dimensions are 4/4 (which finishes down to 3/4, a popular thickness for furniture), 5/4, 6/4, and 8/4. Bohnhoff often carries up to 16/4 of the more popular woods, like maple, oak, and walnut, for those times when—you guessed it—we're feeling beefy.

In another hilarious twist, dimensional lumber is tabulated in units known as *board feet*. Your home center sells lumber by the *linear foot*, which means that a one-by-four, say, will be priced by the foot, for the ease of the customer. That convenience also costs you money. You can slap a tape measure on a board, see that it's nine feet long, multiply that number by the price per foot, and know what you're paying. Easy, right? This is how those establishments make more profit on wood of lesser quality.

A board foot is another animal altogether. It takes into account the thickness, width, and length of a board. The rule of thumb is as follows: One board foot is equal to a board one inch (4/4) thick by twelve inches wide by twelve inches long. A $1" \times 12" \times 12"$, in jobsite parlance. If you multiply those numbers together, you get 144 cubic inches—and that number is your key to understanding board feet. Given the basic unit of $1" \times 12" \times 12"$, now imagine a board that's two inches thick by twelve inches wide by four feet long. Can you tell me how many board feet it contains? If you said 96, you are not right. You might want to check out the charismatic craft of glassblowing. If you said eight board feet, however, then you get it: $2" \times 12" \times 48" = 1,152$ (in.)^3 / 144 = 8 bf.

Sorry to get so mathy on you, but this is a powerful piece of knowledge in unlocking your woodworking destiny. So, one more time: We know that one board foot equals 144 cubic inches. With this number we can discern the number of board feet in any stick of timber, and here is how: Let's take a piece of ash, 8/4 thick by ten inches wide by seventeen feet long. Blorf. I just got exhausted typing even that. Okay, suck it up, Nick, magic time—we need to find the mass of the board; just as how we arrived at the number 144 for a board foot, we now want to multiply the thickness (8/4 or 2") by the width (10") by the length ($17' \times 12" = 204"$), or $2" \times 10" \times 204"$. That math gives me 4,080 cubic inches. Damn, this is going to be an expensive board. Now, to find the number of board feet in this ash board, I divide that number, 4,080, by the board foot number (144), or 4,080 / 144, which equals, if my math is sound, $28\frac{1}{3}$ board feet. Phew. Now you can be strong like bull *and* smart like tractor.

Lee searches for just the right needle.

Here follows some lumberyard etiquette for you. Adhering to this sensibility in a neighborly fashion is very important to the longevity of your relationship with your supplier, so pay close attention.

The next step in chasing smartness involves calling the lumberyard and, using your Sunday manners, kindly inquiring about their board foot prices. You have presumably already determined the pieces that you need for your project and added some dimension in every direction for slop. (Always add thickness, width, and length to your finished dimensions so you can then mill your material to perfection, and give yourself a cushion to make small errors. On top of this, buy an extra stick or two so you can make test joints and/or bigger errors.) Let's say you're buying that ash board from a couple of paragraphs ago. You call the nice lady or fellow and say you're looking for an ash board, 8/4 by ten inches by about seventeen feet. They'll tell you if they have anything in that neighborhood, and also the board foot price. Let's say it's four dollars a board foot, or $4/bd.ft. Rounding up (always round up when pricing wood, or you'll just repeatedly break your own heart) from 28 $\frac{1}{3}$ board feet to 30, that means your ash board will run you about $120 before tax.

Before you even leave your shop, devise your strategy so that you'll know what you're looking for when you arrive. Be ready to ask the yard workers for a size, species, and type of cut, for example: "Hello, Jocephus. Pretty smoggy today, right? Hey, can I please look at some 5/4 quarter-sawn white oak? Then I also need a couple sticks of mahogany, 8/4 flat-sawn, if you have it." The reason for this is because the workers are going to have to disassemble giant towers of wood stacked on pallets and organized by species, just so that you can find your few perfect boards. Do your best to make them stack and unstack as little as possible.

Once you have prepared your grocery list, then make sure you have put together your lumberyard kit:

- gloves for handling splintery surfaces on heavy boards
- chalk/crayon for rough marking
- measuring tape
- block plane
- beverage (Non-alcoholic. Trust me, you'll want your wits about you.)

Once you arrive, make sure you stay out of the way of the big spenders—the contractors who are ordering thousands of board feet instead of your measly seven pieces of carefully chosen wood. After the nice person in the forklift brings you the stack from which you will choose your piece, work quickly and efficiently. Using your tape measure, zero in on the boards that are the right size for your project. Examine every side of them;

don't let a slight twist or a flaw escape your notice at this stage, because you don't want to pay good money for that board only to discover that it's unusable once you have cut it open. An extra set of hands is very valuable at this point, since you may end up sorting through an entire stack to find what you need. Be sure to leave the stacks *better* than you found them. This will keep everybody safe and let the employees know that you respect the hard work they do.

Now that you have chosen some candidates, it's time to up the scrutiny. Mark off the lengths that you like and use your block plane to shave away small sections of the rough surface so you can see what the grain is doing.

You can also use your plane on the end grain to see how the grain lines up in the pieces you have in mind. In this case, Lee is selecting some rift-sawn sections to be used as bedposts. Use your crayon to mark out your choices so you don't lose track.

Once you're ready to check out, the nice lumberyard person uses a special ruler that measures board feet, known as a "lumber rule" or "board rule," to add up your bill by randomly placing dots on a tablet of graph paper. This is not a joke—the tabulation system is inscrutable, which is why it's important to do your math at home beforehand, so you know if it's you being taken for a ride, instead of your lumber. Speaking of, here is Lee's load safely conveyed back to the shop in our trusty Ford F-250 Super Duty diesel. Sometimes it's hard to know whether the truck or the load of hardwood cost me more.

We get our slabs and larger-quantity chunks from a variety of sources, mostly in Northern California. My main source for years was an incredible character named Harold Seward. Now retired, Harold was a juggernaut of a man, who *single-handedly* wielded an ancient Stihl chainsaw with an eight-foot bar and Alaskan mill (an aluminum frame attached to the saw blade, which allows it to make consistent slices like a monstrous cheese slicer). He knew every nook and holler in the low, redwood-covered mountains of Sonoma and Napa Valleys, and kept a mental inventory of which trees had fallen where, and also of which ones were being removed because of construction or sickness. He'd show me a stack of walnut slabs, and I'd ask him how dry they were, and he'd raise his eyebrows and rub his face and say with certainty, "Oh, these are dry as a bone. . . . I just cut 'em a month ago, but the tree was sittin' on the ground for seven years at least." I couldn't tell if Harold was 100 percent sure about the dryness of the trees, given the amount of territory he covered and the number of trees he had lying about in any given month, so I learned to carry a moisture meter, an inexpensive implement that can tell you relatively how much moisture the tree is retaining. That said, he never missed by much. Ol' Harold knew his stuff. At OWS, we look for a reading of 11 percent or lower to trust that the wood is ready to play nice.

Lately there has been a wonderful development in our neighborhood—our pals Jeff Perry and Charles DeRosa have launched an urban tree milling outfit called Angel City Lumber. Sorry, I know I'm pretty low-key, but I am chuffed about this. ANGEL CITY LUMBER!

We're amazed that no one has really officially been doing this in Los Angeles before now. There are a couple of guys with Wood-Mizers around, but no business is centrally located so conveniently, milling up fallen trees in the city so that they might be used by woodworkers, as dimensional lumber as well as table slabs. Sure, we'll miss the eight-hour drive up the 5 Freeway North to Healdsburg in the blistering heat of the Central Valley, but sometimes life is about accepting change. *Chuffed.*

The fellas picked up a Lucas Mill a few months ago and have not stopped cutting up trees all over the county. By taking away the middleman (not to mention the commute to get to the middleman), they are able to offer their material at more affordable prices than larger companies. Most importantly, they are giving these noble hardwood trunks a second life as beautiful furniture, boats, flooring, stringed instruments— you name it. What's more, when the huge masses of wood are saved for another noble round of service, that also keeps them out of the landfill, so if my scorecard is up-to-date, it reads: Win, win, win.

We love what Angel City is doing, not only because we now have a local source of quality furniture woods, but because of the benefits such outfits have on the environment. If concerns both public and private can come to understand the benevolence of tree salvage, then many valuable trees across this fine nation can be saved from the pulper. ACL has been well-served by an earth-conscious relationship with municipalities like the city of Burbank, and we're optimistic that more Los Angeles–area towns will follow suit. You might look into your own locality to see if they are doing anything positive with their fallen trees.

We had acquired a couple of gargantuan trunks of a coastal live oak (talk to Thomas) that were sitting outside the shop for some many, many months. They were awfully good-looking, and left the bystander no doubt what it was we were doing in this warehouse (making trees into smaller pieces), but the landlord was charging us for the parking spots they inhabited, so they were getting less handsome by the month . . .

Charles and Jeff showed up with their super-portable mill and forklift, and together (but mostly them) we sliced those bad boys up into some utterly gorgeous and damn near usable slabs of oak. If my dad had been here he would have undoubtedly paid them his highest compliment: "By god, those fellas were workers." There were so many colors running through this oak, plus a good deal of intensely graphic spalting, that I took to calling it "Ham Fudge," which became the victorious holler of the day, and quite possibly the title of my next book. Here's what that looked like:

Charles sharpens the chain teeth by hand.

Jeff is a rabid Boston sports fan
but paradoxically still seems to know what he's doing.

Charles explains "forward" to me.

Jeff more gently describes "forward."

Ham Fudge, y'all.

MATTHEW MICUCCI

Hear this: I love Matty Micucci (so dubbed when the name "Matt" was already claimed in the shop by my brother). Some years ago, my good friend the master deadpan comedian Tig Notaro contacted me to ask if we might have room at the shop for her friend's brother. He was moving to Los Angeles from New York City, where he had lately been building scenery for the Public Theater. Besides owing Tig a debt of blood that is best left unremarked upon, I must admit I'm a rather soft touch when it comes to anyone who has spent time working in my church of choice, the live theater, and so we corralled young Matt in to get a good look at him. Was he enthusiastic? Sure. Did he seem capable and somehow strapping despite his pole-vaulter's build? Goddamn right. Were we completely freaked out by the devotion he professed for making and operating puppets? We were not. We love puppets; what do you take us for?

He may have arrived with only basic tool skills, but not only has Matty become a vital member of the shop's day-to-day operations, he has become a company leader in productivity. His dependable work and eye for detail, in addition to his elfin sense of whimsy, impress me as well as his customers with great consistency. Every batch of his Pop Tops sells out easily, but it is the popularity of his other, more musical offering that has caused him to be labeled the "Kazoo Tycoon."

NAME: Matty Micucci

FAVORITE TOOL: Lie-Nielsen No. 4 smooth plane

FAVORITE SPORT: Catch with Gus the shop dog

INSTRUMENT: Ukulele, kazoo

PASTA: Rigatoni with meat sauce
(Mamma Micucci's family recipe)

SPIRIT ANIMAL: Buster Keaton

BOOTS: Red Wing

POP TOP

MAKING THE POP TOP

At the time of writing this, I am thirty-three years old. Some people refer to this age as their Jesus year.

However, few people can say they are a thirty-three-year-old woodworker with a beard from Nazareth. Okay, it's Nazareth, Pennsylvania, but still. We have a cheese shop called Cheeses of Nazareth. Get it? It's my super Jesus year.

I never planned on being a woodworker. I'm not "Matt Micucci: Woodworker." I've got a lot of ideas before my time is up (which I hope is longer than Jesus's). But for now, I'm loving making a life by creating with wood.

I grew up working with my dad, Mike. Mike's an electrician by trade but also a skilled welder, mechanic, carpenter, and generally handy guy. He can do anything. He used to take me on jobs as a kid. I handled tools, developed a work ethic, met a multitude of characters known as contractors, and learned about craftsmanship. It wasn't a conscious education. There was a job to get done, and my dad expected me to do it his way—the right way. One of my first jobs was to make all the screws on switch and outlet plates straight and horizontal, to learn precision. The small details are important, just like in art.

A few years ago, Pop, as I call him, came out to California to visit and spend a few days with me at the shop. It was a terrific feeling having him there, working side by side. I've gained a lot of skills since my days leveling switch-plate screws in Pennsylvania. I wanted to develop a new product to sell on the OWS website, and I knew my pop would be able to help. We came up with the OWS Pop Top.

Why make a Pop Top? Bottle openers are a dime a dozen. There are a lot of great designs out there, mass-produced with business logos as promotional knickknacks. I wanted to create something that was simple in design that any layperson could fashion. Since the late 1800s, when William Painter invented the modern-day bottle cap, workers have been cracking open bottles of suds with scraps around the jobsite. Pop and I created a tool: a piece of wood with a hole and a nail. It's a highly simple device. There are small bits of engineering, but it's minimal. The aesthetic of it allows for whatever wood you're using to be featured without screaming out its purpose. It's just a cool piece of wood with a nail. Watch how it opens a delicious craft beer with ease. Bam.

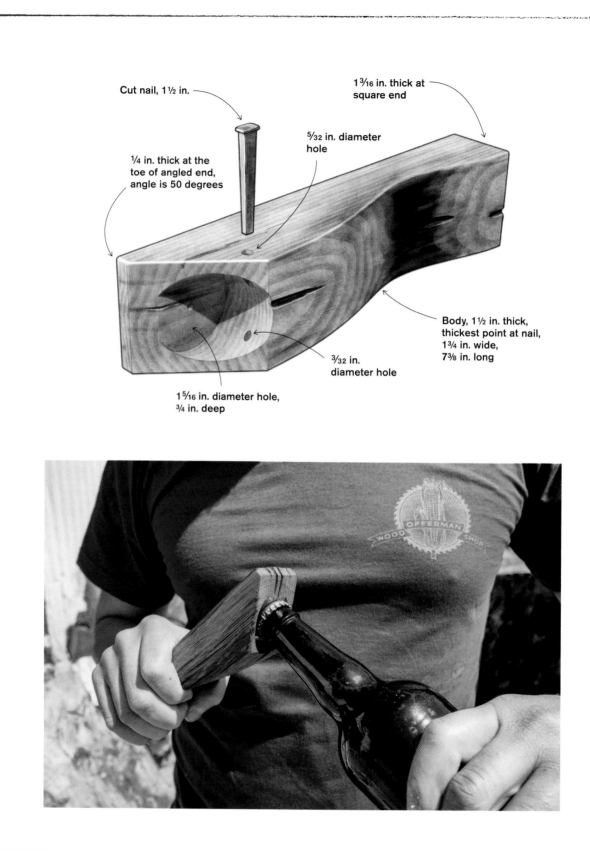

Cut nail, 1½ in.

1 3/16 in. thick at square end

5/32 in. diameter hole

¼ in. thick at the toe of angled end, angle is 50 degrees

Body, 1½ in. thick, thickest point at nail, 1¾ in. wide, 7⅜ in. long

3/32 in. diameter hole

1 5/16 in. diameter hole, ¾ in. deep

1. Choose a piece of sturdy wood. Some kind of hardwood. Oak, walnut, maple, and ash are all good options. I chose a piece of reclaimed white oak. I think the piece has a lot of character, with its natural patina and oxidized nail holes. Plus, it's always nice to recycle instead of tossing an offcut into the trash.

2. Lay out the design with the grain running the length of the piece. You want something that will fit nicely in your hand. I used the natural grain contours of the scrap piece of oak to help inspire the layout. Of course the design is up to the maker, but I wouldn't make it any shorter than 5". You'll want enough leverage to "pop a top."

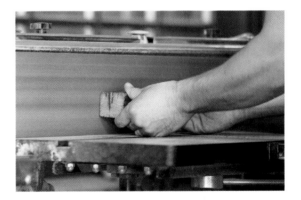

3. When it's time to rough cut your shape, you have two options. Here at OWS we have a beautiful band saw to use. However, a jigsaw works just as well. If you choose the latter, make sure your piece is securely clamped to a sturdy work surface.

4. Horizontal sand next to square up the sides. It doesn't have to be perfect, but it's nice to have at least one flat surface for the upcoming steps. A block plane will also do the trick.

5. Draw a centerline along the length of the bottom of your piece, then make a mark ⅞" from the business end. Using your mark as a center, use a 1 ⁵/₁₆" Forstner bit to drill a hole to a depth of ¾". The idea is to make a hole large enough to fit a bottle and cap along with some extra wiggle room. If the hole is too shallow, you won't have enough clearance to get a bite on the cap to pry it open.

6. Make a mark ¼" down across the top front of the opener. Below the mark, use the chop saw or band saw with miter gauge to cut off an angle somewhere in the neighborhood of 50 to 55 degrees. Again, it doesn't have to be a precise 50 degrees. If it were a truck, you'd be cutting off the front bumper. You'll just want enough of an angle so the cap doesn't get trapped inside the hole. Other options for cutting this angle would be a jigsaw or crosscut handsaw. Whatever gets the job done proficiently and safely. As Nick says, "It's not furniture!"

7. Measure back 1 5/16" from the front of the piece. Using a square, drop a line down the side of the opener and make a mark ¼" from the bottom. Drill a 5/32" hole only on the side of the opener for the nail. I use a square-cut nail since it looks "old-timey." You can use any nail that will give you a bite on a bottle cap—so nothing too fat in diameter. You see, the nail is acting as a prying device and is not actually securing anything. You want to drill a hole on the side large enough to accommodate the circumference of the nail. If you were to just hammer it through this close to the edge, it would most likely crack or break the edge.

8. Sand and ease the edges of the bottle opener. I like it to have a nice hand feel, so I make sure there are no sharp edges and that it generally feels comfortable. How well it should be sanded and shaped is entirely up to the maker.

MATTHEW MICUCCI: POP TOP

9. Place the nail through the hole you drilled on the side and tap gently to mark where it lands.

10. Using pliers, trim the nail to length, about ⅛" shy of the full width of the piece. You don't want the nail to poke out the other end, so be as precise as possible. Always wear your eye protection. The bits of metal can go flying.

11. Using the mark you made with the nail point, use a ³/₃₂" bit to drill out a hole to receive the end of the nail. This prevents blowout when you tap the nail home, but be sure not to drill through the other side. Choose a bit size slightly smaller than your nail tip. This hole is also smaller than the first hole since I'm using square-cut nails and they have a taper. I want a tight fit so that the nail doesn't pull out when there is stress applied.

12. Apply a dab of two-part epoxy to secure the nail tip.

13. Hammer the nail fully into place. Tap it in gently. You want it seated snugly.

14. Apply finish. You'll want a durable finish, as it's likely the wood will get wet. I would stay away from any lacquers—lacquer is a great finish, but it's dissolvable by alcohol. I like to use some kind of poly. It's easy to apply and leaves a hard finish. Two coats should do the trick.

The Best Way to Fell a Tree

STEP 1: You'll want a friend. Burly, if possible.

STEP 2: Now you need the proper gear.

STEP 3: All geared up? Better get some fuel in the tank.

STEP 4: Head for the unknown.

STEP 5: Get your kit on. You need to look the part.

STEP 6: Actually, before you get suited up, make sure you put on some sunscreen.

STEP 7: Now you're ready to have some fun.

STEP 8: Sharpening your axe can be pleasurable.

STEP 9: Photo time!

STEP 10: Seize the moment.

STEP 11: Pay the Lady.

STEP 12: A job well done.

KRYS SHELLEY

I'll tell you right to your face—I love Krys. As you'll soon learn, we have our perennial scout Lee to thank for finding our newest champion, recognizing her talent and desire to do good work, and wooing her to stay at the shop.

Hailing originally from nearby Cerritos, California, Krys had seen some rather unusual twists in her life's path before arriving at Offerman Woodshop to brighten our days. I'm charmed by the fact that our book's contributors represent the people of California, Northern (Lee, Josh) and Southern (Krys); New Mexico (Michele); Kentucky (Thomas); Pennsylvania (Matty); New York (Jane); and from Illinois, a trio of well-meaning Offerman mules. No matter where a body grows up, one can find a happy and productive career in the realm of making things with one's hands.

Ever an example of sunny morale, Krys is always at the shop before me, and that's pretty impressive when I arrive at six A.M. During those quiet morning hours (when we're not on the planer), with coffee or tea, Krys tells me how her "Honey" is doing, and then I tell her how mine is faring. There is something comforting about Krys, in her immediate affection for anyone, even a person's family members she hasn't met. We also often share our gratitude for the gift of good work with which to fill our days. In both of our lives we have come to understand that making something that we like—whisky coasters or canoes or the many things in between—can keep us on the path to a fruitful time on this earth and help us to avoid the pitfalls of vice (which is more in reference to myself than Krys), and that will, in turn, keep our Honeys satisfied as well.

NAME: Krystal "Krys" Shelley

PETS: I used to and I want one, but I don't have one . . . HELP!!!

RAPPER DJ NAME: Prince "Pum Pum"

FAVORITE SPORT: Velodrome racing, tennis

SPIRIT ANIMAL: Butterfly, hummingbird, tiger

FAVORITE FOOD: Homemade pizza with BACON

FAVORITE THING TO DO: Cook and sing

PENCIL HOLDER

MAKING THE PENCIL HOLDER

Hi, my name is Krystal Shelley. I am a thirty-two-year-old gender-nonconforming person who goes by Krys, and I've been working with OWS for close to three years now. In the year 2000, at only seventeen years old, I was sentenced to twelve years in prison for second-degree carjacking as a juvenile. While inside I obtained my janitorial license as well as my high school diploma, so I felt I was ready for the challenges of the world upon my release.

During my time in Valley State Prison for Women, I was introduced to Colby Lenz, who is a legal advocate/volunteer with the California Coalition for Women Prisoners (CCWP). Colby came to visit me for eight years, and through those visits Colby and I became friends—actually more like family. Upon my release in 2012 Colby played a huge part in the lives of my partner and me, and still does. CCWP helped us with housing, job searching, and all the other necessities needed to survive out here on these mean LA streets. Ha ha!!!

In the summer of 2012 I attended a community event where I met Lee (one of Colby's good friends). We talked for a while, and upon ending the conversation I asked if they had any work at the woodshop we had talked about. Lee said she would check, and soon she got back to me and said yes. My first job was pulling nails (which was also my first time working with wood, lol)—so simple but so satisfying. I was excited about going to the shop, but I wasn't called back for a while, so immediately I thought I had done something wrong. It wasn't until one year later that I was called back into the shop to work with Lee on making pencil holders. . . . Boy, oh boy, was I excited to be making pencil holders with Lee!

One thing I love about making them is the different images that appear in the grain and the colors of each individual wood chunk. One time there was a scene that looked like Halloween, with a scary moon that jumped out as I cut the piece and prepared to drill it. It keeps me engaged to find the best side for flattening (pencil holders can't wobble!) while still featuring the most beautiful side for viewing.

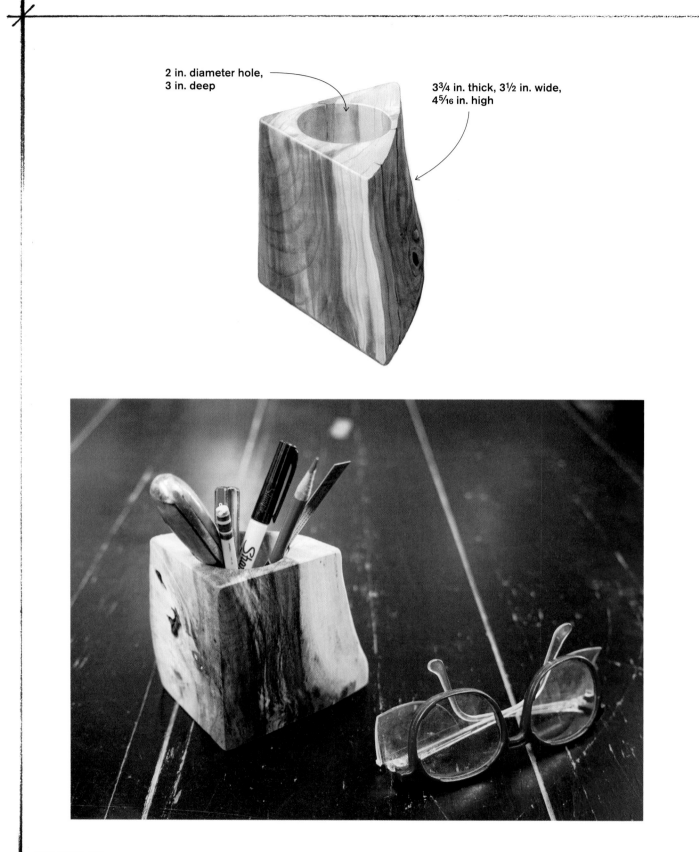

2 in. diameter hole, 3 in. deep

3¾ in. thick, 3½ in. wide, 4⁵⁄₁₆ in. high

2. Mark cut lines at around 3½" wide.

3. Rip strips at 3½" wide on the band saw.

1. One blank should be around 3½" square by about 4½" tall. I make several at a time, so I start with a length of rough timber and cut my blanks off one at a time. Rough cut your piece, cutting off unusable edges and ends. You'll be hogging out a big hole, so choose a relatively soft wood. Italian poplar, cottonwood, or buckeye are our faves.

KRYS SHELLEY: PENCIL HOLDER

4. Crosscut strips on the band saw to 4½" chunks. If you don't have a band saw, you can cut the blank with a hand saw; just make sure you clamp it securely.

5. Drill a 3"-deep hole in the center of the flat top with a 2" Forstner bit in your drill press. If you have no drill press, you can use a vise and a hand drill with a large spade bit or a small hole saw. **NICK: You can make several smaller holes instead of one large one that will still handsomely hold your pencils.** Be sure to clamp your block securely. Turn down your drill speed and raise the bit often to clear chips from the hole.

6. Using the horizontal sander, sand sides along the grain at 150 grit.

7. Flap sand the live edge using a sanding star.

8. Sand all sides and edges to 220.

9. Finish with poly. I do two coats, with a light sanding between coats, and then paste wax.

LAURA ZAHN

One of the big questions frequently put to me is how can a body make a living as a woodworker? "Sure, it's the finest possible pastime known to mammals with opposable thumbs, but how can I have woodworking as my full-time job?" Well, I would confidently answer that I have no idea. It's probably a more competitive field, with many fewer sources of lucrative remuneration than even showbiz, which everybody knows is one of the most foolish vocations to pursue. Before the Industrial Revolution (and Amazon), the human race

necessarily depended upon a lot more hand skills to supply their households with life's necessities: clothing, furniture, alcoholic beverages, etc. The vast majority of these men and women were not woodworkers, per se, nor tailors, nor brewers or distillers, yet they still successfully provided themselves and their families with the required implements of daily life. Like beer.

I then proffer this notion: Let's not, as a people, aspire to become professional makers. Let us instead endeavor to reclaim the honest skills of our forebears, those of the needle and the hand plane, the stewpot and the still. We can then still hold down the jobs that make the world go 'round, whilst occupying our leisure time, as Ben Franklin would have it, in the pursuit of self-

improvement. If all the butchers, bankers, candlestick makers, brokers, and bloggers would begin to hand-make some useful items in their spare time, I vow that every neighborhood would become much healthier than they now appear. When one of us produces eggs and dairy products and barters them for a sewing chore, and another bakes pastries to be swapped for tomatoes and an Offerman Woodshop cutting board, we are enriched not only by the material exchange, but by the caring engendered by the codependence. The more we care about our neighbors, the less likely we are to commit violence toward them, of any stripe. As Wendell Berry says, "It all turns on affection."

Many woodworkers, myself included, come to

LAURA ZAHN

the practice in something of a vacuum. In many cases, those of us who catch the obsessive bug for crafting things from wood have been left to our own devices to find instruction and sources for tools and materials. Of course, the advent of the Internet has made all of this much easier to accomplish, but even if one gleans a great wealth of information from the online community of makers, woodworking can still be a lonely pursuit. As I have often stated, learning any physical discipline will always be much easier to achieve under the in-person guidance of someone who has been down the road before you.

Enter Laura Zahn. A redoubtable young lady (b. 1981) who grew up in a military family with its very solid roots in North Dakota farming and lumber work, she hails from dependable traditions of self-sufficiency that make me swell with pride even just having her for a neighbor. Between her parents and their parents, they indoctrinated in her a love of homespun superpowers like mechanical repair, woodworking, needlework, leatherwork, painting, upholstery . . . you know, homemaking.

Because of her dad's itinerant military lifestyle (moving to a new home every couple of years), she felt disconnected from her solid, extended family in the Midwest, and so "working with my hands was my way of keeping that connection. . . . I've been around woodworking (and that ethic/mind-set/way of life) my whole life."

Her collegiate accomplishments bespeak the fact that her heart is soundly in the right place. This winning young American got her BA from the College of William & Mary in Human Biology, Health and Society, then went on to receive an MA from UCLA in Urban Planning with a concentration in Environmental Analysis and Policy, before attending the woodworking school at College of the Redwoods. When she arrived in Los Angeles, she wanted to be around other woodworkers in a collaborative environment so she could continue learning and growing. After a year of fruitless searching for such a place, she found our own Offerman Woodshop and rented some bench space. Even though she used the shop mostly at night and on the weekends, she fell in love with the space itself and the quietude it brought to her life. So much so that the face of LA woodworking was about to get a lift:

Being at OWS was dreamy, but I had this idea kicking around in the back of my head to be able to offer to other furniture makers what I was looking for when I first moved back to LA—bench space, access to machines, and a community of like-minded people. I saw a space I liked on Craigslist, I visited it, and soon after I was handing over a large wad of cash for a security deposit and first month's rent. I took out a very small business loan and got two credit cards that didn't have interest for eighteen months to finance the operation. I was working a full-time job, and Allied Woodshop was born on a very limited budget with the time that I had to work on it—early mornings, evenings, and on the weekends.

The 3,000-square-foot space she secured was on the tenth floor of a building from the 1920s in Downtown Los Angeles called the Allied Crafts Building. A real go-getter by the name of Florence Casler had built it, and several others like it, at a time when such an accomplishment by a woman was unthinkable in America. She was an innovator of "vertical manufacturing," in which all the processes of any given industry, like printing, would be housed on different floors of the same building, for as she put it: "Why, Los Angeles is to be a big city, and we've got to have space for our industries to grow." Florence Casler was forward thinking and dauntless, just like our Ms. Zahn.

Walking into the expansive space, I am aware of a timeless quality, as it's easy to imagine rows of sewing machines and textile laborers set against the backdrop of enormous windows. The views showcase a vast expanse of sky and city, promoting a feeling that Zahn describes as "inspirational and aspirational," which she says is very important in a creative space. "It's such a lovely place to be and it really takes on the mood of the city around it. On gray, overcast days the shop feels quiet and pensive. The spectacular, cool sunny days of winter impart a real energy. Everything slows down in the summer when the shop is filled with the heat from the pavement

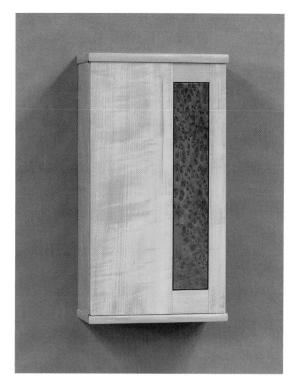

below. My favorite time in the shop is just as the sun starts to recede and the space glows with the colors of the setting sun."

Speaking further about the shop's setting in the Garment District, Laura said that she is afforded two main inspirations: First, the other businesses sharing the Allied building, in which a Spanish-speaking labor force works way too hard for way too little pay, inspire her to maintain her own work ethic; and second, all the absolute garbage for sale down in the storefronts lining the streets—garish hats, short-sleeved cowboy shirts, knock-off designer shoes, cheap bras, you name it—reminds her to remain steadfast in doing her part to keep from adding any further fodder to the landfills.

The Allied Woodshop collective sports

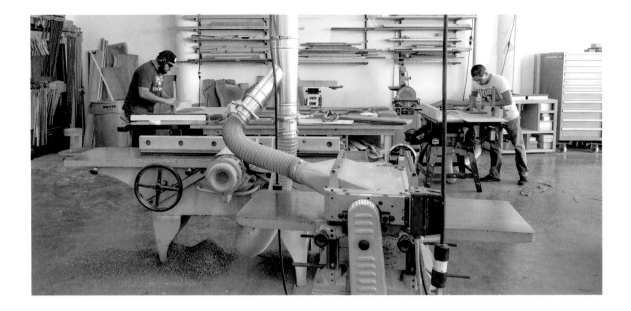

benches for five full-time and four part-time woodworkers, with a second room loaded full of vintage cast-iron machines, like a 20" Davis & Wells band saw and a 12" Yates-American jointer, both more than eighty years old. As fellow captains of woodworking collectives, we commiserated about the ups and downs of having many hands sharing space and machinery. You can see from the meticulously maintained tools and neatly organized benches that she has her ducks in a row, and those ducks know where to find the dustpan. With her collective neatly organized and all the machine tables properly waxed, Zahn then has time to pursue her own furniture work, doing business as Off the Saw, which is also the name of a popular woodworking blog she has been writing since her days at College of the Redwoods.

Laura also supplements her own woodworking habit with jobs teaching woodworking classes, both at the Allied Woodshop and at California State University at Long Beach, and consulting on climate-change policy. She does a lot of very good quality thinking, and I was very inspired by our conversation about the state of the modern woodworker and her/his ability to make a livable income. She told me that the joke about the venerated College of the Redwoods program is that "they take perfectly good carpenters and ruin them. . . . The program at CR is more like an amazing escape from the real world, where people can learn what is possible when you take your time in woodworking—I mean, you spend your first four days learning to sharpen, and flattening a board with hand planes." Now she designs pieces on a budget of time and money, and sees how much of that fine Krenovian detail (as in James Krenov, the founder of the school) she can work into her furniture. A table base that she just made is sitting next to me, and I can attest from the delicate stretcher tenons protruding from the legs, complete with twin blonde wedges, that she is still manifesting the fairylike detail of CR in her Los Angeles practice.

If you've been paying attention so far, the gratifying part of running a shop like hers should be pretty easy to discern: You get to use a bunch of nice, tuned-up machines and hand tools and benches to make beautiful works of art and craft from plain old wooden boards. You also get to do it with like-minded folks, who are usually kind of weird but generally respectful of the craft.

The challenges are more insidious and tough to get a handle on. Laura says that a lot of people have the desire to learn woodworking but lack the price of admission for a workshop or class. She said it's especially heartbreaking when someone's child wants to learn to work in the shop but the tuition is  not at hand. She also voiced her desire to educate the American people as to the *value* of this work. One thing she loves about her classes is that after one nine-to-four day of Intro to Woodworking, the newbies are *astonished* at how much work goes into preparing a simple rectangular "cutting board," from rough milling to squaring to surfacing and finally finishing. Only then do they comprehend why custom work must be so expensive when compared to factory-made items.

This launched us into a vitriolic conversation on one of my favorite gripes: the ignorance of the American people to blinding consumerism. We hit on the fine analogy of our bovine populace's willingness to shovel in fast food even after reading the clearly written reports of journalists like Eric Schlosser and Michael Pollan, enlightening us to just exactly what sort of poisons these charlatans put into their burgers and fries. Laura said that she would like to see such a piece written on furniture and home goods and clothing, informing us all of the impact that this cheaply made landfill fodder must be having on our planet. Often enough, if a woodworker hasn't yet thrown in the towel but is still producing work, then she seems to come down on the side of optimism, and Laura Zahn is no exception. "I feel like there is a growing awareness of this problem, and that's why more people are looking to learn to do things and make things for themselves."

I am tickled that spaces like Laura's Allied Woodshop are springing up all over the country, where folks from all walks of life can scrape together a few bucks to learn woodworking and other crafts. If you are interested yourself, either find a group near you or start your own. You'll be amazed at how much better two heads can be than one, especially if that one is rather melon shaped and grows a good set of whiskers. If Offerman Woodshop were the Ingalls family on *Little House on the Prairie*, then Laura Zahn would be our Mr. Edwards (Victor French)—the most valued and dependable neighbor to whom we can turn when we want to see our community grow and prosper by the labor of our hands.

KAZOO

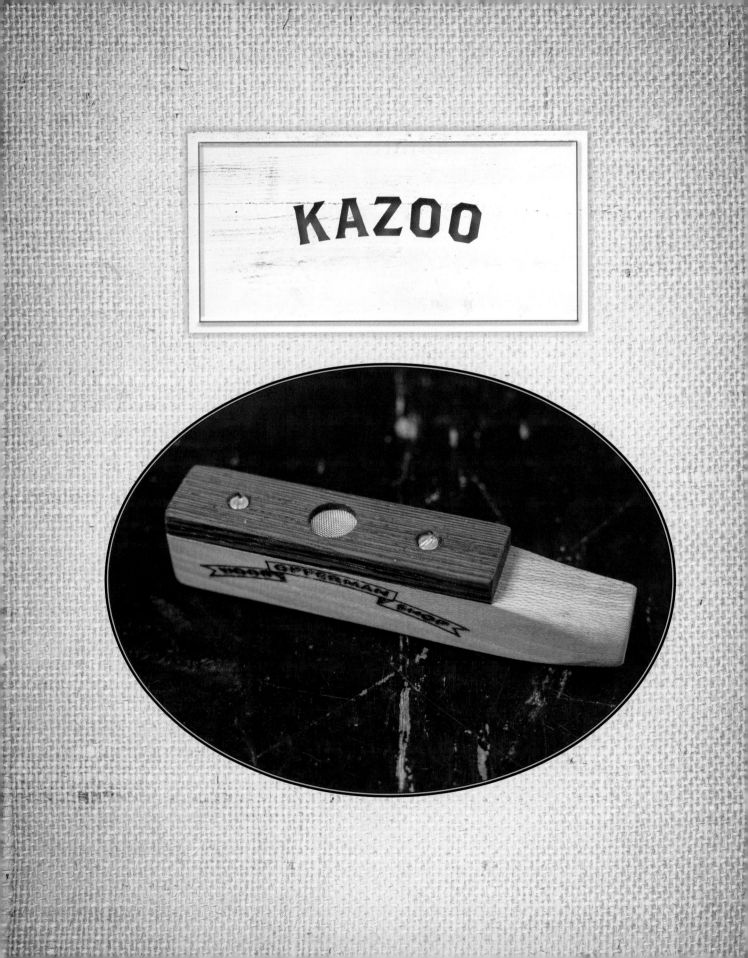

MAKING THE KAZOO

For years I've kept a red plastic kazoo in my ukulele case. I think kazoo solos are funny. Kazoos themselves are funny instruments. If you can hum a tune, then you can play a damn fine kazoo solo. Five minutes of practice and you could give Kenny G a run for his money. Of course, there is very little respect given to the "miracle pocket saxophone" for that very reason. It's easy. So what? Nothing in life is easy! Why can't we appreciate the simple joys of something so small and delightful? The kazoo demands some respect! Gosh darn it!

I'm sorry about that rant. You see, the kazoo hits very close to home. Not to talk too much about my little hometown of Nazareth, Pennsylvania, but wouldn't you know it, they hold a kazoo parade every Fourth of July. That's right. Talk about RESPECT! Hundreds of folks gather at the local high school wearing red, white, and blue, and they march through town playing patriotic music on kazoos. It's a sight to be seen and heard. My sister, Kate, was even the grand marshal one year, complete with an Uncle Sam costume. Sometimes when you embrace the silliness of something and take it seriously, you can find a lot of joy.

I started making wooden kazoos at OWS back in 2012. There wasn't really a job for me, so I was hanging around the shop for a few months, just cleaning the bathroom, sweeping the floors, and occasionally sanding. I quit my restaurant job (they hated me anyway) and started tinkering with making a wooden kazoo. When I had a prototype, I showed Nick and Lee. I believe Nick said, "That is so stupid. I love it!"

Years later I have graduated to helping make furniture here at OWS, but if it weren't for the kazoo, who knows where I'd be today? Respect.

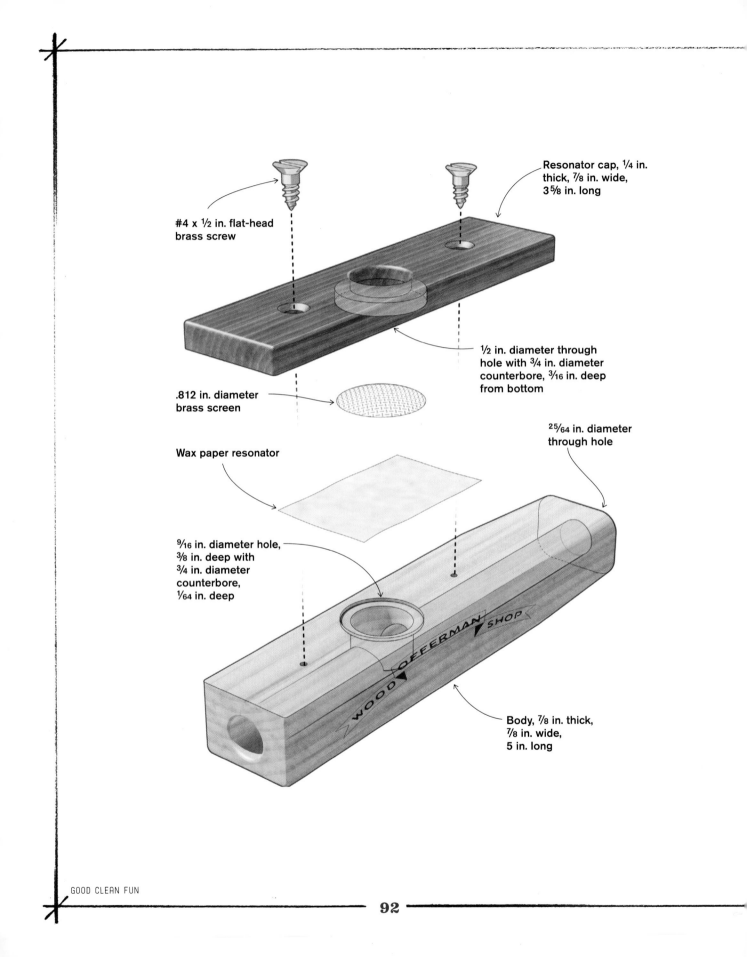

Resonator cap, 1/4 in. thick, 7/8 in. wide, 3 5/8 in. long

#4 x 1/2 in. flat-head brass screw

1/2 in. diameter through hole with 3/4 in. diameter counterbore, 3/16 in. deep from bottom

.812 in. diameter brass screen

25/64 in. diameter through hole

Wax paper resonator

9/16 in. diameter hole, 3/8 in. deep with 3/4 in. diameter counterbore, 1/64 in. deep

WOOD OFFERMAN SHOP

Body, 7/8 in. thick, 7/8 in. wide, 5 in. long

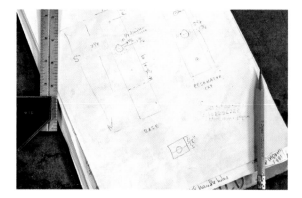

1. Sketch your design. I found a cheap plastic kazoo and took it apart to get the idea.

2. Select your wood. I went with sycamore and wenge for the nice contrasting colors, but I also like to use poplar for the body. You can really use any wood you like.

3. Mill the body (sycamore) ⅞" × ⅞".

4. Crosscut the body piece to 5".

5. Mill the wenge—or whatever you're using for the kazoo's resonator cap—to ¼" × ⅞".

6. Crosscut the wenge to 3⅝".

7. Draw diagonals on the end of the sycamore blank to find center.

8. Now you need to lay out the location of the sound hole. Draw a centerline, like a spine, down the top of the sycamore blank. Measure 1$\frac{13}{16}$" from the far end (not the mouthpiece end) of the sycamore, and make a mark, which will be the center of your sound hole.

9. Now similarly make a mark at 1$\frac{13}{16}$" on the center of both the top and bottom of the resonator cap. On the top you'll also want to make a mark $\frac{3}{4}$" in from either end for your screw holes.

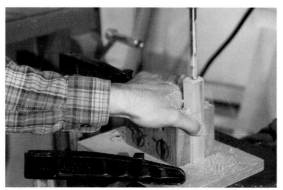

10. Using a safe setup, drill out the center of the sycamore with a $\frac{25}{64}$" brad point bit. If you don't have a $\frac{25}{64}$" drill bit, you can use a $\frac{3}{8}$" instead. Be very careful that your blank is perfectly plumb in both directions.

11. On the 1¹³/₁₆" center mark of the sycamore blank, use a ¾" diameter Forstner bit to drill about ¹/₆₄" deep. This just makes an indentation to allow the resonator (wax paper) room to vibrate.

12. Now, using the same setup, change over to a ⁹/₁₆" Forstner bit and drill to a depth of ³/₈".

13. On to the resonator cap. Using the top center point, drill a ½" Forstner hole halfway through your wenge resonator cap (about ⅛").

14. Using the same setup, flip the wenge over and use a ¾" Forstner bit to drill to a depth of ³/₁₆". This creates a recess in the cap for housing the brass screen. Drilling the two resonator holes in this order will reduce the chances of blowout in your pretty topside.

15. Place the wenge cap in the correct position on the body and use either double-stick tape or a right-angle jig (like me) to hold the pieces together in place for drilling. Predrill and countersink the two remaining holes marked on the surface of the wenge for two #4 × ½" flat-head brass screws. I like to drill pilot holes slightly shy of the thickness of the screw's shaft, which I measure between the threads with a dial caliper. These screws have a shaft thickness of $^5/_{64}$", so I use a $^1/_{16}$" bit before countersinking.

16. Assemble the chassis using your brass screws to make sure everything lines up. Brass is soft, so don't use a screw gun, and add a little wax to the threads.

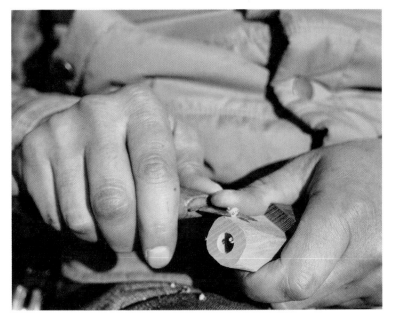

17. Carve and shape the mouthpiece. Use caution when carving, always directing the force away from your body.

18. Hand sand the whole kazoo and ease the edges, starting with 120 and working up to 220 grit.

19. Brand your logo or initials (optional).

20. I like to sand the inside of the body to smooth out any rough spots left from the machining steps. An easy way to achieve this is by wrapping a piece of sandpaper around a dowel that is chucked into a drill.

21. I finish both pieces top and bottom with Emmet's Good Stuff. Once it's fully dry, I give the mating faces of the wenge and the sycamore a coat of wax so they won't stick together after assembly.

22. Almost done! Here I insert a .812"-diameter brass screen, which you can purchase at your local head shop, by pressing it into the hole in the bottom side of the resonator cap. This screen is a handsome way to protect the wax paper resonator. **NICK:** The Offerman Woodshop kazoo is not designed for use as a smoking implement for any tobacco products or other smokable goodness. Use an apple.

23. Carefully disassemble the kazoo. Now cut wax paper into a large enough rectangle to cover the kazoo hole. You can also use thin plastic from a shopping bag, etc. This membrane will serve as the kazoo's resonator.

24. Place the resonator cap on and trim the resonator (wax paper) with a razor blade.

25. Play your heart out.

JIMMY DiRESTA

In 2007 my wife, Megan, was hired to perform the role of Elizabeth in *Young Frankenstein* on Broadway for Mel Brooks himself (she was astonishing, and the show was top-drawer), so we moved to New York to allow our marriage to accommodate the run of the show. I was excited, since I had not ever gotten to live there for more than a week or two at a time. I brought a bag of hand tools with me, hoping to use the time away from my shop and my client base to finally build my first canoe. The first requirement was finding a shop space large enough to house the

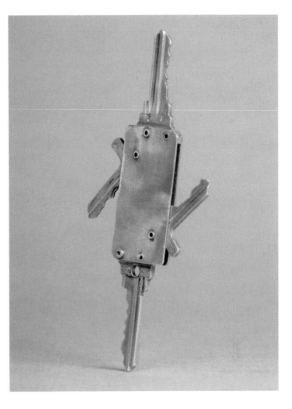

construction of an eighteen-foot-long boat, and so I set off to find the perfect barn in the middle of our country's most expensive real estate market.

My first stop was at the Lower East Side shop of Jimmy DiResta, whom I had heard about from his brother John "Johnny Two Shows" DiResta, with whom I had worked on a Comedy Central program called *American Body Shop*. I made my way down ancient stone steps through a trapdoor in the sidewalk to find Jimmy's wonderland of tools and materials. I was smitten immediately, like any shop rat would have been, by the clear evidence that this dungeon-like setting was home to an impressive amount of creative productivity. Before long, we were jawing away

like we had known each other forever, excitedly discussing our histories with tools and projects and triumphs and mishaps. His curiosity and enthusiasm are infectious, especially because, although others know him primarily as a woodworker, he claims no specialty—beyond "making," that is. He'll discuss an intricate job of welding a display case with the same fervor as weaving a basket out of recycled cloth strips. What was immediately clear was that he just loves to make things.

Born in 1967, Jimmy grew up on Long Island under the guiding hand of his dad, Joe, a hard-working blue-collar handyman. His early education is still paying off because the handyman (or -woman) can claim no

specialization. He or she needs to have the tools and know-how at the ready to deal with any problem a job site might effect: plumbing, electric, roofing, masonry, carpentry, stained glass, landscaping, heating, you name it. Jimmy took to these skills naturally, finding himself obsessed with every sort of material and how it can be used to create anything and everything in the physical world. His bedrock knowledge was that of a handyman, but it was his sculptor's heart that altered his life's pursuit from mending pipes and construction timbers to turning those materials into works of art. In 1990, Jimmy graduated from the School of Visual Arts in Manhattan and found himself working as an inventor and designer of toys, which makes a lot of sense. He has an innate talent for concocting clever and whimsical notions out of thin air, which makes him the perfect mad scientist for thinking up new toy ideas. Suddenly he was back and forth between the States and China, overseeing production of his different toy creations.

Unfortunately, as you might imagine, the toy business is not unlike show business in that *business* is the root word of the phrase. Jimmy soon left the unpleasantly fast-paced world of commercial toys for the comparatively idyllic life, however sweaty, of a New York City artist. In 1998 he began teaching at SVA, his alma mater. His class, which he continues to teach as of the time of this writing, is entitled 3D Design. In it he simply passes along his knowledge and inspiration to his students: "Imagine that shape in space, and fill in

Before

After

that shape in space. If you use wood, you use wood; if you use paper, you use paper. Papier-mâché, Styrofoam, whatever." In this day and age, armed with a seemingly limitless wealth of information and materials, one can find instruction on how to make a vast array of items. Jimmy is very inspiring in his class (which I have crashed) when he encourages us all to let go of convention. The students were making lamps when I visited, and they were devilishly crafty, which made each and every one of them uniquely delightful.

Every time I visit Jimmy in New York we (a) get coffee, (b) catch up on our ladies and our pups, and then (c) he teaches me something amazing. I went to see him a month ago to chat about this chapter for my book, and I gave him a Swiss Army knife that I had had made up special for all the book's contributors. The knife has a beautiful view of Yosemite National Park in California and the word *PITH* engraved on it. *Pith* is a favorite word of mine, and its definition is not

unrelated to another fave: *gumption*. Not only does pith refer to the heart of a tree trunk, but it also means "essence, core, heart, strength, or mettle."

Jimmy thanked me, then looked at the printed image on the knife and said, "Oh, this is hydrographics." As usual, I grinned and asked what in the Sam Heck hydrographics is. He neatly explained it to me and then showed me a couple of amazing YouTube videos in which the rim of a car wheel and an electric guitar were printed upon using the process. I won't take up space here explaining it; you can YouTube it for yourself, and you should—it's super cool—but the point is that Jimmy knows how *everything* is made, and what he doesn't know, he finds out. Then he tucks it into his cranial filing system for later use—so that when he's brainstorming any future project, he has all the possible options of fabrication available to him.

He combines this encyclopedic knowledge with an easy facility for using tools, all tools. Watching the aggressive way he works on his band saw held yet another great lesson for me: Don't be so precious. Once he decides how to make whatever it is that has caught his fascination at the moment, he then seems to say, "Okay, now how fast can I do this?" Jimmy cuts wood and metal on his band saw as though he's testing the blade to find its breaking point. It reminds me of my early years building houses and scenery—I was pretty sharp with a circular saw, and I recall the sensation of pushing a long cut along a chalk line to see how fast I could execute it while still nailing the line. Jimmy has never lost that sense of urgency—no part of the process is precious, it's simply a means to an end; whether it's a die grinder or a carving gouge, he just throws himself at it until he has achieved the shape he sees in his head.

(It must be noted that a couple of years ago Jimmy nearly lost a pinky to his table saw. After so many years of skilled tool use, he finally got a very lucky wake-up call. Now he has a SawStop! The key to safety is knowing your tools and your own skill level, adding in the proper equipment, and then throwing in a little natural caution/distrust.)

The lesson I take away from his intrepid approach is that, while meticulous work is pleasantly indulgent, time really *is* money, and so I do my best to pursue a happy medium between enjoying my time in the shop with a tool in my hand and expeditiously getting to the finished product—to feel the pleasure of the resolution and the client's delight (hopefully) before plunging forward into the next adventure. Jimmy ever reminds me that there's no need to wallow in the making of anything—there will be plenty more to make once the current project is out the door.

Jimmy has dabbled in television a few times,

with his aforementioned brother, the amusing and ruggedly handsome Johnny Two Shows. One of their programs boasted that "Jimmy could make anything and John could make anything funny." While this certainly holds true, the brothers were to discover some of the painful truths about trying to combine creativity and commerce.

Without indulging in the foul language that Jimmy and I tend to favor when discussing working with television and cable networks, let me just say that the bankers and salespersons running TV channels don't tend to give a rat's fanny about how amazing a talent like Jimmy's can be to watch. These folks were not in the business of selling furniture or anything else the DiResta brothers could create—the TV people were in the business of selling soda pop and pharmaceuticals via advertising time, while Jimmy gamely built works of art between commercials.

Naturally, Jimmy grew tired of chasing this crappy brass ring, and the timing could not have been better. He had already been shooting and editing and posting online his own shop projects when we met, attesting to his desire to not only make things, but to share his knowledge with others as a teacher. Jimmy agreed to shoot the entire build of my first canoe (you can read more about this in the Bear Mountain Boats chapter, and even purchase a DVD online). It was in a sweet shop space on a pier in Red Hook, Brooklyn, during the many hours of that build that we became attached for life. Even though he claimed to have very poor woodworking skills at the time, at every turn he would suggest improvements to the many steps of the build. I remember specifically when I was sanding the curved hardwood stems, which I had steam-bent into shape, he effortlessly invented three different implements out of leftover MDF (medium-density fiberboard) to help me sand a curve. He can't help but look at the challenge at hand, examine every scrap of detritus lying about, and then MacGyver together some solution (or three).

Back to the video side of things, Jimmy began to really invest in making his YouTube videos around this time. He has a hypnotic style in which there is never any talking—just the project, start to finish, sped up in time so that a job spanning several hours can be viewed in as many minutes. Those of us who like to make things especially love to watch his creativity manifest itself in any number of techniques and shop tricks as he builds

incredible custom items before our very eyes. We are not alone—at the time of this writing, his YouTube channel has 566,000 subscribers and his Instagram has 40,000 followers.

I have to mention another character or two in this chapter. Since I have known him, Jimmy has had a right-hand man by the name of David Waelder, who is every bit the weird Robin to Jimmy's Batman. They thrive on making things together and collaborating on a lot of their video work. Waelder has his own channels as well, and they are committed to growing the online community of "makers," so that everyone with access to a computer and the Internet can give and take from the wealth of the global pool of tool knowledge. Jimmy said, "This YouTube community is amazing. We've got friends all over the world now, and we've never met them in person."

If Waelder is Robin, then there is also a Wonder Woman in the picture: Jimmy's better half, Taylor Forrest. Taylor is a fabricator and artist who works mainly with heavy-gauge leather and welded steel, and who also happens to be a smart young woman, further exploding the stereotype that one needs to be a hirsute fellow to work with any tools or materials. She makes really handsome and sturdy furniture and shares the same curiosity that fuels our whole community. When we all get together, I know the conversation is going to be delectable—full of questions that are then answered by experience: "Have you ever worked with horseshoes?" "Oh man, that is an art *and* a craft *and* a science. You can't screw up—you're forging the perfect shape, because if you miss, that's going on an animal who will be injured by your mistake."

Jimmy is a sweetheart who gives away his knowledge freely in many forums (he also is one-third of the podcast *Making It*), lending him a very urban, grease-stained Robin Hood quality that I adore. We often just send each other pictures of beautiful vintage tools that we come across, like soldiers in the war sending pinups of movie starlets. Trust me, nobody was ever half as inspired by Betty Grable as Jimmy and I are by a Northfield jointer from the 1960s.

WHISKY COASTERS

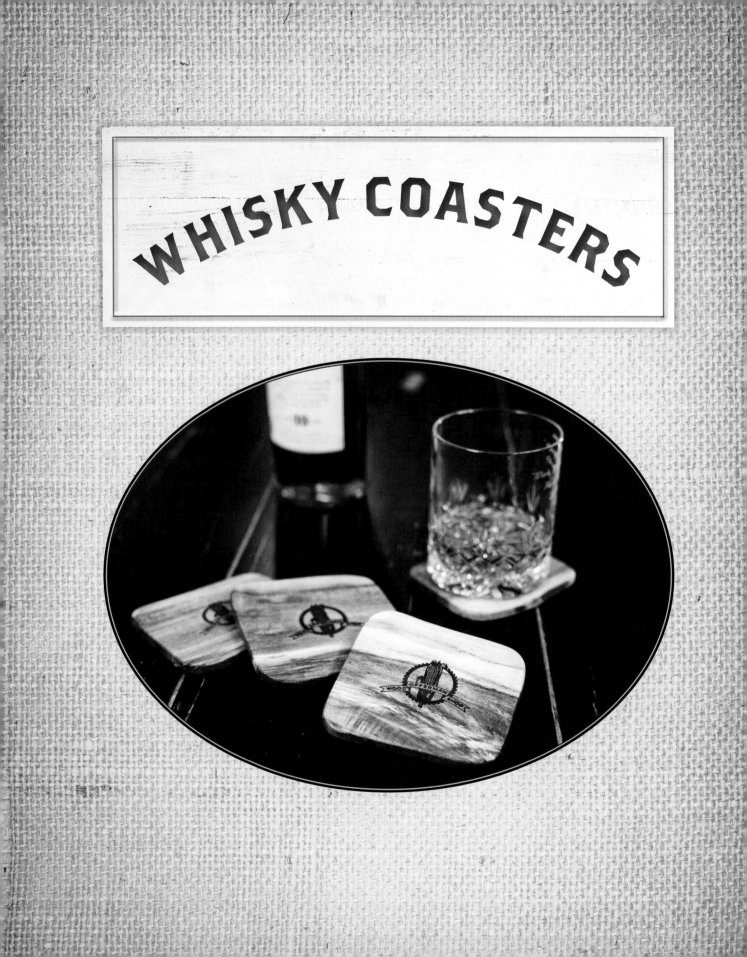

MAKING WHISKY COASTERS

After making OWS pencil holders for about a year, I was approached by Lee about making my own web product. I thought long and hard but couldn't come up with anything when suddenly a light bulb came on. Growing up in my home, we used a lot of coasters, so I thought about my design and went for it (you can make these any shape you like, avoiding any dangling parts like a clover stem). Just size your coasters big enough to fit under a glass or mug. Now I have a top-selling item at OWS, and my god, I am so grateful and thankful for the opportunities given to me. Aside from my coaster making, group projects are my favorite at OWS. I love it because I get to spend lots of long hours with the team and we all have a wonderful time together and I get to learn so much.

Since working at OWS, I've come in contact with lots of different species of wood. I'd have to say my favorite is buckeye. I would pick buckeye because of the color contrast (navy blue and gold) and camphor because of the smell. However, I try to use a hardwood for the coasters so they can take a beating. Cherry, oak, eucalyptus, mahogany, maple . . . really whatever cutoffs come my way from the larger projects.

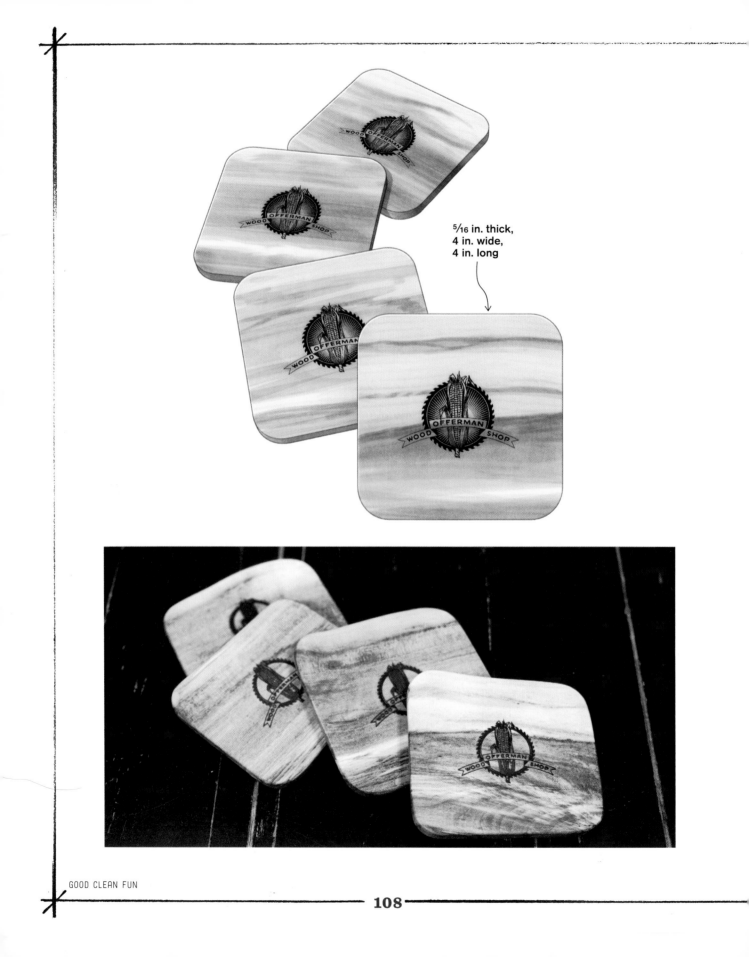

5/16 in. thick,
4 in. wide,
4 in. long

1. You'll want a board that will yield four coasters, around ⅜" × 4" × 18"—unless you want to make multiples, like a dozen, then you can resaw three of those boards from a piece of ⁶/₄" × 4" × 18". I'm using the middle strip from my buckeye pencil holder slab to slice off some coaster planks.

2. I rough cut an 18"-long piece of wood about 3" to 4" wide.

3. Pass two adjacent faces over the jointer to make them a square 90 degrees.

4. On the band saw, resaw a ⅜" thickness from that piece. Using the two jointed faces on the table and against the fence will yield a consistently cut piece.

5. Mill your strip to ⁵/₁₆" thick in the planer with the jointed side facing down. Take care to plane with the grain, not against it.

6. Crosscut with the chop saw to 4" lengths. I set up a stop block to do away with the guesswork and any margin for error.

7. Round the corners with the stationary disc sander at 120 grit.

8. Sand all sides to 220 grit with the orbital sander.

9. Use a custom drill press iron to brand your awesome logo on one side.

10. Clean up and break the edges by hand using 220 grit sandpaper.

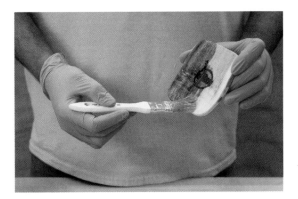

11. I finish with a sturdy polyurethane, two coats with a light sanding between. Now enjoy these coasters with your family and friends!

SHOP FASHION

Featuring

OWS STYLE ADVISOR AND CONFIDANTE,
MEGAN MULLALLY

WHAT YOU BUILD IS FUN, but it's what you wear while building it that really counts. You'll find that a daring color combo, asymmetrical bias cuts, or the latest in Belgian footwear will lend your woodcrafts an ineffable quality of je ne sais quoi.

When people say to you, "I love this table, but there's a poignancy to it that I can't quite put my finger on," just wink, throw on your sawdust-embroidered capelet, and turn away. After all, they don't have to know *all* your secrets . . .

Thomas's timeless Carhartt pant is paired with
a designer-distressed T-shirt and arms.
The splash of green on his breathing filter adds
a touch of whimsy, perfect for daytime or evening.

So many shoes, so little time! Get ready to be the envy of
all when you step out for a stroll in any of these well-
heeled prancers. (And the slight platform and designer
sole will keep your feet smiling all day long. Arf!)

Nick is on-the-go in these booty-hugging stone-washed
jeans and this slimming dirt-washed navy jersey.
His fashion-forward beanie and handy sander complete
the ensemble. Whichever fun and flirty path you're going
down this time, Nick, we'll be sure to follow!

This gal-in-transition transitions us right into summer
in her Fourth of July–inspired long shorts, exposing
just the right amount of calf above the indispensable
white tube sock, topped off with that staple
of every sensible dresser: the gray tee.

We'd follow this gal anywhere with her take-charge, no-nonsense denim frontispiece and multiuse paddle accessory. Hmm. Provocative. Is that cap crimson, Lee . . . or bloodred? We'd be happy to find out "firsthand"!

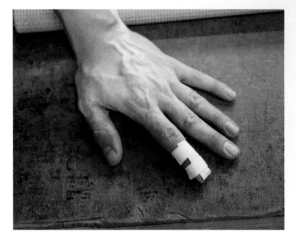

White is the new black, and the new jewelry trend this season is the finger wrap, or "bandage." Wear it with your Herve Leger bandage dress, or simply pair it with jeans and a T-shirt for a more casual look.

Bangs are a must to pull off this Middle East–inspired fez; everything old is new again—large frames and a humorous, extra-wide-collared mint-green top. Our model is kickin' out the jams—share your playlist with us, Jane!

Dust is a must but headgear is the headline here. Matty proves that more is more with his breathing filter (wear yours frequently to get this well-worn look), nerd-chic safety glasses, extra-large—and extra-funky—ear protectors, and cap with a light-pink stripe for just a hint of the feminine.

BEARD LENGTH
Virility Chart

Beards are the real power tool. If you know your stuff, you'll be sporting some facial finery of your own. Remember: It's okay to go at your own pace. It may be that no two chin-dusters are alike, but they're all equal in allure.

12 days

23 days

23 days

37 days

6 weeks

1 epoch
(The Offerman whiskers are actually elvish tendrils drawing us ever home to the Grey Havens and Valinor.)

NICK OFFERMAN

Having turned the lens on myself and my middling statistics plenty enough already in this volume, I'll briefly inhabit a copse (a small thicket or woods) in this here biographical real estate to mention to you a little bit about why this book came to be. I am writing this on the evening of May 28, 2016, a date which finds my extremely well-proportioned wife, Megan, and me in London on vacation (as soon as I finish this writing—ahem). This afternoon we had the unlikely pleasure of High Tea at the venerated and historically redoubtable Fortnum & Mason on Piccadilly (home of Fortnum's Beef Extract—"spread on toast, it is incredibly moreish"). Our host for a light meal of ridiculously savory lobster omelet was one of my absolute favorite writers, Bill Bryson, pals with whom I had the pleasure of becoming when I played a small role in Robert Redford's 2015 film adaptation of *A Walk in the Woods*, Mr. Bryson's most popular volume (a must-read).

Bill and I were in a bit of a daze in the company of a woman as rarefied as my wife, in such a fancy joint no less, and we three spoke enjoyably of work and pleasure, and how to balance labor with time in the garden, park, or woodshop. I mentioned to him that this was just the tidbit I needed for my "bio" section.

So I will now share with you, in this somewhat educational text, that no matter how much we love our time at work (those of us lucky enough to love what we do), we can still find it detrimental if we do it too much. For optimum health, leisure must be held in a regard commensurate with labor. Woodworking serves that function in my life— it inhabits a place where I can go and slow down and do things deliberately, which invariably gets my head turned straight back around from the cockamamie angles at which showbiz can leave it tilted. By focusing one of my day jobs, book writing, on my shop, I have then additionally tricked my calendar into even more slow shop/wood time. And so here we are.

NAME: Nick Offerman

FAVORITE SAUSAGE: Bratwurst

PARTNER: Comedy legend Megan Mullally

MOST RESPECTED ILLUMINATUS: Benjamin Franklin

FAVORITE TOOL: Shovel

INSTRUMENT: Guitar, saxophone, nunchaku

MODE OF TRAVEL: Tesseract

FAVORITE HOBBIT: Samwise Gamgee

MOST EFFICACIOUS SPOT: G

SAVIOUR: J. R. "Bob" Dobbs

BERRY
STOOL

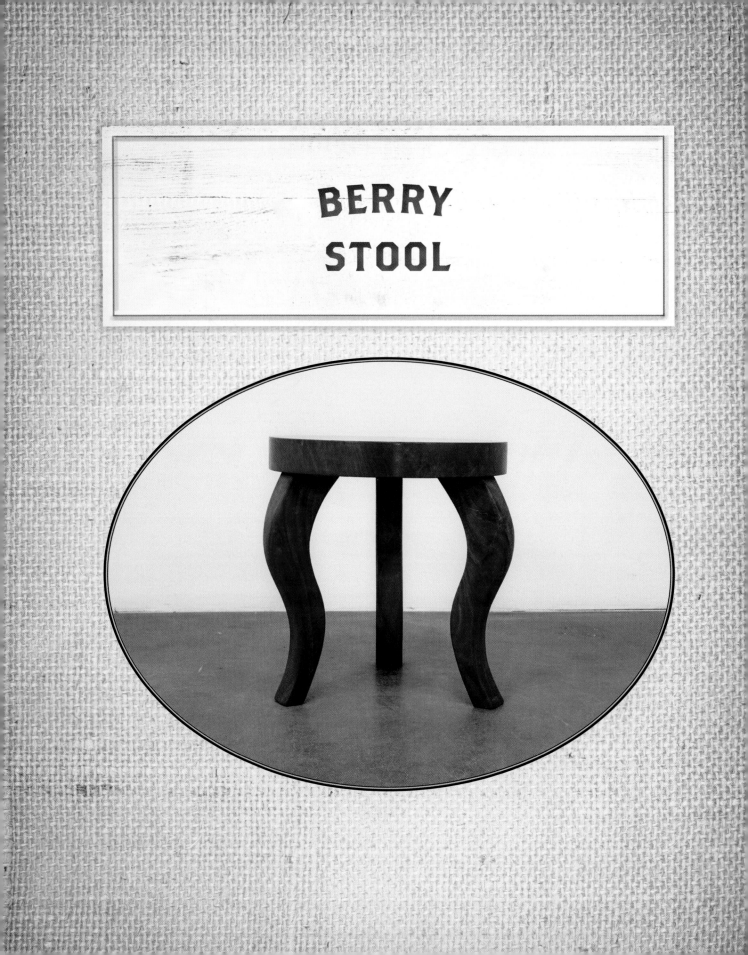

MAKING THE BERRY STOOL

I was already tickled beyond belief to be a cheerleader and coproducer of my pal Laura Dunn's documentary on Wendell Berry, *Look and See*, but imagine my elation when she asked if I would make a stool so that they could film it for the documentary, to underscore a section in which Mr. Berry (my all-time favorite writer) speaks in a moving way about people who make things, specifically artists:

> *We all come from divorce, now. This is an age of divorce. Things that belong together have been taken apart, and you can't put it all back together again. What you do is the only thing that you can do: You take two things that ought to be together and you put them back together. Two things, not all things. That's the way the work has to go. You make connections in your work. I reckon, I'm no filmmaker, but you'll put this film together by seeing how the parts of it belong together. The film, the made thing, becomes a kind of an earnest of your faith in and your affection for the great coherence that we miss, and would like to have again.*
>
> *Well, that's what we do, we people who make things. If it's a stool, or a film, or a poem, or an essay, or a novel, or musical composition, it's all about that: finding how it fits together, and fitting it together.*

Clearly, since he said "stool" first, Mr. Berry holds that art form above the lower, or more base, creations such as poetry and music. Therefore, Laura thought it appropriate to film my hands and tools crafting a stool, and I do believe it may be the peak of my career in film, especially because my face is never seen.

I love to make a three-legged stool, or anything with three legs, because a tripod cannot wobble. You can be as clumsy as, well, me, and screw up your legs six ways to Sunday and that thing will still sit sturdily upon the ground. That is why I chose to craft just such a stool for Laura's film, since we were hustling a bit to get it done during postproduction. I wanted to remove all the possible chances for error.

I chose a piece of walnut slab that had been ravaged by termites, which had caused an organic pattern of hieroglyphs to be excavated that would normally qualify the wood for nothing but the firewood pile. The Swiss cheese quality of the wood's appearance, however, struck me as beautiful, so I cut the stool's seat to feature the damage.

I'm also a big fan of the wedged through-tenon, for if you get the joinery even close to decent, its permanence is idiot- (or Nick-) proof. Finally, I have recently been indulging in projects with curved details that require not so much accurate measuring as they do eyeballing for "fairness." Laying out, measuring, cutting, and shaping wood with acuity are very enjoyable skills to learn, but then, once those activities have been mastered and repeated enough times, cutting loose with some freehand techniques can provide a refreshing sense of liberation.

With that in mind, I whipped up a leg design that I liked and went to town. I'm sure that a person with talent could craft a nicer stool, but I'm afraid that this model, inspired by a call to illustrate Wendell Berry's language, will always be my favorite, as making it was one of the greatest privileges I've had on my bench. For the book, I have simply replicated the techniques in a couple more versions of the stool, and I do hope you enjoy building it.

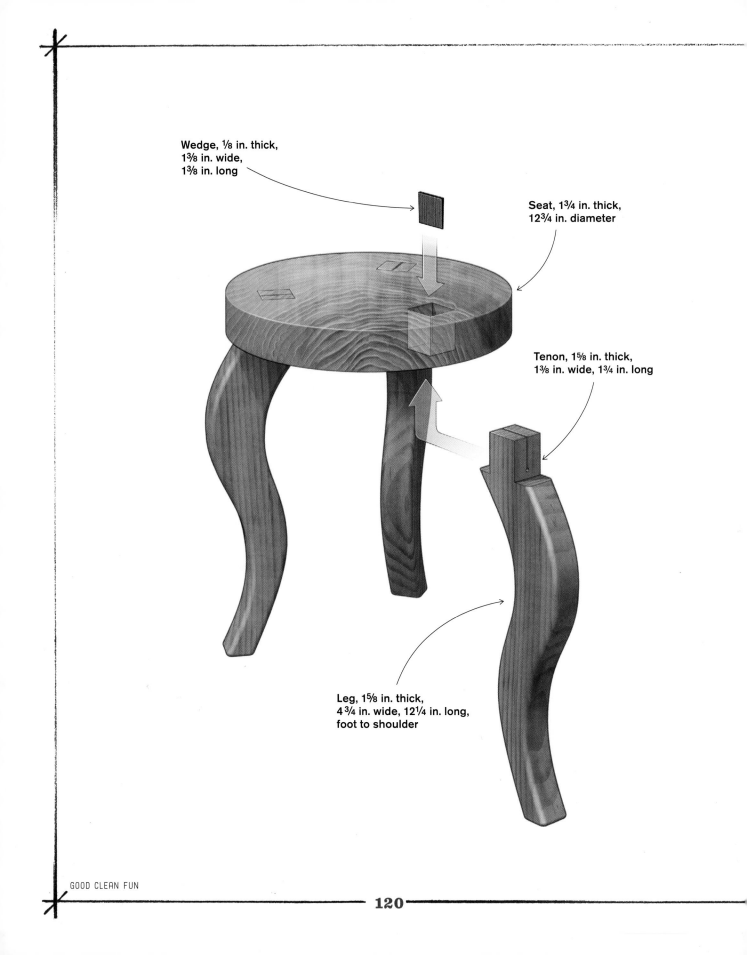

Wedge, 1/8 in. thick,
1 3/8 in. wide,
1 3/8 in. long

Seat, 1 3/4 in. thick,
12 3/4 in. diameter

Tenon, 1 5/8 in. thick,
1 3/8 in. wide, 1 3/4 in. long

Leg, 1 5/8 in. thick,
4 3/4 in. wide, 12 1/4 in. long,
foot to shoulder

1. Choose your wood—this is a really fun place to use weird or irregular items from the scrap pile, since you need only a 12" disc, and not necessarily even that, because you can use any size or shape piece within reason that will support the joinery and your fanny. I am using some gorgeous (but difficult) red eucalyptus for one stool's parts and a nifty slab of California myrtle for another, with eastern black walnut legs. Use your common sense to determine seat thickness—my smaller stool is 1⅝" thick, and the myrtle slab will finish out at 2". If your stool is for a toddler, a stuffed animal, Adam Scott, or any other supermodel, you can get away with a much thinner seat, but if it's for a professional wrestler or a Sasquatch, then you'll likely want to beef up your dimensions, although good luck getting Bigfoot to sit still (they tend toward skittish in my experience).

2. Choose your shape, like a 12" disc, an octagon, or a weird heart (or a flower—who cares?), and cut it out on the band saw or with a jigsaw. Lay out the locations for your three mortises by eyeballing the inset you want underneath the seat from the edge of the stool to the leg. Find the center of your seat and mark a straight line wherever it makes sense—now you have a centerline. I use a protractor and the centerline to mark off the circle into thirds, or 120 degrees per mortise. No matter what shape your seat ends up as, it's good to use the circle system for layout if you want equidistant legs. Or not! Do as you please on a three-legged stool!

3. As wood contracts and expands with the humidity of the seasons, sometimes the cells can't keep up and so cracks occur, known as "checking." These most often happen along the grain, and they can be thin, hairline cracks, or they can be wide gaps. Dealing with checks is a different conundrum every time. Depending on factors like comfort of use and aesthetics, I do my best to leave checks alone when I can, maybe just easing the edges so that they're not uncomfortable to touch. If I want to arrest any further cracking, I inlay a butterfly key, which is effective and also a cute detail. However, in a tabletop, maybe I don't want to leave any crevices that will collect gravy and subsequently be a drag to keep clean. In this case I will make a mixture of two-part epoxy, microfiber filler, and sawdust from the wood I'm working on (or something contrasting if I want it to become a design detail) and fill the gap. This red eucalyptus had some small checks that were jagged and sharp, so I decided to fill them. The tape saves me a great deal of laborious cleanup. Mix in your filler and dust in equal parts until you like the color—doing tests ahead of time can help with color matching. Once your paste feels like peanut butter, pack it into the crevice, making sure there are no voids or air bubbles left. A scraper makes quick work of cleanup after curing.

4. Next, I designed my legs, which in this case I had already done—but I wanted the Wendell Berry stool legs to be the right scale for my other two stools of disparate sizes, so I enjoined our trusty Jane to use the computer and scanner to scale the template to several other sizes so that I could dial in the best one for each new stool. We'll focus on the eucalyptus stool from here on out for simplicity's sake.

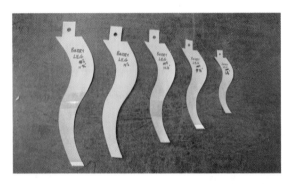

5. For furniture legs, you generally want a hardwood that can put up with a person's weight and also get banged around a bit. Once again, I depend upon my eye to determine a good thickness for the leg. I like the thickness of the original leg, but I want to thin it down a bit for the slightly smaller version, so I mill my material until it looks right, which is at 1¾". I use our planer, but you can also do this with a hand plane.

6. It's very important to align the leg design with the long grain so that you don't have short-grain weak spots. Some of my walnut legs are guilty of this very deficit, but I make the top curve, or "thigh," beefy enough to hopefully withstand breaking. The leg curves are marked from the template, but then I go back in and more anally dial in the tenon layout, to ensure accuracy and squareness at the top of the curved form, so the joints will be friendly. Once I'm satisfied with my lines, I cut out the legs. Leave an extra ¼" of tenon length to protrude from the mortise for later flush trimming.

7. I cut my tenons close to the line, then use a chisel and/or a shoulder plane to pare them just right. Once I like the tenons, I use them to lay out the mortises in the seat. In this case, I cut some excess off the tenon end (I had left extra length) and used the block to lay out my tenon locations. A marking knife is ideal in this application, as you want to get these mortises cut as perfectly as possible. All three joints *should* be identical, but I always seem to manage to screw something up just a bit, so I mark the tenons and their respective mortises as A, B, and C. Mark the top of the seat to make the joints as pretty as possible where folks can see them. If it's going to get ugly (and with red eucalyptus, it *will* get ugly), you want that to happen on the bottom side, where it will pass undetected. Once I have cut the lines in with a knife, I double down with a chisel to reinforce my clean layout and protect against tear-out.

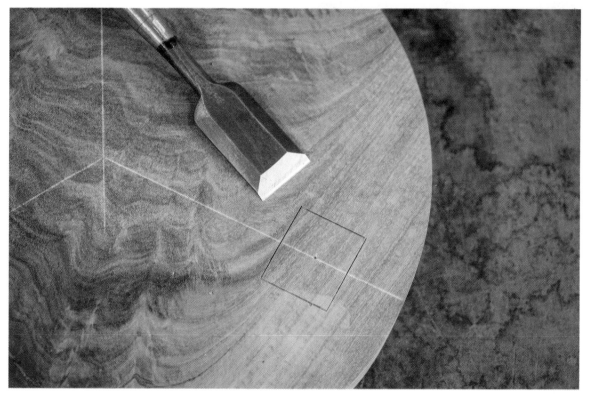

8. You can use a bit and brace (which is really fun—you should try it) or a hand drill, but I'm spoiled, so I drill out most of the waste from the mortise with a Forstner bit on the drill press. I chisel the rest, taking my time to keep my chisel 90 degrees to the surface of the seat. No matter how careful I am, this ornery eucalyptus begins to crumble in places, leaving me with some less-than-perfect topsides and ugly blowouts below.

NICK: **Don't ever work with red eucalyptus.**

9. Once you are satisfied with the mortise-and-tenon joints, you'll want to cut a saw kerf in the tenons, into which a wedge will be driven once the joint is assembled. Mark out your kerf to a depth ¼" shy of your seat thickness. (Drill a ¼" hole at the bottom of your wedge kerf line to relieve the leg-splitting force once the wedge is driven in.) I cut mine with a Japanese pull saw. One kerf thickness is fine unless you want a thicker wedge for aesthetic reasons. Align your kerf and wedge perpendicular to the seat grain. If your kerf is parallel, your wedge is likely to split the top. Ideally, I would cut the kerfs before shaping the legs. There should still be ⅛" between the drilled bottom of the kerf and the leg tenon shoulder.

10. Time to shape the legs. To me, this is the funnest part. I draw a centerline down the front of the leg, just eyeballing, then freehand a reference curve along each of the two front edges, drawing it on each side of the leg. I taper the curve from nothing at the top corner to a width of ½" or so at the protruding part of the thigh. These lines are just to give me a loose guideline as I remove material from both edges. I want them to be relatively symmetrical and "fair," but it can differ from leg to leg, since you can never really look at more than one leg at a time from head-on. I start with a drawknife, but the grain is so ornery that I quickly turn to spokeshave and rasp. Remove material from both sides until you like the curves. Eventually this godforsaken red eucalyptus would not get along with anything but a card scraper, and then I finally won the argument thanks to that noble scrap of thin steel. A little hand-sanding and these legs were ready to go to work.

11. I mill a scrap at the exact width of the tenon (length of kerf) and at the length of the tenon minus ⅜" or so. I cut my wedges on the band saw (at an angle of 3–4 degrees), then clean them up with a chisel so both sides of the wedge will be good glue surfaces. I make the thin end about ¹⁄₃₂" less than the kerf width, which allows me to leave ⅛" to ¼" of space below the wedge when I drive it home, which gives the glue a place to go. I glue up the seat mortises and the leg tenons, gently knock them together, then glue up the wedges and tap them home. I wipe up my glue with a wet rag, since I know there is sanding yet to come. Once the glue dries, I cut off the tenon tops with a flush-cut saw.

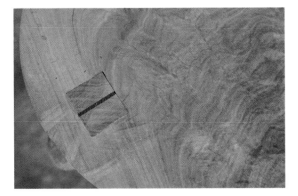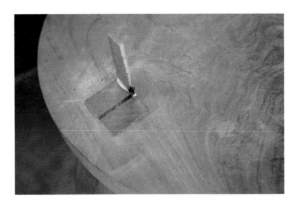

12. Now look at this mediocre work. That's called a gap. One of the best things about working with wood is that you can do a job this crappy and still get away with it. Cut some thin wedges in the appropriate species and tap them in with glue. Nobody's the wiser! Suck on that, eucalyptus.

13. Bringing the tenons flush with the seat is a great place to use a card scraper. If you try sanding an end-grain tenon, the long grain surrounding it will usually be abraded more quickly, resulting in an uneven surface. Scrape the tenon flush with the seat until it requires little to no sanding.

14. Now you can sand the stool for finish, starting with 120 and working up to 220. When you think it's close to done, wet the whole piece with water to raise any possible grain, then sand with 220. This red eucalyptus is such a pain in the keister that I end up needing the card scraper for most of the seat as well. I finished the stool with a couple of coats of tung oil.

NICK OFFERMAN: BERRY STOOL

MIRA NAKASHIMA

In 1991 I spent the better part of a year acting in a tour of a Kabuki theater adaptation of *The Iliad* entitled *Kabuki Achilles*. The lion's share of this time was spent at a venerable regional theater outside of Philadelphia: the People's Light and Theatre Company. The theater subsists peacefully in the pastoral town of Malvern along what is referred to as the Main Line—a string of "old money" communities lining the original vein of the Pennsylvania Railroad. The wealthiest Philadelphia families knew what they were doing when they scooped up large estates in

the region, because it is jaw-droppingly gorgeous country: softly rolling hills draped in a proliferation of deciduous forest. (As you'll learn later in the book, Pennsylvania is from whence Christian Becksvoort selects his cherry lumber stock.) I had an absolutely idyllic time living in the region, performing (for pay!) at a respected theater and exploiting the local Yuengling brewery's sixteen-ounce-returnable-brown-bottle policy by the case. Delicious living indeed.

A goodly portion of life in my early twenties was also very Japanese flavored, artistically and aesthetically. Because of the profound influence that my sensei, Shozo Sato, had upon my life and career (*Kabuki Achilles* was his production—we had already toured Japan and Europe), I was rather invested in the colors and design details of

traditional Japanese arts. Among the many artistic gifts he had bestowed upon the University of Illinois at Urbana-Champaign was the funky and resplendent "Japan House"—a two-story clapboard farmhouse that he had gutted and refitted with all the trappings of traditional Japanese teahouse culture.

All this background information came solidly roiling back as I rolled into the Nakashima Woodworker Studio in April 2016, about an hour northeast of Malvern in the sleepy little town of New Hope, Pennsylvania. April fourth it was, to be exact, because the cherry tree in the middle of the compound was in verdant blossom. Because of the area's resemblance to the wooded hills around Malvern, I felt a strong sense of nostalgia as I parked my rental. Once I poked my head into

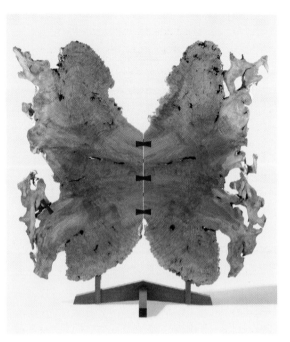

the office, the déjà vu kicked up tenfold because of the overwhelmingly Japanese flavor to the design of all the buildings. How strange that my experience in the hills of Pennsylvania should always be rife with my reverence for Japanese culture!

I have long been a fan and student (via his writing and his actual furniture work) of the late George Nakashima, best known for his unique style of Japanese-flavored design, often utilizing live-edged tree slabs and organic lines and textures. In fact, I wrote a chapter about him in my last book, *Gumption*. I had been quite familiar with the bullet points in his life story, including the establishment of this eclectic compound of buildings in which I now stood, enjoying the damp quiet and the sweet, occasional birdsong. For some reason—and I guess this is a testament to the fact that virtual

or secondhand information can never substitute for the real McCoy—it had not occurred to me in my reading just how familiar it all would seem. Perhaps my laser focus on the furniture in the rooms in the photographs had occluded the peripheral views of the setting, architecture, and décor, which were just as powerfully executed by George himself. After all, he was a talented and accomplished architect long before he ever picked up a dovetail chisel.

Because of my rich and specific personal history in the very small middle of a Venn diagram overlapping the terrain of Chester and Bucks counties with woodworking with green tea incense with wabi-sabi with traditional Japanese tatami mats, the sense of homecoming that struck me as I entered the small Nakashima showroom/office was profound. My sensei, Shozo, had been such a unique character in the midst of the cornfields of Illinois that I had always attributed his incredible style to his own idiosyncrasies, which were indeed prevalent; but what hadn't occurred to me, because I am generally ignorant (a.k.a. "blissful"), was that Shozo's brand of magic was also dripping with tradition. Sheepishly greeting the benevolent workers at the Nakashima Studio, I was surprised to find that I felt very emotionally warm, and so much more acclimated to the people there than I would have expected. It felt so familiar that I wanted them to put me to work.

Sadly, they did not allow me to get my hands dirty. Instead, I was offered tea or coffee by George's daughter, the matriarch well-versed in woodshop comportment upon whom this chapter relies: Mira Nakashima. I was quite moved by her generosity in touring me about the buildings and grounds and fascinating me with the historical lineage of each structure.

Born in 1942 in Seattle, Washington, Mira got a very early lesson in American fear and racism. Not long after she came into this world, her parents were sent, with her in tow, to a Japanese internment camp in Idaho during World War Two. Shortly after regaining their freedom, the young and plucky Nakashimas were able to set up shop on a piece of wilderness in New Hope, where they lived in a tent until her dad began to construct the shop and other buildings (he built the shop before the house!). Young Mira's intention was far from following in her father's footsteps by becoming a woodworker. She said that she had really wanted to study music or languages, but her overweening father insisted that she should study architecture instead, so she attended Harvard University, where she

could "still do choral society and dance group, so it was okay." She then followed that up with a master's degree in architecture from Tokyo's Waseda University before returning to the States.

In hindsight, it's easy to examine the arc of a person's life or career with a discerning eye, but when we are actually living through that life-span, its destination is not so clear. Luminaries and legends as well as abject failures are often just trying to make their rent or get kissed (or both). Looking back on Mira's history, I see less of a future American furniture scion and more of a valued young daughter at the family's studio furniture operation—an operation that just happened to catch the nation's fancy in a very big way.

In 1970 her dad built her a house across the road from the studio and offered her a part-time job. She told me that she started out as more of a gofer, juggling three little ones and the random needs of the other studio employees. In an interview with *Craft in America*, she said, "I was pretty much the understudy. He never told me the way to do things, he would just change a [drawn] line without telling me why. . . . I can't count the number of times I was fired while Dad was alive. It was very good discipline." Thankfully the firings were never permanent, as Mira continued to doggedly learn how to design her father's tables, chairs, and consoles.

One thing that really struck me upon visiting was the disparity between the fantasy and the reality of what I had imagined the Nakashima Studio must be like. I suppose all those years of admiring their work in books and magazines and museums conjured a vision in my mind's eye of a wizardly woodshop deep in the forest. An eldritch place where the very trees flexed themselves into majestic burls, emblazoned with ponderously spalted hieroglyphs and the most dazzling of quilted figures, then inexorably shambled to the shop door upon which a stiff breeze would cause them to knock, presenting themselves as an offering to the sawyers of the great Halls of Nakashima.

In reality, here was a shop that required no magic at all, beyond a father's exquisite vision and philosophy and his daughter's adherence to those qualities. A daughter who said, "Dad really believed that there are spirits in the wood that enhance people's lives, and you know not everybody can live in the woods, but they can live *with* wood and stay connected to nature and to the divine in that way." Here was the woodshop I have been emulating all my woodworking life: one where they fully respect the concept of wabi-sabi. In a 2012 interview on the189.com, Mira said that "we depend entirely on the natural shapes and colors of the wood to inspire and determine the course of our work and never apply artificial colors or shiny finishes." Neither do we! Ha ha. I knew glossy finishes were for the birds! Sorry, I got excited. Of course glossy finishes have their place. In 1987. I kid.

My enthusiasm, however, to see every nook and corner of this elfin compound was no joke. A business that remained successful despite designing furniture pieces one at a time in a painstaking way that was true to the particular qualities of the wood itself and also to the client's needs. "It is actually very problematic to respect and honor natural forms, so that each piece is individual and different from the next," said Mira,

again in 2012. "As this artistic process is not at all cost-effective, we have historically sold only directly to clients, eliminating the middleman markup of modern entrepreneurship." Well, this was something incendiary indeed to inspire all of us little shops who are striving to profit by the same business model. If you're not aware, when you sell a piece for $100 at a show, the gallery will usually take fifty of those dollars from you. Showing your work in a gallery is a luxury that can prove very dear.

What further struck me as I drooled over the 1965 Hornbach-Zuckermann 32" planer and the 1964 Hornbach 25" jointer was this: So many of us woodworkers have been emulating this style for decades—I have simply arrived at studio-furniture Nirvana. This is where they made it this way first, and it is where they make it this way best.

George may have built this ship, but it is Mira who now stands confidently at the helm. The thing is, she is sailing on very different seas nowadays, twenty-six years after George's passing in 1990. Her dad once said, "If we end up with something that pleases us and pleases others, then we feel that the destiny of a piece of wood has been fulfilled." Mira says that she just sort of "picked up the pieces where [George] had let them fall—that [she's] tried to continue his tradition and explore it a little further." Well, that is an understatement very representative of the humility with which she has donned the captain's hat.

As you might imagine, a lot of the clientele lost interest in new Nakashima commissions once her dad was no longer around. This served as quite a wake-up call to Mira, who had become

a talented, fully skilled designer in her own right by this point. She was grateful that family friend Bob Aibel of Philadelphia's Moderne Gallery encouraged her to have a show of her new designs, sponsored by him. Up until that point she hadn't understood the importance of PR and creating proper slides of one's work in the pre-digital age. With Aibel's support, she debuted her new line of Nakashima Studio pieces, entitled "Keisho" (which in Japanese simply means "continuation"), which I think is as touching a title as it is apt. Public interest in the continuing production of the studio called Nakashima Woodworker blossomed once again and has yet to abate. Mira may have unintentionally backed into the stewardship of the Nakashima line, but once she found her feet, she has taken to it like a duck to water.

I could go on for many more pages about the Nakashima woodshed alone. I spoke to the woodworkers there of canoes and joinery and tools, and yes, of course, television. I was nothing short of besotted with Mira's grace and strength as the figurehead of this groovy furniture concern in the woods of Pennsylvania. Her dad was an intrepid trailblazer in twentieth-century American furniture, a gene that has clearly been passed on to her, here in the twenty-first. There is perhaps no better representation of the enduring mastery passed from father to daughter than the perpetuation of their Altars for Peace project. In Mira's words:

In 1984, a huge and beautiful walnut log appeared, and my father dreamed that its most perfect use would be to construct peace altars for the world from its enormous planks. He designed, built, and installed the first one at the Cathedral of St. John the Divine in New York City in 1986, and was hoping to send one to Russia when he passed away in 1990. Since then, we have installed one at the Academy of Arts in Moscow in 2001 and sent one to Auroville, India, in 1996, where it was finally dedicated in the Hall of Peace, Unity Pavilion there in 2014. We were able to establish a global connection between these three sacred tables in 2011, 2014, and 2016, and hope to send a fourth one to the Desmond Tutu Peace Centre in Cape Town, South Africa, sometime in the future. We are open to suggestions on other continents where a very large altar/table might be placed and put to use by an organization devoted to world peace.

"In India, they believe that beauty is man's connection to the Divine," Mira said in her *Craft in America* piece. I can then safely say, in my piece, that I experienced a great deal of beauty during my visit to Mira's studio. Ignorantly, I emailed Mira later to ask if that had been a cherry or a dogwood tree in blossom when I visited. She replied, "Yes, that is indeed cherry . . . the single-petal variety called Yoshino in Japanese." Give it up, people.

JOSH SALSBURY

"I'll be honest with you. I love Josh. In 2009, shortly after Lee and I had decided to make a go of developing a collective of woodworkers, I was in Pasadena, shopping for a bicycle at an excellent bike shop called Incycle. It was a pretty badass ride I was looking into, a Cannondale CX9 Cyclocross, so the young man helping me was really employing his best bedside manner, talking me through all the cool features of this bike designed for street travel as well as light trail riding, perfect for my beloved route of LA River bike path to Griffith Park dirt trails and back out again.

As I was checking out, purchasing the sweet ride, thanks in no small part to the young man's generous efforts, it somehow came up that he was just graduating from a renowned woodworking program down at Cerritos College. I said that we were looking for woodworkers, so he should come by and check out the shop. He did. His name is Josh. Josh Salsbury, which is why I immediately nicknamed him "The Beef." Since the beginning of our time together, Josh's work has been known for its meticulous details and fine finishes. He is on the quiet side, but he allows us to make him smile at times, so long as he's not embroiled in the sweating of a mortise that's off by $1/128''$.

His work emphasizes honest craftsmanship, and he is especially influenced by Shaker, Arts and Crafts, midcentury modern, and Asian design. When not at the shop, Josh enjoys cycling, snowboarding, and drinking IPAs, some of which he brews himself. Five stars.

NAME: Josh Salsbury

NICKNAME: The Beef

FAVORITE WOOD: Walnut

FAVORITE TOOL: Lie-Nielsen bevel-edge socket chisels

PREFERRED LUNCH: Turkey sandwich

COLLEGE MAJOR: Music (BM Eastman School of Music, MM UCLA, trombone performance)

FAVORITE SEASON: Winter
NICK: I believe this refers to "California winter"— an important distinction.

JUPITER SIDE TABLE

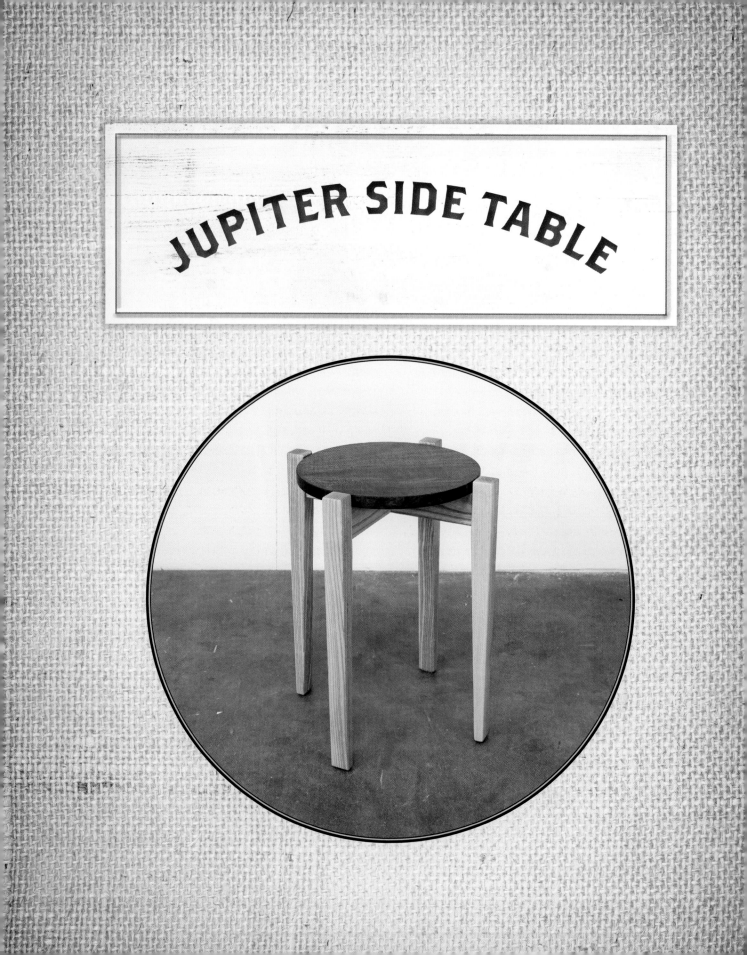

MAKING THE JUPITER SIDE TABLE

I've always enjoyed building tables, especially side tables. They're relatively quick to build, don't use a ton of material, and provide an opportunity to experiment with different designs. Easy to move around, their smaller footprint also makes them particularly versatile, allowing them to seamlessly fit into a room with any décor. They also make a perfect spot to rest your beverage of choice as you read your favorite book.

The Jupiter table is influenced by the round tabouret tables of Gustav Stickley (1858–1942), a prominent furniture designer and manufacturer from the Arts and Crafts movement, which thrived in America from around 1880 to 1910. The table utilizes traditional woodworking construction methods, including mortise-and-tenon joinery. I decided to take a more minimalist approach to this side table by not including a lower stretcher or any exposed joinery—elements that are typically found on Stickley designs. While I enjoy a pinned through-tenon as much as any woodworker does, I felt that such a detail could distract from the simple form of the Jupiter table. NICK: Despite his naming this table after a planet, I feel compelled to reassure you that Josh is not, in fact, a hippie.

For this piece in particular, I wanted to draw attention to the nice figure of the claro walnut top, reminiscent of the planet Jupiter, so I used a lighter wood—ash—for the base. In addition, I chose to expose the top of the legs and taper them, giving the table a lighter, slightly more modern feel. There are no hidden parts on the Jupiter table. You can see everything. It's stripped down to the essential components needed to make the table both functional and strong. There are only seven pieces, yet the use of exposed legs and mixed wood still makes it interesting.

Building the Jupiter table allows the woodworker to practice standard woodworking techniques, such as mortise-and-tenon joinery, half lap joinery, tapering legs, and cutting a circle. Although jigs are not required to build this table, they can be quite handy. I often make multiples of one design at a time, so the use of jigs allows me to be more efficient, accurate, and repeatable. For this project, I created jigs for both cutting a circle on the band saw and tapering legs on the table saw. All these practices, procedures, and concepts can apply to other projects, giving you the confidence to tackle more complex woodworking in the future.

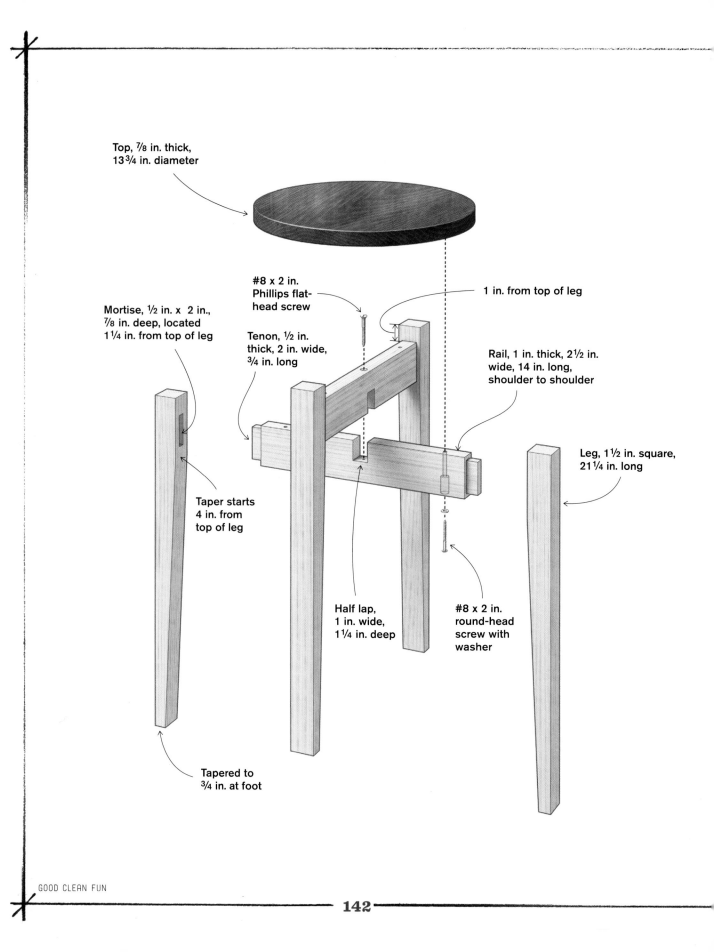

Top, ⅞ in. thick,
13¾ in. diameter

#8 x 2 in.
Phillips flat-
head screw

1 in. from top of leg

Mortise, ½ in. x 2 in.,
⅞ in. deep, located
1¼ in. from top of leg

Tenon, ½ in.
thick, 2 in. wide,
¾ in. long

Rail, 1 in. thick, 2½ in.
wide, 14 in. long,
shoulder to shoulder

Taper starts
4 in. from
top of leg

Leg, 1½ in. square,
21¼ in. long

Half lap,
1 in. wide,
1¼ in. deep

#8 x 2 in.
round-head
screw with
washer

Tapered to
¾ in. at foot

TABLE BASE

1. **LAY OUT LEGS AND RAILS**: Begin by inspecting the rough lumber that you will be using for the base and determine where to cut out the legs and rails. I used a single board of 8/4 ash from which to "harvest" all my parts. I always buy more wood than I need, to ensure that I can select the best-looking grain from a board. Try to avoid knots and other defects if possible, and use straight grain for the legs. At a minimum, you will need to map out four legs and two rails, but it is also a good idea to cut extras to test your joinery (or to have on hand if you screw up). As you can see, I harvested my legs from the outer edges of the board to take advantage of the rift-sawn grain orientation, so I'll have straight, vertical grain visible on all four sides. Measure approximate dimensions of each part with your measuring tape and mark them out with chalk or pencil. Keep your marks oversize from your final dimensions so that you have some wiggle room when you are actually cutting.

2. **ROUGH CUT:** Because the board is still in a rough state (not flat or square), I used the band saw and chop saw to cut out the oversize parts. I cut the legs to about 2" × 2" × 26" and resawed the rails to about 1 ¼" × 3" × 20". Keep in mind that, depending on your board, you may need to rip it first before crosscutting to shorter lengths, as I did for this particular project.

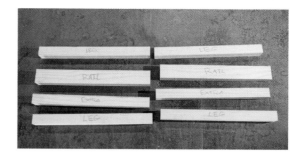

3. MILL: Now that the parts are roughly cut to size, mill them to your final dimensions. At this point, you will need to go through the process of squaring your stock.

For the legs, I milled two adjacent faces straight and square on the jointer, ripped them to 1⅝" × 1⅝" on the table saw, then finished them to 1½" × 1½" in the planer and continued milling the two opposing faces flat, using an arrow on the end grain to keep track of passes during rotation. Then, using a stop block at the chop saw, I crosscut them to 21¼" long. This method gives me four identical legs to work with.

For the rails, I flattened a face on the jointer, then established a parallel face in the planer, ending at 1" thick. I then straightened an edge on the jointer, then ripped them to 2½" wide on the table saw. Use a stop block again and crosscut to 15½" long.

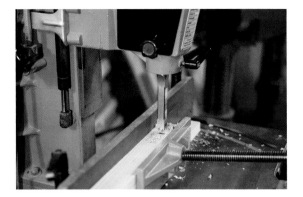

4. LAY OUT MORTISES: Now that the base parts are milled, you're ready to lay out the joinery. Take a look at the legs and decide how to orient them, keeping in mind which faces are most visible. Mark the ½" × 2" mortise locations 1¼" down from the top of each leg using a combination square and pencil or marking gauge.

5. CUT MORTISES: Using a ½" bit in the hollow chisel mortiser, cut the mortises ⅞" deep in each leg. If you don't own a hollow chisel mortiser, you can use a drill press to make a series of holes close to your lines, then clean up the mortise walls with a chisel.

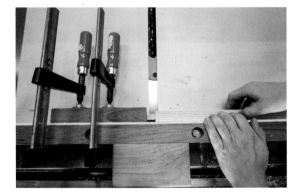

6. CUT TENONS: Using a dado stack and a stop block on the table saw, cut ¾"-long tenons on each end of the rails. Sneak up on the tenon thickness by gradually increasing the blade height, checking the fit in the leg mortise until it's snug but not tight. When cutting the edges of the tenon, I leave about 1/64" of what is known as the "cosmetic shoulder" to pare away by hand later. This ensures an even shoulder all the way around and a tight joint.

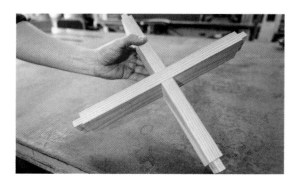

7. FIT JOINTS: Now that all the mortise-and-tenon joinery is cut, pare away the leftover 1/64" from the end shoulders with a sharp chisel. Double-check the fit and make sure that each joint will fully seat.

8. LAY OUT HALF LAPS: Mark a centerline on each rail edge, then lay out the 1" wide × 1 1/4" deep half lap joint with a sharp pencil and combination square.

9. CUT HALF LAPS: Back at the table saw, cut the half lap joints using a dado stack and two stop blocks, one for each side of the joint. Again, gradually raise the blade and adjust the stop blocks until the fit is snug and the rail edges sit flush when dry fitted. I fine-tuned the fit with a chisel and sanding block.

10. **LAY OUT LEG TAPER**: Now that all the joinery is complete, it's time to taper the legs. On the inside face (same face as the mortise), mark a line 4" from the top of the leg. Mark another line on the bottom of the leg (end grain), ¾" in from the same face. Connect these lines with a long straight edge to establish the taper.

11. **CUT TAPER**: I made a jig for the table saw to cut the leg tapers. It's a safe and easy way to cut repeatable angles, ensuring four identical legs. The jig rides in the table saw's miter track and uses an angled fence with toggle clamps to keep the workpiece firmly secured. If you don't want to take the time to make a jig, you can simply cut the taper on the band saw, cutting outside the line, then remove saw marks on the jointer or with hand tools.

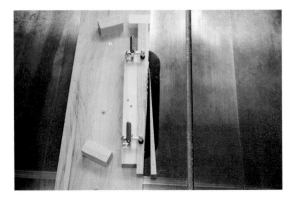

12. **CLEARANCE HOLES:** Lay out the placement for clearance holes in the bottom edges of each rail for attaching the tabletop with screws. Mark 1½" in on center from each shoulder. At the drill press using a fence to center your marks, use a ½"-diameter Forstner bit to drill 1"-deep counterbore holes into the edge of each rail. After drilling the four holes, switch to a 7/32" brad point bit, but don't move the fence. Drill all the way through the previous holes, creating a centered clearance hole for the top attachment screws. The hole is slightly oversize, allowing the screws to hold the top firmly while still adjusting laterally with seasonal wood movement.

13. **DRY FIT:** Using clamps, assemble the table base without glue to make sure everything looks good. Double-check that all loose joints are seating fully.

14. SAND: Disassemble the base, then sand all the parts and ease edges so that they don't feel sharp. Be careful when sanding near the mortises and half laps so that you don't ruin the fit of the joint. I use a hard sanding block in those areas to maintain flatness and use a random orbit sander on the rest. Some people call me crazy, but I like to sand to 400 grit if time allows. **NICK:** He is crazy.

15. ASSEMBLY: Before spreading any glue, I like to do a practice run of how I'm going to assemble. This ensures that I'll have all the right clamps, cauls, and brushes, and prepares me for a successful glue-up. The table base is assembled in two stages. First, apply glue inside the mortises and on the tenon faces and clamp together. Try to avoid squeeze-out as it can be a pain to clean up later. Leave these two frames in clamps overnight.

Once the glue has cured, unclamp the two frames. Now, glue the two frames together. Apply glue inside the half lap joint on both frames, then clamp together. Let sit overnight again. After the glue has cured, I install a screw from above to lock the half lap joint, since the half lap doesn't provide much face-to-face glue surface. The screw will be hidden by the top and gives me some additional peace of mind.

TABLETOP

16. MILL: Mill the top to ⅞" thick, but keep it oversize in width and length, about 14¼" × 14¼". I had a wide piece of claro walnut left over from an earlier large-slab dining table project, so I was able to get the top out of a single piece of wood. If you don't have a wide board, don't worry—you can glue two or three smaller ones together to obtain the required width.

18. CUT CIRCLE: There are many ways to cut a circle in woodworking, but I like using a band saw because it's easy to control and isn't prone to tearout when the grain direction changes as it does sometimes with a router. The circle jig rides in the miter slot of the band saw and has a ¼" dowel that the material rotates on. The center of the dowel is placed at 6⅞" (radius of 13¾" top diameter) from the front of the saw blade. A screw protruding below the jig catches the table saw and stops the jig in the correct position. Place the top on the indexing dowel and cut straight in. Once the screw stops the jig from moving forward, start rotating the workpiece past the ½" blade to complete the circle.

17. FIND CENTER: To cut the 13¾"-diameter circle top, first find center on the underside. I drew an × from corner to corner with a straight edge and pencil. After finding center, drill a ¼"-diameter hole ½" deep to index the circle jig.

19. SAND TOP: Sand the round top, removing any saw marks left from the band saw. Wiping the wood with a damp cloth between grits, known as raising the grain, will help you see if you've gotten rid of mill marks as well as give you a preview of what the wood will look like with finish. Raising the grain also helps to achieve a smooth finish later on.

TABLETOP AND BASE

20. APPLY FINISH: Once everything is sanded, blow off any excess dust in preparation for finishing. I prefer an oil finish for its grain-enhancing characteristics as well as ease of application and repairs. (This particular finish was a 50/50 mix of Epifanes Clear Varnish and BioShield Hard Oil.) Apply the oil with a clean cloth, letting it sit for a few minutes, then wipe off the excess with more clean rags. Monitor the wood after wiping clean as the finish can continue to weep out of the pores. I usually put a minimum of three coats on the base and five for the top, applying once a day. Never leave oil-soaked rags wadded up, as they can spontaneously combust! Lay out the rags flat or draped over a trash can so that they can off-gas safely. Once they feel dry and crusty, they're safe to throw away.

21. ATTACH TOP: Once the oil is dry, it's finally time to attach the top to the base. Set the top on the base, checking that it's centered between all four legs. Clamp in place using cauls and rags so as to not mar the surfaces. Flip the table over and stick a 3/16" drill bit through the clearance holes to mark where to drill in the top. Unclamp and, using a 7/64" bit, drill 1/2" deep into the marked locations on the underside of the top. Place the top back on the base and attach with four #8 × 2" round-head screws plus washers. Stand back and admire your handiwork!

CHRISTIAN BECKSVOORT

Fans of my former television program *Parks and Recreation* might recall this venerated woodworker from episode nine of Season 5, entitled "Ron and Diane," in which Ron attends the Indiana Fine Woodworking Association Awards. Shortly before receiving the annual award for "Achievement in Chair," Ron spots this personal hero of his and utters, "Mary, Mother of God . . . it's Christian Becksvoort, modern master of the Shaker style!" while giggling and brimming with childish glee. This is a prime example of Ron's life hewing quite closely to my own interests. I consider this episode to have been a great gift to me, since it allowed me to invite not only Mr. Becksvoort but also Asa Christiana (former editor of *Fine Woodworking* magazine). We even had my two favorite makers of hand tools, Lie-Nielsen and Veritas, set up their trade show booths— rendering me (and Ron) a veritable kid in a candy store.

My own personal history with Christian Becksvoort began with an extensive tutelage at my self-imposed homeschooling courtesy of the University of *Fine Woodworking* Magazine. (A note on woodworking publications—*Fine Woodworking* is the magazine that was handed to me by a contractor pal when I expressed an [obsessed] interest in learning to cut mortise-and-tenon joints, but there are other very worthwhile and enjoyable publications out there, like *Popular Woodworking Magazine, Wood* magazine, *Woodworker's Journal, ShopNotes* magazine, and *Woodcraft Magazine,* not to mention *WoodenBoat, Canoeroots* magazine, and plenty of other delicious maritime periodicals.) The most prolific of all contributors to *Fine Woodworking* across its forty-one years of history, Mr. Becksvoort has been responsible for twenty-seven years' worth of instruction of many different stripes, in seventy-some articles

ranging from building full Shaker furniture pieces to excellent fundamentals and techniques like cutting joinery and applying finish. Especially important to him are his articles about wood expansion, as he has logged more than fifty years of experience in woodworking backed up by an education in forestry and wood science.

Of course, I didn't realize at first that I would come to so fully revere this fellow's massive contribution to my education. I began to catch on by noticing his name cropping up again and again as I worked my way through the archive of *FWW* back issues. I was familiarizing myself with the basic hand tools like chisel, block plane, marking gauge, and card scraper, and I had grown comfortable with mortise-and-tenon joints and finger joints on the table saw, but I was too intimidated to attempt dovetails. The moment of epiphany occurred when I read an article with a set of plans for a Shaker blanket chest that had just appeared in the most recent issue of *Fine Woodworking*, by Charles Durfee. The piece included some clever ways to fix dovetails that had been screwed up or poorly made. Well, this was something. I took this information as tacit permission to perfectly cock up my dovetails and then fix them! I quickly practiced on cutting a few pins and tails (I should have practiced on many more).

By specifically targeting dovetail methods, a few different Becksvoort articles presented themselves as I searched through my back issues of the magazine. Time after time he would pop up with yet another reassuring feature on hand-tool tricks. By this point I began to realize that this unassuming gentleman from New Gloucester, Maine (winner of the Maine Crafts Association Master Craft Artist Award, 2009), was a veritable encyclopedia of building furniture in the Shaker style, many details and techniques of which are utilized in all styles of quality handmade furniture. I sought out his books, *The Shaker Legacy* and *With the Grain,* and soaked up every other article I could find, since his instruction also appears in many other collections of furniture books. Unbeknownst to him, he had become rather a Yoda-like character in my training, and to this day I still hear his Jedi voice in my head as I begin to cut pins for a dovetail: "... a little heavy to be on the safe side always cut them, then on it rub some graphite, to get a good fit, away slowly pare them you must ..."

Mr. Becksvoort, who goes by Chris, was drafted into servitude at age twelve by his father (a cabinetmaker who trained in Germany), then took four years of woodworking in high school and then a couple of years of wood technology in college. He found this knowledge to be invaluable, as his work focuses squarely upon the natural seasonal movement of wood and the effect this has on solid wood furniture. After college he saw a show of Shaker pieces at a Washington, DC, gallery that resonated with him enough that he returned to see the work several times. When he moved to Maine and opened his own shop in 1985, he had stopped by the last remaining community of Shakers, at Sabbathday Lake in Maine, and told them he would be interested in repairing any furniture that might be in need, for the cost of materials. The Shakers agreed, and a relationship of sincere artistic passion was born that has yet to abate, as the Shaker style became the primary focus of Chris's practice, which at the time of this writing has yielded over eight hundred pieces.

Some of his catalogue items, such as the lamps or the music stands, he says the Shakers would never have made, but he has allowed the inherent functionality in their design aesthetic to positively flavor all his Shaker hybrids. In his book *The Shaker Legacy,* he avers, "I not only value the Shakers' considerable craftsmanship but also respect their insistence upon utility as the first tenet of good design. With the Shakers, there is no ego involved, no conscious effort to produce works of art. Austere utility is beautiful in and of itself, and often works of art are inadvertently produced." I can certainly attest to this, having spent time in his shop and his showroom, where the simple honesty of his designs lends the furniture a charisma that comfortingly says "heirloom." Evidence abounds that these items are handmade by a master craftsman, lending the furniture a sense of warm familiarity that had me itching to make a purchase. His signature piece, a fifteen-drawer chest, includes 190 individual pieces and requires nearly 300 dovetails.

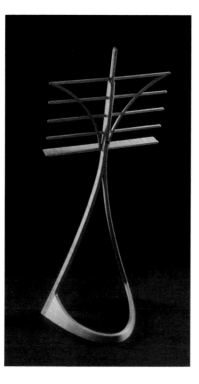

Another aspect of his line of goods that I find terribly charismatic is that they are all made of American cherry, top to bottom. He took me up to the loft in his shop and showed me a shipment of lumber that had just arrived—gorgeous planks all around sixteen inches wide. In a podcast interview with Trevor Green, Chris said, "I get my cherry from Kane Hardwood in Pennsylvania. They've been in business since about 1858, they own about 130,000 acres, and everything is sustainably harvested. As someone who's been in forestry, that means a lot. It's not a cut-and-run operation. What makes cherry such a nice compromise wood is that it's got great color, it's strong enough to use for table legs and bedposts, it wears well, it colors in nicely, and lastly, it's well behaved. It moves about thirty percent less than oak or maple, and that's a huge advantage when you're fitting drawers or doors."

His shop is built from the ground up, like a sweet little barn out behind his house in the woods of rural Maine. There are few places I love to hang out more than a workshop where great work is being done. You can see and feel the efficiency and economy that have developed over years of experience and trial and error. I drooled all over his classic wall cabinet containing the perfect kit of hand tools, and his bench by Lie-Nielsen, with custom drawers beneath, and at floor level a two-inch pullout step for climbing up to gain a little extra leverage on the bench.

Screwed inside the door of his tool cabinet is twelve inches of one of those planks of quilted bird's-eye maple that looks like some sort of expensive marble or really intense pink maple fudge, with this idiom burned into it:

"Productivity is nothing without Craftsmanship—Craftsmanship is nothing without Productivity." Then Chris walked me through the speed-tenon technique on his SawStop, and I giggled nervously, excited to get home and try it out. Cutting your tenons by hand is a joy, and you can hear every sweet chord in the Neil Young song playing on the stereo, but sometimes (often) you have to hustle, and that's when the machines can buy some time. Becksvoort spends sixty hours a week at work, but thirty of those hours are spent away from the bench. They are occupied with customer relations, writing proposals, making drawings, dealing with advertising, doing taxes and keeping the governor happy, rounding up hardware, going to the lumberyard, and any of the other miscellaneous tasks that are also billable hours, as it were. He says that if you want to make a living at it, you just have to throw yourself into the effort, to get dirty and make mistakes, so that you can learn how to avoid the mistakes as quickly as possible.

This is such great advice, since people don't think about the business end of things when romanticizing about woodworking. It's all visions of maple shavings and linseed oil and band saws and beeswax, but if you want to make a living you have to cover every aspect of the operation. This is very specifically what I admire most about this particular sliversmith: He found a niche in which he could prosper, building fine Shaker-inspired furniture pieces combined with some writing and teaching, and with hard work and talent and a proper domestic frugality, he has seen a very dependable success rate.

He keeps an old card catalogue with one index card for every piece of furniture he has built. On each card is the name of the client, the date(s), the piece being built, and a daily tally of hours and procedures undertaken. This meticulous record allows him to compare his speed and efficiency against himself over the years, since so many of his pieces are repeatable. The furniture he produces now commands a healthy price because of the mastery he instills in each and every piece. Not only are you getting a handmade article from a renowned craftsman, but he goes so far as to hide a silver dollar in a secret compartment in every large furniture piece, coined the year of the furniture's construction. That kind of thoughtful touch makes any custom commission that much more special, and the steady stream of orders on his calendar is the result.

We drove down the road to Lie-Nielsen Toolworks, the hand tool mecca of American woodworking, where so many of the finest woodworking tools are made on-site by honest, hardworking Americans: chisels, planes, saws, spokeshaves, and many, many more dreamy accessories. It's the tool-porn headquarters, and I was much enlarged to meet all the redoubtable employees, including Thomas Lie-Nielsen himself, whom I had only interviewed from afar for my last written effort, *Gumption*. They welcomed Chris Becksvoort like he was a local dignitary, which I suppose he rather is—it was like visiting the Louisville Slugger plant with Sammy Sosa. Not only is Chris a great hands-on spokesperson for their line of tools, but he actually has designed an expansion washer, several router bits, and a redesigned lock chisel for the august tool fabricators. His proximity to this institution of quality, combined with his idyllic one-man shop in the woods, made Maine look pretty attractive to this denizen of Los Angeles.

Probably my favorite thing among many about Chris is his matter-of-fact practicality when it comes to tool choice. One of his first articles in *Fine Woodworking* suggested using a belt sander to flush up your drawer fronts to the surrounding case sides, a method that is certainly practical but might be considered sacrilegious to the devotees of the jack plane. Becksvoort makes no bones about using the right tool to get the job done quickly, and that is more important to a woodshop's success than any romantic vision of a quaint, unplugged "woodwright's shop" ever could be. He's quick to point out that it was the Shakers, after all, who invented the circular saw. The less time one spent on woodworking, the more one had for the pursuit of spiritual endeavors, by which I assume they meant drinking beer and playing euchre.

CHRISTIAN BECKSVOORT

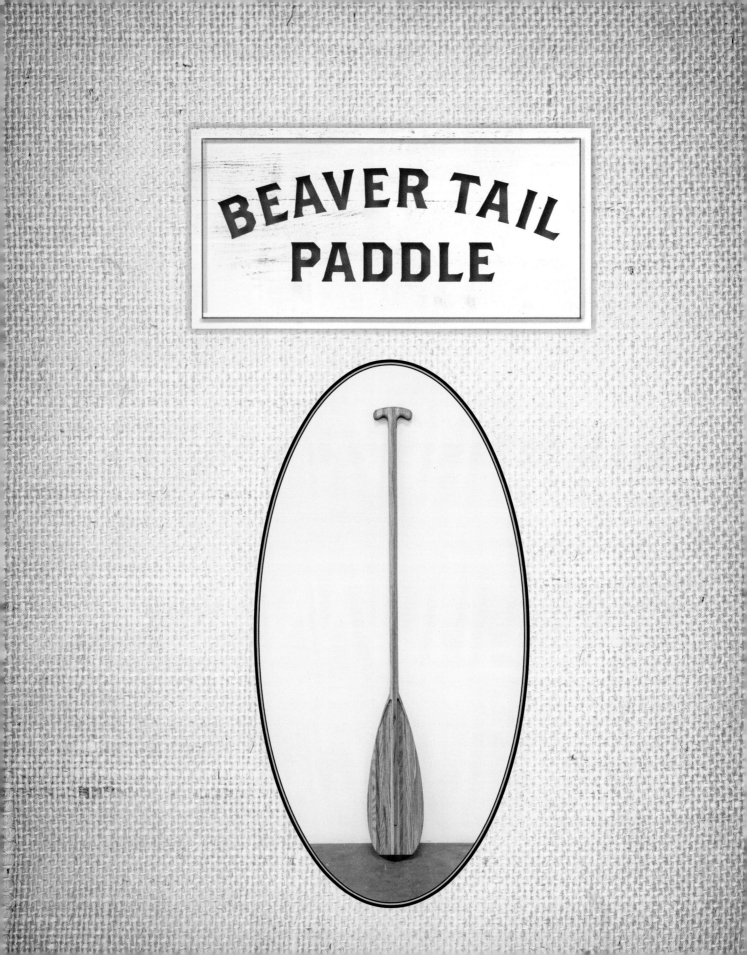

BEAVER TAIL
PADDLE

MAKING THE BEAVER TAIL PADDLE

Okay, friend, you have arrived. A canoe paddle is a great project in which to become comfortable with some of our most useful hand tools. This is my absolute favorite item to make in (or out of) the shop, unless I have time to make the whole damn canoe, which would then certainly take the cake. On one hand, you can trace this legendary shape on a plank of suitable wood and cut it out. On the other, you can glue up a blank from otherwise useless shop scraps and head for the very same finish line. I can think of few finer manifestations that a plank of wood can undergo than beginning life anew as an outdoor accessory so indispensable that an idiom was created saying as much. Everybody knows that if you are in trouble of any sort, then you, my friend, are up a creek without one of these handy water-shovels.

The fact that so much of this implement is fashioned with hand tools allows me to sit on a porch, or a nice patch of grass beneath a tree, preferably in earshot of a burbling stream or a neighborhood of finches, or both, and shave away at my blank until my paddle is ready to see me propelled upstream to the place where the deer come to drink. Of course, many of my paddles are made in my slightly less-than-pastoral shop in Los Angeles, but between Jeff Tweedy on the stereo and the sycamore glade in my head, I am still able to get to a happy place.

Please note that I am not an expert paddler, or an adventure enthusiast of the ilk who likes to paddle a fully loaded boat for eight hours a day into the wilderness. My paddles are not designed for a marathon, but very much for the effective motoring and steering of a pleasure jaunt on a river, lake, or stream. The nifty thing about paddles, though, is that with a little research you can choose the style that suits your needs/tastes/arms the best, and simply change the original template accordingly. The subsequent steps remain the same, by and large.

I first learned to carve paddles from Ted Moores's seminal treatise *Canoecraft*, and, as with so many repeatable shop projects, have made my own tweaks to the design and build methods, but there are only so many ways to skin this particular cat. Something I love about the project, however, and so many similar moments in boatbuilding, is that you are relying less upon the combination square and the caliper and more upon your eye and your judgment. Since there is hand carving involved, every paddle will turn out a little different, which is completely fine—all you care about is if it works well. It's not a drawer that needs to fit into a case just so, for the optimal opening and closing. A paddle is not furniture. It's a long-handled, flat wooden spatula that you will use to move and navigate a canoe through water. Learning to trust your own eye to determine whether a shape or line is "fair" is a very empowering moment in woodworking, and chances are—if you like it? Then it's perfect.

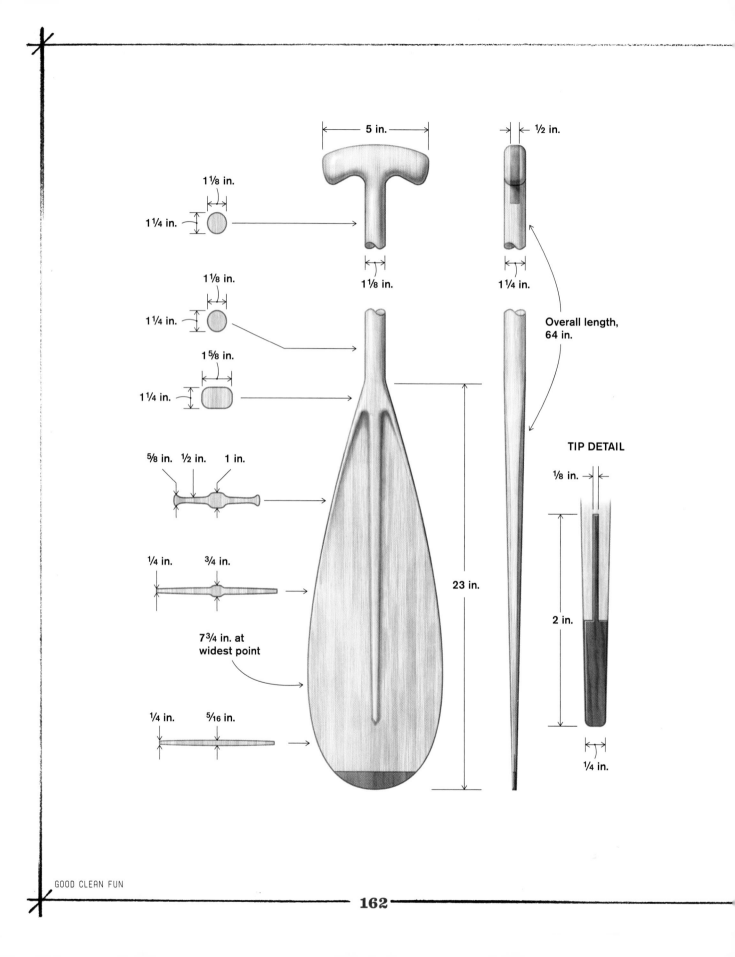

5 in.

½ in.

1⅛ in.

1¼ in.

1⅛ in.

1¼ in.

1⅛ in.

1¼ in.

1⅛ in.

1¼ in.

1⅝ in.

1¼ in.

Overall length, 64 in.

⅝ in.   ½ in.   1 in.

TIP DETAIL

⅛ in.

2 in.

¼ in.   ¾ in.

23 in.

7¾ in. at widest point

¼ in.   5/16 in.

¼ in.

1. Select your wood. You have some choices here—softwood or hardwood, for starters. Softwood paddles are easier to carve and much lighter in weight—but guess what the downside is? That's right, they're soft. So if you choose a pine or a cedar, you either need to be very careful not to break it, which is not easy to do when you're suddenly shoving off of submerged rocks in fast-moving water, or you have to reinforce it with epoxy and fiberglass. If you go with hardwood, the tool work is slightly more difficult (like carving ice versus butter), and it ends up a bit heavier, but you can go with a thinner blade to lighten it up a touch. I started out making cedar paddles, mainly because I had some extra red cedar planks lying around, but also because I like to carve details on my paddles and cedar is really easy to carve. Because the fiberglass-and-epoxy process is not the most pleasant or organic experience, however, I have since switched to oak, both red and white, for my paddles. Choose the clearest and straightest grain you can, avoiding any grain run-out in the length of the blank. When the grain "runs off" the edge of your paddle, the paddle is much easier to break at that spot.

For this paddle I am using some blanks made (by Matty) from all the red oak trim that was stripped from the set of *Parks and Recreation* when the show ended. Between the windows and doors and baseboards and more . . . that was a lot of custom-milled trim that was going to end up in a landfill. That this wood should then have randomly fallen off a truck in front of my particular shop, out of all the woodshops in the world, is an astonishing coincidence for which I am deeply grateful.

2. Create your blank. The dimensions for this design need to be 8" wide by your length* by 5/4" thick. As mentioned, you can use a solid plank, but cutting out the shaft section leaves some pretty large areas of waste. A more economical method is to glue up strips or pieces of scrap to accommodate all the paddle's dimensions. Be sure to mill everything to 5/4" before glue-up since your planer won't be friendly to the blank once you have opposing grain directions in the alternating strips. Once the glue has dried, plane or sand the blank nice and smooth so you have a friendly surface on which to draw lines.

---

*Find your paddle length by measuring from the floor to your chin, or from fingertip to fingertip of your outstretched arms. Most people like paddles between 56" and 62", but preferences vary. When paddling with a basic stroke, if the paddle is perpendicular to the water's surface, the blade should be in the water and the height of the grip should be in the neighborhood of your shoulder or chin.

3. Choose your design. I have read a lot of books about canoes and seen lots of paddle styles. I like to eyeball old photos and then draw my own versions freehand until I like the cut of their jib (not a literal use of *jib*. Paddles and jibs are usually not found in close proximity). The design I'm building is based on a traditional beaver tail, combined simply with my mental image of the ideal canoe paddle. Based on the narrowness of their blades, I imagine the indigenous paddlers of Canada would find my design silly, but it works fine for me. "To each his/her own," says me. Create your own template by drawing a centerline and then laying out half of your paddle's shape. To create your curves, use a thin strip of wood as a fairing batten, which is a common method of laying out pleasing lines in boatbuilding. For my templates I use 1/4" MDF, and I drill strategic holes in the two ends so I can match the template's centerline with the centerline on my blank.

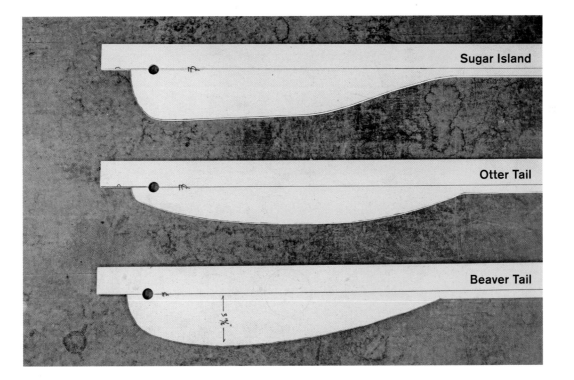

Sugar Island

Otter Tail

Beaver Tail

4. Draw a centerline on your blank upon which to register your template. As per Ted Moores, I use a black ballpoint pen to make the lines more indelible and easier to see than those of the pencil. Trace your half template, then flip it over the centerline and trace the other side. Eventually, I'll use a smaller template to lay out the carving details, but that's a few steps away.

5. Cut out the profile on the band saw or with a jigsaw, or if you're in the woods with no juice, use a coping saw. Stay just outside the line so you don't shoot yourself in the foot. One little slip and you've ruined your beautiful curves.

6. Trim/shave down to your line using a block plane and a spokeshave. Be sure to keep the edge square to the faces.

7. Now you'll want to transfer your centerline to the other side of the blank, and also use your pen and a combo square to draw a centerline around the outside edge of the blank. On the blade edges (not the shaft), draw two more lines denoting the finished thickness: ¼" for softwood, ³/₁₆" or even ⅛" for hardwood. If it's softwood, you'll draw a line ⅛" to either side of the centerline, etc. I now trace the template I made for my carving details in the throat area at the top of the blade.

8. As you proceed to shape your paddle, bear in mind that you'll be removing areas of thickness and therefore stability when it comes to clamping it down. For this reason you'll want to operate on the blade first since the shaft can be clamped right to your table or bench—be sure to use the appropriate clamp pads so as not to damage your blank. Even a small dent will bother you later as your fingers catch on it between every stroke.

9. Use a block plane to remove a wedge of material from the throat to the thickness line at the tip, creating a flat taper. Flip the paddle and repeat on the other side, so the tip, or "toe," should now be at your finished blade thickness. Once you have removed this material you can insert shims beneath the tapered blade to support further work. Your blade should now be a tapered wedge lengthwise from shaft throat to tip. You may need to reapply your carving details if they got planed away. I also carve a raised spine, tapered in height from the throat, down to 3–4 inches above the tip (optional).

10. Redraw your centerline on the blade and draw in a tapered spine (optional), then plane from that center ridge to the blade-edge thickness line all the way around, taking care to leave the center material alone for your carving if you choose. Unlike the last step, this tapering goes from the thick center to the thin blade edge all around.

11. Now remove the remaining blade material with a spokeshave or scraper. This step can go smoothly, or if your blank is made of laminated strips, the alternating grain can make this removal difficult to achieve without some grain tear-out—this is where a scraper comes in very handy. Whenever I run into opposing grain orientation or else just highly figured grain such as quilted maple or burled wood, I reach for the scraper.

12. I carve out my custom spine and throat details simultaneously with the removal of the rest of the blade material. Flexcut makes a really nice little set of hand-carving tools that gets a lot of use in our shop. I am personally not great at carving, but I know how to execute this shape from lots of practice with difficult grain directions. Every paddle ends up a little different based on what the wood is telling me. If it's an extremely hard wood or a squirrely grain pattern, then I trim the details down to minimize the amount of carving. Once the blade has been reduced to the proper thickness, I take care to transition all the details smoothly into the blade so there's nothing to catch on out in the woods.

13. Next I shape the grip end. You can choose from a few different styles here as well. Serious paddlers tell me they prefer the knob or "pear" style, since they don't want any hooks or corners to catch their hands as they smoothly transition their strokes from one side of the boat to the other. I tell them that sounds fine and I wish them a good day. Me? I like having hooked ends on my grip, as I often take out friends who are novice paddlers, and they invariably drop their paddle in the drink at some point, which is when I quickly hook their paddle with my own and save us a lot of trouble trying to retrieve the errant one. Because the hook design creates sections of short grain, I cut out a mortise and glue in a thick spline with the grain running perpendicular to that of the paddle. This is a very strong solution that prevents the little hook knobs from snapping off. Whatever shape you prefer, just be sure it feels good in your hands and has ergonomically shaped curves for guaranteed comfort during a long day of paddling. I mainly shape my grip with a spokeshave and a rasp, another amazing shaping tool for sculpting wood—this is a Nicholson #49.

NICK OFFERMAN: BEAVER TAIL PADDLE

14. You already have centerlines on all four sides of the shaft. Now use your sliding combination square to scribe lines dividing all four sides into thirds. The front and back should be 1⅛" wide, so your new lines will be ⅜" in from each edge. The shaft sides are 1¼", so your new lines are ⁷/₁₆" from the edge, or you can do ¹³/₃₂" if you're feeling anal. Don't try to go all ²⁷/₆₄". Please. That will just upset me. That's not what this is about. If you need to indulge in precision of that ilk, put this book away and jump straight into geometric marquetry.

There are two reasons that the shaft is thicker front-to-back than it is wide. One is that the human hand likes to grip an oval more than a perfect circle, and you can then use the shape to feel the correct alignment of the blade without looking. Secondly, it's good engineering considering the direction of the stress that's being placed upon the paddle, for the same reason that rafters and joists stand on edge rather than lie flat.

15. When you are ready to round off the shaft, you can clamp the blade in a vise, properly padded (we use yoga mats folded up—we also put them down for sanding pads—very handy for many shop applications), and support the grip end

if necessary. Take your new favorite tool, the spokeshave, and shave away the corners of the paddle shaft between your new lines until you have created a slightly oval octagon. Then shave away those eight new ridges, adjusting your shave angle slightly until the faceted shapes are virtually round. Check your work often by feeling it with your hand. You can leave the slight facets or make them perfectly smooth by sanding.

16. Run your hands over this magnificent new stick of power you have created. Feel the action and valor coursing through its very fibers. It should feel an awful lot like a canoe paddle by now. Using the old "blind man's test" method, let your hands tell you if there's anything wrong with the shape, or the location of the grip. Sand everything you care to, to the degree of smoothness you think is right. I rarely go above 180 grit on a paddle. It's not furniture.

17. After wetting your paddle to raise the grain and performing a final sanding, it's time to apply finish. If it's hardwood, I use linseed or tung oil, and I maintain the oil over years of use. Some folks use varnish, but I have found that my tender little paws tend to blister after some tenacious paddling into a headwind. One good finishing trick: Drill a tiny hole in the center of the grip end, then wax a screw eye and insert it. This allows you to hang the paddle while the finish dries so that you can coat the entire piece at once without needing to set it on blocks. You can whittle a piece to fill the hole later, or sometimes I just pack it with wax so it's available for eventual refinishing. Always dispose of oily rags properly; lay them spread-out to dry so the solvent can all off-gas. As we learned from The Beef (Josh), once the rags are stiff and crunchy, they are safe to toss. If you crumple them up wet and throw them out they will spontaneously combust! I have seen this happen, and we were very lucky that our jobsite didn't burn down.

18. For a softwood paddle, I use a couple of coats of West System epoxy for an extra level of protection, and I also fiberglass the blade. When the epoxy has cured glossy, I give it a brisk rubdown with 0000 steel wool to knock down the shine, which leaves a nice, soft matte finish. Now get the heck out on the river and enjoy your new paddle. Just keep 'er 'tween the banks!

BONUS SECTION: TIP TIPS

If you're anything like me ("hobbit" handsome but clumsy as an O. J. Simpson alibi), the tip of your paddle will be the focal point of possible damage. Despite my best intentions, I occasionally end up shoving off the rocks or muscling my craft along shallow water over gravel. These actions can batter and crush the end grain of your wooden paddle, leaving the area susceptible to the invasion of water. After repeated use and weathering, these contusions and their subsequent water damage will become exacerbated by seasonal movement and render the paddle a liability, as the blade can split on you and leave you stranded and heartbroken, the laughingstock of the woodland population. To guard against such an indignity, here are a couple of defensive techniques to help your paddle tip stay strong in the face of adversity.

OPTION 1. HARDWOOD SPLINE TOE: Before you cut out the curved paddle blank, cut off the last inch of the paddle toe. Cut a ⅛" × 1" deep dado across the center of the tip's width. Create a toe insert out of the hardest wood you can find. I used African padauk for my red oak paddles. It's very oily and dense and will therefore resist water damage and withstand a beating when it gets banged on rocks and the end grain can become vulnerable to water damage. My insert starts at 2" × 7" × ⅝", but you can adjust the dimensions as you see fit. It will end up 3/16" thick, after the blade has been shaped. Cut a long, thin ⅛" × 1" tenon along the toe plug to fit the dado. I keep the grain of this toe piece running parallel to the paddle grain so that I'm

still depending upon the tougher end grain to take the beating. Before gluing it in, wipe an exotic wood like padauk with acetone, which removes the oils from the surface and allows the glue a much better chance of adhering to the wood fibers. I used epoxy again (or Titebond III is also good here) for its waterproof qualities. I'll shape the paddle as usual, leaving just 1/16" or so of the oak blade material on each side of the padauk insert. People are regularly astonished by this joint, as it looks nigh impossible to achieve in the finished product.

OPTION 2. EPOXY TOE: Once you have cut out your paddle shape from the blank and trimmed/sanded it nicely to the template line, lay it on construction paper, mark the centerline, and then trace the curve of the toe. Now use a compass or a fairing batten (or a spackle bucket) to trace a curve slightly larger than that of the paddle tip, so there is at least ½" between the two arcs at the centerline. Cut out the pattern of this new curve, always keeping your centerline for reference. Now trace the new, larger curve on a piece of $^5/_4$" scrap at least as wide as the paddle blade. Cut it out and make it nice; but not too nice—it's just a form for casting epoxy. When you place the new scrap curve on the line you've drawn on the paper, it should leave a space between it and the paddle blade that resembles a crescent toenail. I also cut my mold in half to make removal easier, in case my wax fails me and something gets stuck. The curved space between the scrap and paddle toe is about to be filled with epoxy, so you'll want to put down foil or wax paper, then cover the inner curve with tape and wax the mold, but leave the paddle tip itself nice and clean and dry so the epoxy adheres to it well.

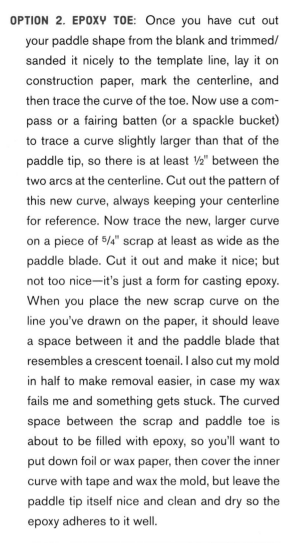

Clamp down the paddle so it stays put while the epoxy cures. I used a large weight here to that end. Clamp your mold in place and make sure you have no leaks where the form contacts the paddle.

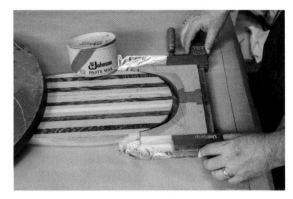

I use two-part West System epoxy with some special ingredients added in. I measure out my two parts—three pumps each of hardener and resin—and mix them clear for a full minute. Now I take a goodly portion of sanding dust from the same wood as the paddle (or I use dye tints if I have no sawdust yet) and mix it in until I like the color; then I mix in West System microfibers until I like the consistency and it pours like molasses. If you care about the color match, do some tests ahead of time and keep track of your ingredient proportions. Since I like to mix species in my paddles, I usually just go dark brown or black so the toe is complementary to almost any wood species. No, it's not lazy—it's because I'm classy. Not lazy. Classy.

Once the epoxy has cured, I clean it up and shape the blade as usual, using my second-best planes and scrapers, although the curve now extends an extra ½" or so at the tip. I just taper it back to the wood sides of the blade as pictured, so that the curves are still fair. You can use all your wood-working tools on hardened epoxy, by the way. This tough epoxy toe will take a lot of damage that would otherwise be inflicted upon your pretty wood, and it's a cinch to repair as well. Always wear a respirator when dealing with epoxy dust, as it's carcinogenic, which means super bad for your lungs and whatnot. Enjoy! (The paddle, not the dust.)

After copious stirring, pour your mix into the crescent-shaped void, taking care to keep it in the mold as best you can. If you get a drip or two on the blank, it's okay because you still have to remove a lot of material when you shape the blade. I then let it cure overnight at 65–70 degrees.

PS: I have seen this epoxy tip executed with a mold shaped from Play-Doh, but that is more messy and also only good for one use—I prefer the wooden mold because I can be more accurate, wasting less epoxy material, and also get countless reuses out of my mold.

BEAR MOUNTAIN BOATS

TED MOORES AND JOAN BARRETT

*The way to make a small fortune
in the boat business is to
begin with a large one.*

—TED MOORES

I have written enough words by now about enough people whom I love and admire to tell you right here at the outset that this chapter is going to feel terrifically incomplete to me. Nonetheless, I will press on, in hopes that I can succeed in doing even partial justice to these charismatic Canadians, providing you with a satisfying meal even if the portions might seem to me more scant than ideal.

It all began when I decided to build my first canoe. That magnificent periodical *WoodenBoat* informed me that the aspiring canoe builder need look no further than Ted's institutional tome *Canoecraft*. As was (and is) my habit, I bought the book and read it repeatedly, as if I was going to be tested on it (which I suppose I was—tested by my own demanding self). It's a beautifully crafted book, loaded with clear instructions, photos, and a heaping serving of wisdom. Early on, Ted informs the supplicant that he/she need not

worry about the project as a whole. One needs merely to focus upon the first step, then the second step only, and so on, until voilà! Thar she floats. This gentle positive reinforcement was just the nudge I needed to say, "What the hell. I'm going to take a crack at this."

One thing I really enjoyed about the experience was how inclusive the book was in helping me to source blueprints, foreign materials like marine epoxy and fiberglass and brass hardware, and even the specialized cedar strips required for a canoe hull. Many of these items are available through Bear Mountain themselves, but they were also quick to point me to the Builder's Forum on their website, my first substantial run-in with the generous community of online assistance. This globally available FAQ support group is especially priceless, I would think, to prospective builders in places more far-flung than California (like Australia . . . or

Topeka). I contacted Bear Mountain to ask a few questions about my order and was handled very graciously by Joan Barrett herself, Ted's partner in business and in life.

At this point, our relationship took a great advance forward thanks to three leaps of faith:

1. Because I was a woodworker with a lot of on-camera experience, Joan and Ted asked me to shoot a video of my canoe build, the point of which would be walking the viewer through the process as I experienced it myself for the first time. Joan floated this project to me about five minutes into our first phone conversation (this was 2007—pre-*Parks and Recreation*, so I was definitely unknown to her as a giggling moustache wearer).

2. My very new pal Jimmy DiResta not only agreed to drive me to Peterborough, Canada, to meet the couple and receive all the materials for the build, he also committed to shooting and editing the entire video, which we accomplished during those memorable salad days in Red Hook. If he had known then how slow I work, I wonder if he would still have signed on.

3. My own leap of faith was simply that this whole scheme would work out—driving to Canada in the dead of winter, meeting an impressive couple who build canoes and sell the accoutrements necessary for canoe building, driving back, finding a shop space, actually building the damn thing whilst communicating each step clearly

to an audience, then finally launching the finished bark in the East River. What could go wrong?

As you may have surmised, it went pretty right. Our video turned out to be engaging and successfully educational, trademark adjectives when it comes to Jimmy DiResta videos. Joan and Ted traveled to New York for the launch, Ted told me my work was "exquisite," I cried, we launched her (*Huckleberry* is her name) in the Upper New York Harbor, we didn't die or sink, and so now I get to write about it in my book.

It's funny, looking back on it, I feel like we should have been nervous about any number of things, but I think we all recognized in one another that dependable attribute known simply as work ethic. They trusted me and Jimmy to simply work hard, and had the feeling that I would repay their trust. I, in turn, feel so grateful for that trust that I want to continue to earn it even today. I have done my best so far in the tests set before me on their behalf, and I will always hope to please them because they are doing the right kind of work and have been doing it for a very long time.

Joan and Ted first began experimenting with wood-strip/epoxy canoes in the early 1970s when Ted noticed a cedar canoe for rent near their home. He proceeded to analyze the construction of said watercraft and decided he would like to try to build a better version. It would have to be argued that he did indeed revolutionize the design and construction, but the project perhaps took a little longer than he anticipated, since he is still at it now, some forty-five years later. Woodworkers and boatbuilders never seem to be

able to finish tinkering with tools and techniques, likely because that itself is the most delicious part—the tinkering. We always yearn to see if we can do better next time.

The key ingredient to this form of wooden boatbuilding is, ironically, the epoxy, which impregnates fiberglass cloth both inside and outside the cedar hull. West System is the brand of epoxy that was specifically developed by the Gougeon Brothers to couple well with wood, and Bear Mountain Boats was in the right place at the right time to benefit from this development. Even more than their actual canoes, which were gorgeous, Ted and Joan found that people were clamoring for their instruction and knowledge of materials. Thus, a bustling mail-order business was born, which has of course greatly burgeoned

since the advent of the Internet. Ted basically runs the shop and the actual designing and building of boats, and Joan runs the office and the shipping, which she really enjoys, as she is the epitome of a "people" person, even though I imagine it gets to be quite a load at times. Her personal touch with all the products they send out makes dealing with them a very pleasant experience.

What Ted and Joan have achieved together in their decades of collaboration is really quite monumental when you think about the numbers. Ted's book *Canoecraft*, considered the veritable bible of cedar-strip canoe building, has sold more than 300,000 copies to date, not to mention his later works, *KayakCraft* (1999) and *Kayaks You Can Build* (2004, with Greg Rossel). Ted and Joan wield a knowledge born of experience and

decades of trial and error. This, combined with their generosity of spirit, makes them a very enjoyable one-stop shop for the amateur builder. They say their success is measured by the thousands of Bear Mountain canoes and kayaks that emerge from home workshops around the world each year.

On top of their canoe/kayak concern, this humble outfit has also quietly logged some other very impressive and magnanimous achievements. Bear Mountain builds all the racing canoes for the Canadian Sprint CanoeKayak Championships (a massively popular sport north of the border).

They have also been involved for many years in a charitable effort at an eco-friendly river resort in Belize called Chaa Creek. Mick and Lucy Fleming, the pioneers behind the resort's humble beginnings in 1981, first contacted Bear Mountain because they actually just needed canoes to actually get to town. Joan and Ted flew in and were very taken with the local people and began regular visits, which included woodworking instruction and gifts of secondhand tools. With the assistance of Bear Mountain Boats, Mick Fleming was able to set up his own shop (which now houses eight woodworkers) and build all the furniture and trim work for his and Lucy's resort. With characteristic generosity, Joan and Ted have now been traveling the woodworkers of Belize up to visit their shop in Canada, to teach them more building techniques but also to expand their scope of the world. They also make educational DVDs for grassroots organizations in Belize on topics like organic cacao production and the preservation of endangered areas. I am continually inspired by the personal approach that Bear Mountain Boats applies in passing along the techniques of the developed world to less affluent communities.

In 2010, Ted and Joan launched *Sparks*, their thirty-foot hybrid electric fantail launch. I have had the extreme pleasure of cruising the Trent-Severn Waterway with them (including experiencing the Peterborough Lift Lock!), and I must say that gliding silently along in a pleasure boat powered by electricity was an awfully convincing argument for avoiding the gas station. The technology for powering the boat was developed with some assistance from the National Research Council Canada, and Ted noticed something interesting about the Research Council's approach. Any part of the operation that seemed successful didn't really hold their interest—it was the failures they were after, as it then furthered the research in their experiments. Of course, Ted wanted to get things

right the first time around, but the research is aided more by the deficits, because they provided more opportunities for learning—as he says, "It's frustration that is actually the mother of invention. . . . If it starts to go off the rails, we are forced to be creative and usually end up with a better solution than we started with."

I have been to visit them a few times now, and I am always charmed by the resemblance of their small farm to the landscape of my own youth in Illinois. Good-hearted, hardworking folks getting together to make something positive— adding to the greater good rather than the national deficit. In 2013, my dad and I had the pleasure of attending a double celebration at Bear Mountain Boats— forty years in business, and Ted's seventieth birthday. Not only were we fed and watered like prize livestock, we had an incredibly rewarding time getting to know some of the gang surrounding this industrious pair.

One such character was Rick Nash, one of the last few remaining craftspeople who know how to construct a birchbark canoe by hand, culling all the necessary parts from the woods and requiring only a "crooked knife," a hatchet, and some matches. That is an education I would very much like to chase—I told Mr. Nash how much I had enjoyed John McPhee's book on the subject of the birchbark canoe, and it turned out that Rick Nash had been there with McPhee when the book was researched in the 1970s! It also didn't hurt that this conversation took place over a healthy bonfire. I really enjoy this kind of serendipity, when like-minded folks end up running into one another as though attracted by some unseen magnetic force. Ted has a great take on this and describes it thus:

> *It is the defects in wood and in people that give them depth and make them interesting. They both take thought and patience to work with, but the rewards outweigh the effort.*
>
> *Let the wood (or people) speak—it will tell you what it wants and what it will let you do to it. Force it and it breaks; slowly steam it and it bends. A wild grain will be ornery to work and unstable, but cut it in half and book-match it and the beauty fills your senses. Straight grain is predictable and will stay where you put it; but aside from the engineering properties, there is nothing that excites. I see people this way— might be why all the people I respect, admire, or love are beautiful people with their own kind of crazy.*

My two favorite things about experiencing Bear Mountain Boats are aligned with the two main buildings: the house and the shop. First you go into the house and receive whatever cozy refreshment is appropriate to the time of day—a muffin, a coffee, a lunch, or a beer. Then Joan explains how ineffectual she is, even as you watch her handle the website and the telephone and the calendar and the shipping and several other sundry items. She'll assemble an order for a customer from the delicate and precious paper goods in the office, like the boat plans that are framable works of art, and then head out to the shop to prepare a quantity of fiberglass cloth for a customer by rolling it carefully around a cardboard bolt—like fabric should be handled, so it doesn't suffer any creasing (creases in your fiberglass are nigh impossible to get rid of).

When Joan takes her cargo back into the house for wrapping, I then stay in the shop for my second favorite Bear Mountain pastime—Ted's classroom. Wherever we're standing, there is something to discuss, whether it's the current canoe on the strongback (the long sawhorse-like mold), or a new jig for routing out mortises, or a hole in the exterior wall to create sufficient outfeed space for milling the extremely long hull strips, or any of the numerous specialized tools and clamps for boatbuilding. Ted is a gifted teacher in that he loves to research the best way of doing a job and then pass along his findings to anyone willing to listen. He's like a Pied Piper of canoe building. Here's yet another example, which I find very moving:

> *Years ago we built a decked Rob Roy–style canoe for [a wealthy client]. He wanted something that was my creation that he could hang in his office. It was a piece of art—book-matched walnut-veneer decks and a lot of handmade brass hardware. I had been trying for years to build the perfect canoe and after building this one*

realized that this was so far past what a canoe should be—that as a canoe, it was a failure.

While Ted assumes the role of the wise man in his shop ("Joan used to tell me that all I thought about was boats and sex. As you obviously know, it is patience that really brings out the true beauty in both, so they have a lot in common"), Joan teaches just as profoundly by her example. She exists at the hub of a community of craftspeople and builders and suppliers, not to mention friends and family (the pair have two lovely and successful daughters). When I asked for some reference pictures for our drawing of her and Ted, she said to me, "But I have no idea why you would want to include me in your book." (Joan, it's because you say things like that whilst bearing a Herculean load upon your shoulders as mother, manager, secretary, navigator, and cheerleader. Just because you don't wield the chisel doesn't mean you're not fully half the operation.) Joan is also the guinea pig—while Ted loves nothing more than to spend endless hours in the shop working on boats, it is Joan who loves to paddle them, particularly her kayak, in the wilderness.

I have been personally grateful for the opportunity

afforded me by projects like this book, to celebrate and promote the lifestyle of woodworking and handcrafting and making things like canoes. Moreover, I am thrilled to introduce you to folks like Joan and Ted, who have found their own quiet spot on a country road in rural Canada, where they strike it rich almost every day—Ted says that the boat business has been good to them . . . if you don't put accumulating wealth into the equation.

It may sound like cornball philosophy but I do believe that connecting and responding to materials and tools has made my life less of a mystery and more rewarding. It has been an exercise in problem solving that relates to everything that interested me. It has been a privilege to build beautiful things the way I think best and in a small way make the world a better place to live.

RIC OFFERMAN

" I love my dad. I also must add that I love my mom. She is about as heroic as a person can be, and my dad will be the first to tell you that in the parade of our family, she is the clear grand marshal. Dad, however, is the one with whom I spent so much time swinging a hammer, so he gets more coverage in the woodworking book.

My dad is very inspirational to me and worthy of much praise and exposition, which is why I have written a good deal about him in my previous books. Here I'll focus instead specifically on what a big deal it has been to indulge in woodworking with my dad. We call him Rico, "Suave" optional.

When I was a kid in school, my dad taught junior high social studies and geography in the neighboring town to Minooka: Channahon. The students from both Minooka and Channahon junior high schools then went on to attend Minooka High School, so called because it was physically located in Minooka, although I suppose it would have been fair to call it Chanooka High School, combining the two names like we did for the youth football league (Chanooka Braves) and the newspaper (*Chanooka Weekly*). I'm afraid my sweet little hometown is as guilty of insensitive sports team names as my fictional television home of Pawnee, Indiana, with their previous team name, the Dishonest Savages. Part of the American experience, I guess—indulging in the nostalgia of traditional team sports versus being decent to all the folks, especially the

ones who got such a deal as raw as that of the indigenous tribes.

Anyway, when I finally arrived in high school, half of the students were from Channahon and so were new friends to me, but they had aleady been in my dad's classes. Now, I had just turned fourteen, that age at which young adolescents tend to bristle and bridle against the authority of their parents, and I was no exception to this rule. My dad really didn't seem to be on the same page with me at this juncture, particularly regarding my slavish devotion to George Michael and the study of the dance—by which I of course mean the break dance. Any given morning before school a passerby might have witnessed me screaming in my cracking pubescent voice things like, "Dad! You don't even understand rap! Ughh! You're totally the opposite of fresh!!!"

You can imagine my surprise, then, when these new compatriots in the halls of high school informed me that my dad was everybody's favorite teacher. Despite my horror to hear of this betrayal on the part of my peers, it eventually became clear to me that my dad, who was legitimately voted as the favorite teacher every year, fomented this adoration by simply caring. He's nice, he's funny, sure, but more important, he just really gives a dang. When I hearkened back to all the effort my dad used to put into his classes, like hand-making these quizzes and tests that always caught my eye because they looked like fun (which they were because he made

them with love), it became clear that he was also my favorite teacher, or he could have been if he had only paid a little more attention to the social relevance of Grandmaster Flash and the Furious Five. Since my teenage confusion thankfully and eventually passed (at age twenty-seven or so), woodworking has been a substantial source of bonding for my dad and me. We love to inspect each other's shops, to ask questions and point out whatever little innovation we have cooked up, even if it's just a cool wall hook that keeps the door open when it's breezy out but doesn't require the bending over of operating a floor wedge.

You'll see in the following chapter that Dad sometimes comes up with his own way of doing things, which is one of the joys of woodworking. My brother, Matt, and I have inherited this trait from him, and sometimes we get it right and sometimes we get it wrong, but even when we are doing something in a way that is best described as "back-assward," the fact that we thought it up—it's our way— fills us with pride in our work. This is another intangible benefit to woodworking. Whether you have made a spoon or a canoe paddle, when you hand it to a person and they say, "How did you do this?" as though you have learning in the ways of wizardry, it brings forth a welling of pride that I can't describe. I can only encourage you to seek out that feeling for yourself, because it feels pretty darn special.

NAME: Ric Offerman

MY FAVORITES

PERSON: Wife, Cathy

TEAM: Cubs

SHOE SIZE: 10¾

MALE SINGERS: Frank Patterson, Ed Ames

FEMALE SINGERS: Kate Smith, Jo Stafford

SONG: "My Cup Runneth Over"

MOUTHWASH: Balvenie

MOUTHWASH I CAN AFFORD: Christian Brothers Brandy with honey

POLITICIAN: He died in 1865, was honest and a man of few words—isn't that something?

RULES: The US Constitution

BIRD: Sandhill crane

COLOR: 40 shades of green

BAIT: Night crawlers (well, actually half a night crawler—use the smart end first)

SCRAPPY BIRDHOUSE

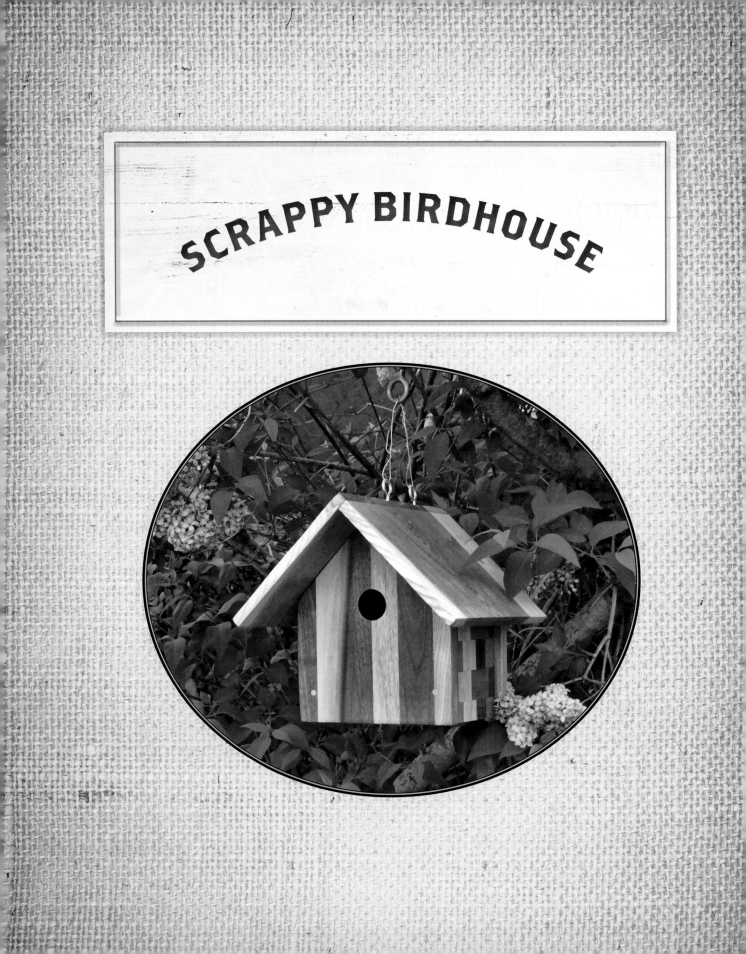

MAKING THE SCRAPPY BIRDHOUSE

I have been lucky and blessed, a nice combination if it happens to you. My first twelve years of life were on farms, the last being a dairy farm where there is always work to do. My younger brother and I had chores every day, with one of us helping Mom with the dishes and the other helping Dad feed and milk the cows. Dishes = fifteen minutes, milking = an hour and a half. It's funny, we'd both rather be in the barn, but at least we enjoyed our chores half the time. My dad, like all good farmers, was a hard worker. He admired and greatly respected anyone he deemed a good worker. He didn't care what they looked like, how they dressed, how far they could spit their tobacco juice, or how many cuss words they used. He looked to see who was with him when the shovel got heavy shelling in a corncrib or when the mow got dustiest baling hay. I never forgot that, never forgot the respect he had for hard work. I guess you could say that shaped my life.

Even after we moved into town (the small town of Minooka—1955 population: 350), we were only two or three blocks from the nearest corn, bean, or hay field. My generation was lucky because if you wanted to work there were always jobs to be had. I was big for my age and was able to go to work at fifteen for a company putting in clay field tile (installed correctly, it helped drain fields so low spots did not drown out the crop in a wet year). I first spied my future beautiful bride while baling hay for her dad, another hard worker, as is the whole Roberts family. Between farm and factory jobs, there was always work to be found; what a blessing—wish it was like that today. While going to college, I got lucky again in my twentieth year by taking what was supposed to be a three-day job with Lamping Blacktop. Eighteen summers later I gave them back their shovel. I doubt any of us will be put up for sainthood, but what a bunch of good workers. My dad would be proud of them.

I began my woodworking career at the age of twenty-eight when Nick needed a step stool to get tall enough to use the toilet, just a simple pine box. It was simple but fun. Next was a bookcase, then a TV cabinet to house our eighteen-inch screen. A few years later we bought an old farmhouse, had it moved to a new location, then spent ten years fixing it up with a lot of projects.

The last twenty-four years of my teaching career found me in a new junior high building that had, among other things, a woodshop, which was available to the teachers after school. That allowed me to work with some tools and machines I could not afford on my own, which helped move me along the woodworking trail. In this shop I also had access to the gut box, the box of discarded wood from the students' projects, and thus began my humble career of making things from scraps. With that said, I am sure, as you look over this fine book, that every other contributor has more technological knowledge and talent, including our two sons, Nick and Matt. That fact does not bother me a bit, as they have taken the little knowledge I gave them and built on it. My bride and I are blessed with four good kids, hard workers. Two of them happen to be woodworkers, one a library director, and one an outstanding teacher. We are proud of them all. The bottom line is I like to make things, be it out of wood, a quiz or worksheet for my students, or a pile of fish fillets at the lake (yep, ya gotta catch 'em first). I also spend a lot of hours in the garden. Mother Nature has a way of keeping you humble, but if you keep the weeds down, she almost always rewards you with something good to eat. It's kinda like raising kids: You keep removing the weeds around them till they can stand on their own. And speaking of raising kids, Nick thought, as this is his book, I might include a few words about raising him: "HE WAS A CHALLENGE." How's that for a few words? He also had more confidence in himself than any youngster I've known, taught, or bred, and it was more confidence than cockiness.

Anyway, I was talking about birdhouses. I make mine out of scrap. Some people end up with more scrap wood than others. The amount of scrap produced is usually in direct proportion to your level of craftsmanship. The better your work, the less scrap wood you end up with. I, on the other hand, end up with a lot of scraps . . . sad, but true. We had better describe scrap wood as it relates to this project: It is any piece ¾" thick by 1" to 8" wide by 6" to 11" long, depending on your design. If working with rough-cut lumber, you will need to cut and trim so that you have two parallel smooth edges (for gluing) and one other finished (smooth) side to face out. Almost all my purchased wood comes from Dan Daly's sawmill outside Minooka, Illinois (2016 population: 11,000), and it is rough-cut with two finished faces. The raw outside edges, when trimmed away, find their way into my projects. If your material is finished on four sides (planed and jointed), you are ahead of the game. Make sure your board edges are square (90 degrees) to the faces for gluing.

For many years I have slapped together birdhouses, some for gifts and some for home use. Thirty-two years ago we moved into a home built in 1905 that had eight mature trees. Since then we have planted or transplanted (thanks to the squirrels) four more, so we have many good birdhouse locations. As the years have passed, I have tried to improve the design of the home for birds. A few years back I began selling these through Nick's woodshop website, and I have continued to read and study different methods to improve the end result. If you bought one of my earlier efforts and read the following plan, you will see a slightly different, but I believe better and stronger, birdhouse. I wish I had gotten smarter quicker (my kids have the same wish).

In this plan we will be using hardwoods, which offer a good variety of colors, shades, and textures. In the photos you may notice red oak, ash, walnut, hackberry, and cherry, among others. I have been known to sneak in some red cedar (a softwood), but don't tell anybody, please. If you are just getting started, the sources of wood are many and varied. You may go to the lumberyard and buy what you need. There are online sites that list wood free for the hauling, among other items. Some cabinet shops have a Dumpster they don't mind you going through (check first). My friend Craig Sweeney, a master cabinetmaker, kept me in hardwood scraps for a long time—until he bought a wood-burning stove for his home, that is. Hardwood scraps burn very well, actually really well. Dumpsters at new home or rehab construction sites are another possible source, but, as always, check with the owners or workers first. Another good friend, Terry McDonald, cleaned new houses after construction was complete but before the new owners moved in. Any hardwood scraps a foot or longer he kept for me. I am blessed with good friends.

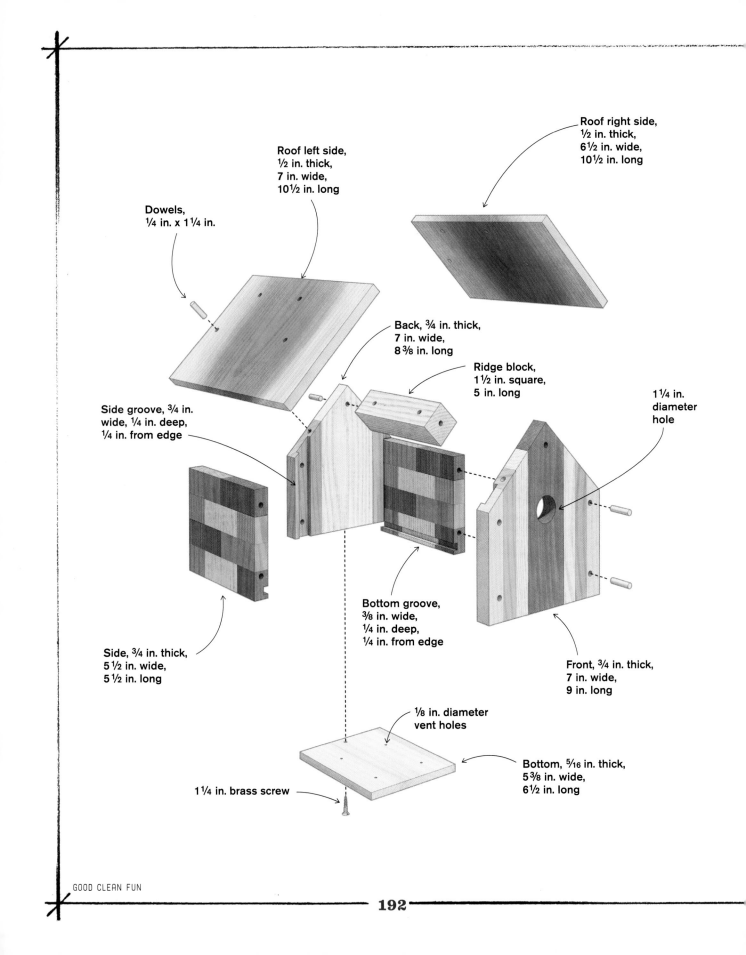

Roof right side,
½ in. thick,
6½ in. wide,
10½ in. long

Roof left side,
½ in. thick,
7 in. wide,
10½ in. long

Dowels,
¼ in. x 1¼ in.

Back, ¾ in. thick,
7 in. wide,
8⅜ in. long

Ridge block,
1½ in. square,
5 in. long

1¼ in.
diameter
hole

Side groove, ¾ in.
wide, ¼ in. deep,
¼ in. from edge

Bottom groove,
⅜ in. wide,
¼ in. deep,
¼ in. from edge

Front, ¾ in. thick,
7 in. wide,
9 in. long

Side, ¾ in. thick,
5½ in. wide,
5½ in. long

⅛ in. diameter
vent holes

1¼ in. brass screw

Bottom, 5⁄16 in. thick,
5⅜ in. wide,
6½ in. long

1. All right, you have collected some wood. For this project, either hand or power tools can get the job done. Hand tools will take you longer, but that's not all bad if you like working with your hands. When I use this plan, I usually make twenty to twenty-five birdhouses, so my table saw, miter saw, planer, drill press, 18-volt drill, and hand sanders get a lot of work. If one or two houses is your goal, don't worry—you'll do fine with hand tools. More than likely you'll make fewer mistakes than I do. I tend to go too fast, skip a step, and end up with a piece I can't use in that section. Oh yeah—I forgot to list "mistakes" as an excellent source of scrap wood.

2. The house I will build is sized for smaller birds such as wrens, chickadees, and nuthatches. This is determined by the hole size and inside dimensions. As you glue your scraps together you will need two blanks for the front and back that measure 9" high and 7" wide, two for the sides that are 5½" high and 5½" wide, and two for the roof that measure up to 11" long and 7½" wide. You will cut the bottom after you put these six parts together. When gluing scraps, it is difficult to find pieces that equal those exact sizes, so make your blanks bigger and then cut to size after the glue sets. What makes these houses unique are the different colors and textures, so look for variety when matching each piece to glue. Many scraps are scraps because of some defect: a gouge, stain, rough-cut side, etc. Glue your blanks so the best side faces out and defects face in. As near as I can figure, birds don't care what the inside looks like as long as it is dry. So, with that, glue your pieces together. Make sure you wipe off excess glue with a damp cloth, especially off the sides that will face out. I usually glue the scraps with the best side facedown on a flat surface. This also makes it easier to wipe off excess glue.

3. The next step after the glue dries is to cut your six blanks to their finished sizes as noted earlier. Among those six are a front and back that measure 9" tall by 7" wide. To figure the 45-degree cuts that hold the roof, I mark the middle of the top of the front and back, hopefully at 3½". Using a speed square helps mark the lines to cut. To check your lines use the 90-degree angle on your square. The bottom of both 45-degree lines should line up on the 90-degree line. If you have a different method that works for you, go for it. As Dad said, "There is more than one way to do a job wrong." I believe he was looking at me. The positive corollary of that is that there is more than one way to do a job right. Keep that in mind always. Everyone has good ideas and different ways of looking at a job. Yours may be the best. Really. **NICK: If the chop saw makes** you nervous, clamps and hold-downs are great for keeping your fingers farther from the blade.

4. Before I connect the front, back, and sides, I vertically dado the front and back to accept the sides. This allows for a stronger bond for the four sides. There will also be a horizontal dado near the bottom of the sides, which allows the bottom board to slide out for cleaning. For years I would, at this point, butt the sides and glue and screw. Nick suggested I use a dado with wood dowels for a cleaner look. He was right. It takes a little longer, but I end with a stronger, more polished look, in my humble opinion. I come in ¼" from the outside edges of the front and back and usually make the dado ¼" deep and ¾" wide. If your sides are of narrower stock, adjust accordingly.

5. It is now time to dado the sides so the bottom may slide in and out. Many bird books state that it is very important to clean the birdhouse each year. You may have noticed in your many years of observing nature that hollow-tree nests do not have a clean-out. I wonder if OSHA and the EPA know about this. Come up the side ¼" from the bottom and cut the dado ¼" to ⅜" wide, depending on your flooring thickness. I do not dado the bottom of the front piece for two reasons. One, many bird experts warn about not having enough ventilation or drain holes in birdhouses. Two, I make the dado cut on the table saw, which would show on the outside edges of the front piece. I personally like the look of a straight line on that edge. If you dado with a router, you can add the extra groove without sacrificing the look by stopping the dado before you hit the end of the board.

6. Before I glue and dowel these four sides together, I need to trim the back piece to allow the bottom to slide in and out. Butting a side wall next to the back, transfer the top edge of the ¼" dado on the side piece via pencil onto the back piece, scribe a square line across the width of the back, and then cut off the part below the mark.

Assemble the front, sides, and back on a flat surface. Cut a scrap that is similar in width and thickness to the bottom. When the scrap is inserted into the floor dados, the back wall can rest upon the scrap for glue-up. Glue the front and back edges of the side walls and the vertical dados in the front and back walls, and clamp the four parts together. Watch for glue squeeze-out and wipe it off with a damp cloth. Make sure your assembly is square, and that you don't have any glue in your dados for the floor piece.

While the glue sets, I measure and cut a 1½" by 1½" scrap piece to go inside the ridge from peak to peak to reinforce the roof. Glue and clamp this in place. If you don't have clamps, just tightly squeeze the pieces for fifteen minutes. Check again for glue squeeze-out. (I was kidding about the fifteen-minute squeeze. Get some clamps.) The top beam helps strengthen the screw eyes to hang the birdhouse.

7. Once the glue sets, it is time to drill the holes for the wood dowels. For dowel size, depending on the thickness of the walls, I like ¼" or ⅜" and a matching drill bit. A sharp (new) bit really helps give a nice clean hole with no tear-out. The dowel hole should be at least 1" deep. On the bit I mark 1" up from the tip with a piece of tape. You may go deeper if you wish. The dowels need to be ¼" longer than the hole is deep, to ensure that you can tap it fully into the hole with glue. You also want to be sure your dowels have grooves running up the side so the glue can get around. That will be two holes front and back into each side wall, plus one hole front and back for the top beam. If my math is correct, that's ten holes, you good kid. Once the glue has dried, I use a flush-cut saw to carefully saw off the excess, and then a light sanding brings the surface flush.

8. You now get to choose your style of roof overhang. Many folks (maybe you) like the protrusions to be equal, front and back. After some research and observation, I prefer that there be only 1½" overhang on the back, with the remainder on the front. Why? Because the front hole needs protection from the weather and predators like the pesky raccoon. That is also the reason my birdhouse has no perch. Birds do not need a perch, and a perch makes a good handhold for a predator. I prefer to construct swinging birdhouses to thwart baby-bird and egg thieves. If you wish to add a backboard (5" × 14" would be a good size) to your birdhouse to nail or screw it (screws are better) to a tree or building, add that now and butt the roof right up to the backboard. You are doing the work, so you choose your overhang and whether to add a perch or not. You won't hurt my feelings a bit. I'm all for you.

9. It is now roof time. I am going to glue and clamp the roof pieces in place, butting the top edges along the ridge peak. To ensure that the length of your eaves comes out the same, mark the thickness of the top board (you pick, it doesn't make any difference) on the bottom board and cut off that narrow strip. Install the short side first, clamping it into place, then do the same with the long side, making sure you have the wider board overlapping the narrow one. Yep, I have done it backward, going too fast, and that kind of makes you look silly. When I am happy with the fit and alignment, I lay out my dowel holes, drill them out, then tap in the dowels with glue. I bet you'll do great.

10. Now you are ready for the bottom. Since this is not rocket science or advanced trigonometry, I wait until this time to measure and cut the sliding bottom piece. The bottom should be $1/16$" less in thickness than your side dado. If you cut your side dado at $3/8$", then your bottom thickness should be $5/16$", etc. Measure between the outside edges of the side dados and cut the width of the bottom $1/8$" less than the opening. For length, measure from the inside of the front wall to the outside of the back wall. I add an inch to that length and trim the back corners, which gives you a tab to grab at clean-out time. Try it, will you, please. If it slides easily but falls out, the floor width is too narrow (yep, done that). If it does not slide easily, it is either too thick or too wide (done those too). The last two are easier to fix. Once you have a good slider, insert your bottom so it is tight to the front. Find the middle of the back's bottom edge, and drill and countersink a pilot hole to accept an all-weather screw. I use a $1\frac{1}{4}$" screw. That is all you need to hold it firm. The folks who write bird books suggest we drill holes in the bottom for drainage and ventilation. Seems like a good idea to me. I drill one hole near each corner, figuring it will be harder for the littler critters to clog those holes with doo-doo. No, I have no proof that this theory works or that four is the correct number. If you are really good at making holes or just love drilling, knock yourself out.

11. I like to use brass or stainless steel screw eyes to hang the birdhouse. They are located along the peak, 1" inside the front and back walls so that they have a bite into the ridge beam. To make drilling a pilot hole easier, I use a small saw and a small file to construct a flat surface on the ridge peak at the 1" mark. Use an awl or nail to make a point for the drilling of a pilot hole for the screw eyes. On a side note, our Midwest weather and prevailing winds usually arrive from the west, southwest, or northwest. With that in mind, we hang our birdhouses with the entry hole facing east whenever possible.

12. The front face, the back face, and their exposed edges get a good sanding before the roof is attached. The roof, its exposed edges, and the slide-in bottom piece are also sanded with a final sanding grit of 180 for all surfaces.

13. The final step is two coats of clear satin spar urethane. Why? Because I had a can of it in my shop, it was marked for outside, and I liked the way the finished job looked. The clear satin allows the true wood colors and grain to show, and the second coat helps me because I almost always find a spot I missed with the first coat— drives me crazy.

Thank you kindly for your attention. It is an honor to be included in this book. Yep, you guessed it, another blessing, by golly.

A Quiz About Wood

___1. Which wood species was used for the hull of Old Ironsides?
   a. Red Elm
   b. Blue Chestnut
   c. White Oak
   D. Raggedy Old Hackberry

___2. Early tennis rackets and the vast majority of baseball bats were made of
   a. Walnut
   b. Ash
   c. Beech
   D. Hazelnut

___3. Which of the following is not a recommended use for sawdust?
   a. clean up oil spills
   b. weed repellent (walnut dust)
   c. filler to add fiber to bread dough
   D. spread on snowy trails for traction

___4. What's the best wood for carving a "tobacco pipe?
   a. briar
   b. hickory
   c. pine
   D. don't worry about it Copper!

___5. The largest tree by volume is a Sequoia at 275 feet tall and 52,500 cubic feet. It has been named the
   a. General Patton
   b. Sargent York
   c. Private Benjamin
   D. General Sherman

___6. A sugar maple produces up to how many gallons of sap a year?
   a. 2   b. 12   c. 22   D. 222

___7. The best month to collect maple sap is
   a. March   b. July   c. September   D. December

200

____8. When boiled down the sap from one sugar maple makes about
a. a pint b. a quart c. a gallon d. 10 gallon of syrup.

____9. The most numerous American Hard wood is the
a. oak b. maple c. cherry d. Norwegian pine

____10. The hardest American hardwood is
a. walnut b. aspen c. hickory d. Costa Rican Teak

____11. The chemical predecessor of aspirin came from the bark of the
a. willow b. hollyhock c. elm d. maple Tree.

____12. In the good old U.S.A. most chopsticks are made from the wood of the
a. aspen b. peach c. pumpernickel d. red wood Tree.

____13. The most important (I think they mean money) American nut tree is
a. pecan b. cashew c. walnut d. pistachios

____14. Some native Americans made their bows out of a tree they
called powcohicora. We call it
a. pondarosa pine
b. pecan
c. willow
d. hickory

____15. The cottonwood tree was thought to be a good sign to
westward pioneers because
a. they could make thread for new clothes
b. turkey's like to roost in cottonwoods
c. the bark was good for sun burn
d. they were a sign of streams and creeks

____16. The native American tree with the largest leaf is the
a. birch b. sycamore c. banyan d. elm

____17. In the U.S.A. the Pine Tree state is
a. Nebraska b. Maine c. Washington d. New Mexico

____18. Our seventh President, Andrew Jackson, had the nickname
a. Mighty Oak b. Pecan Puss c. Old Hickory d. the
Sassafras kid e. the Wild Willow of Whitehall

201

True or False

_____ 19. George Washington's teeth were made of wood.

_____ 20. Cypress trees are found mostly in the mountains of the west.

_____ 21. Norse mythology refers to ash as "the mighty tree that supports the heavens" and "below the earth its roots went down to hell."

_____ 22. In England Sassafras roots were converted into a tonic that smelled like root beer and kept its drinkers youthful and healthy.

_____ 23. Native Americans and early settlers would boil and eat white oak acorns.

_____ 24. From sap to bark birch trees are used to make everything from beer to toothpicks.

_____ 25. "Measure twice, cut once" was traced to the ancient Druids after working on Stonehedge.

"Once you replace negative thoughts with positive thoughts you'll start to have positive results." Willie Nelson

"Remember, a chip on the shoulder is a sure sign of wood higher up."

Brigham Young

"I don't like things that can be reproduced. Wood isn't important in itself but rather in the fact that objects made in it are unique, simple, unpretentious" George Baselitz

"Be yourself, everyone else is already taken." Unknown

Fact

In Romania, brides who wished to delay child bearing placed into the bodise of their wedding dresses one walnut for each year they hoped to wait. There is no record of the success rate of this method.

Extra Credit (1 point each)

____ 1. Oak Tree
____ 2. Blue Spruce
____ 3. Birch
____ 4. Sequoia
____ 5. "Old Ironsides"
____ 6. Andy Jackson
____ 7. Band saw
____ 8. Radial arm saw
____ 9. Environmental President Teddy Roosevelt
____ 10. Humorist Will Rogers

Quiz Answers

Multiple Choice		True or False	Extra Credit	
1. C	10. C	19. F	1. L	6. E
2. B	11. A	20. F	2. N	7. I
3. C	12. A	21. T	3. H	8. B
4. A	13. A	22. T	4. J	9. C
5. D	14. D	23. T	5. K	10. D
6. B	15. D	24. T		
7. A	16. B	25. F		
8. B	17. B			
9. A	18. C			

JANE PARROTT

" You might want to be sitting down for this next bit . . . okay? Comfy? Here goes: I love Jane. She is decidedly our most groovy artist, no doubt thanks to her upbringing in a community of craftspeople in Woodstock, New York. She joined an unruly gang of Bard graduates in San Francisco, which is where Lee first ran across her path. When the two street toughs later moved to Los Angeles, Jane was actually Lee's landlord, although the nomenclature is a bit thin considering that Lee was renting a chicken coop. For real. I'm telling you, these ladies are tough. Although Jane seemed to know everybody in Los Angeles who had ever slung a glue stick, the rest of us came into her circle only when she began renting space next door to the shop to do some welding of her cool lamp projects (www.wavesofwhite.com). As a member of the neighborhood, with obvious talents to be valued (exploited), Jane pretty quickly found herself answering requests from Offerman Woodshop for metalworking needs of one sort or another (table legs, bases, custom hardware, ammunition). As we became friendly, we were tickled to discover that Jane likes welding, but she can make damn near anything with her hands, thanks in part to her BA from Bard College in 1999. Perpetuating our propensity for fraternizing (or sororitizing?) with the theater nerds, Jane also got a dang master's degree from Central Saint Martins in London, where she specialized in designing sets for theater and dance performance. Once she started hanging around on our side of the parking lot, it didn't take Jane long to pick up some slab scraps and see the potential lamp bases in the beautiful wooden chunks. Her efforts quickly became some of the nicest items on our website, and she joined our club of dusty hedonists. Eventually she decided she was having a little bit too good of a time, so she began running our shipping operation in order to put a slight damper on her spirits. It doesn't seem to have worked, however, I suppose because she's so dang good at it.

NAME: Jane Parrott

FAVORITE COLOR: Indigo

BIBLE: *Kids in the Hall*

FAVORITE GAME: Hot Dice

FAVORITE MEAL: Thanksgiving

FAVORITE CONDIMENT: Ketchup and mayo

PIERCINGS: Ears and nose

FAVORITE WOOD: Eucalyptus

FAVORITE TOOL: Hollow chisel mortiser

MAIN MAN: Isamu Noguchi

***PARKS & REC* AVATAR:** April

FIRST CAR: '88 Volkswagen Fox, 2 door/4 gear/no power steering

CRAFTSMAN LAMP

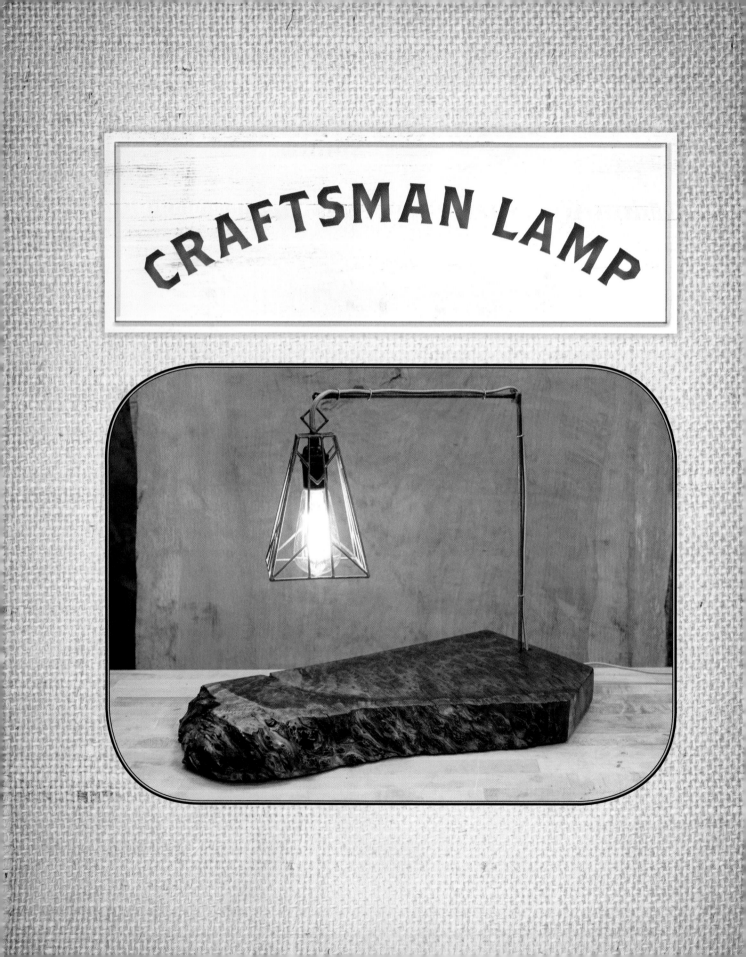

MAKING THE CRAFTSMAN LAMP

I grew up in the Hudson Valley in a small town near Woodstock, New York. It was the early '80s, but the grassroots community established in the '60s was still there. Many people had left more urban settings behind to build a house in the woods and raise a family. Down the road a neighbor had an annual raucous community pig roast. In the summer the Clearwater Festival was full of banjos, bandanas, and giant puppets. "The Green," a small substitute for a town square in Woodstock, was always alive with musicians and motley characters. It was commonplace to pick a trade and make it your own homegrown business. I grew up with the idea that your life builds around what you do, and that can be an engaging and enjoyable endeavor.

From there, through a jingle-jangled career or two in art and making things, I came to making lights. A few years back I started making slab table lamps at the woodshop. Lee suggested using the offcuts from the shop's furniture projects as lamp parts, which meant I was going to be making some badass lamps no matter what I chose to do with those chunky gems. For this project I've used a decent-size redwood cutoff. The availability of this beautiful species is quite novel for me. Not having seen a redwood until my late twenties, I still find them totally majestic and otherworldly. Its dense, chocolaty complexion when finished is trance-inducing.

I've chosen to make a Craftsman-inspired design for this lamp. *Craftsman* refers to the American Arts and Crafts movement, a continuation of the British Arts and Crafts movement started in the 1860s. Its first essential contributors, namely John Ruskin, William Morris, and Augustus Pugin, were responding to the growing popularity of factory-made decorative arts, opting for hand-hewn methods in the face of mechanized mass production in the early part of the Industrial Revolution. It was an aesthetic movement—emphasizing the simplification of design to let its function and materials do the talking, as well as a social movement—honoring the worth of human labor.

In Los Angeles, the Craftsman style permeates many more established neighborhoods. We have the advantage of seeing firsthand homes like the Gamble House in Pasadena, which is a living, breathing sculpture in itself, featuring eye-popping joinery and over a dozen hardwoods. The style uses geometric lines in concert with organic shapes. Japanese aesthetics largely influenced the movement, which imbued it with references from nature, ironed out and left simple, to let you breathe a little and just enjoy the objects around you.

The Craftsman style has clearly influenced a lot of the zeitgeist of design aesthetics today. On a parallel string we have the gaining popularity of handmade goods and backyard businesses. The pendulum has swung back, and we find ourselves in another craft era. We can learn from a movement spawned over 150 years ago, responding to unfair working conditions in the name of profit and speaking to the need for community-based economies. Perhaps our time has even more to respond to.

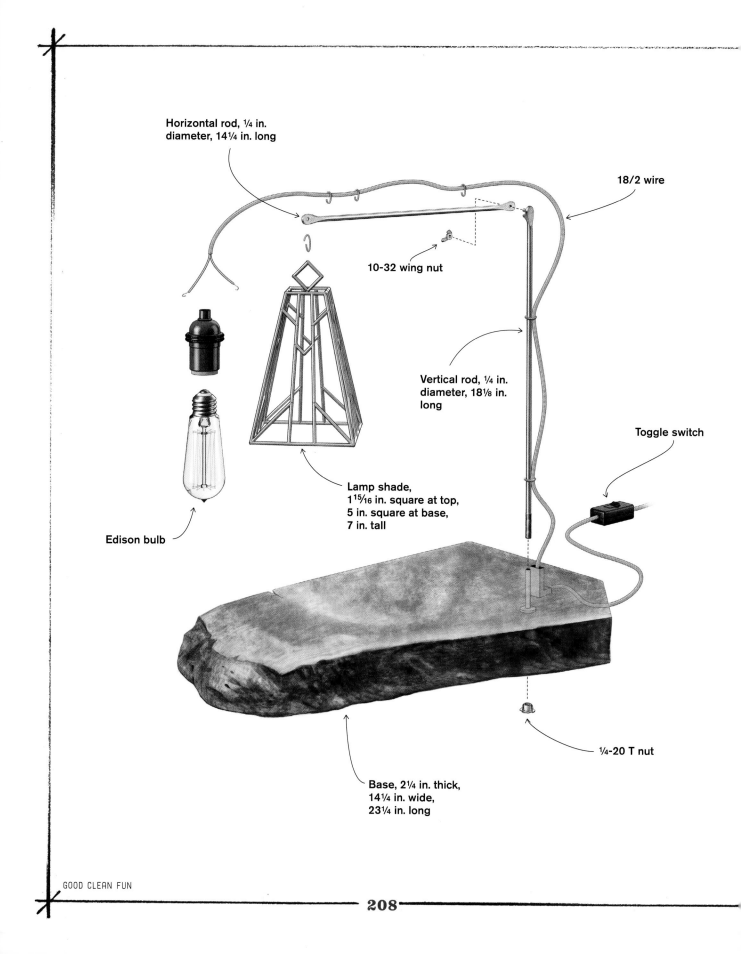

Horizontal rod, ¼ in. diameter, 14¼ in. long

18/2 wire

10-32 wing nut

Vertical rod, ¼ in. diameter, 18⅛ in. long

Toggle switch

Lamp shade, 1¹⁵⁄₁₆ in. square at top, 5 in. square at base, 7 in. tall

Edison bulb

¼-20 T nut

Base, 2¼ in. thick, 14¼ in. wide, 23¼ in. long

WOOD BASE

1. Select your piece. I've chosen redwood burl.

2. Tape off a shape to cut out and trace the lines.

3. Cut out the shape on the band saw.

4. Sand edges flat with a horizontal belt sander at 60 grit.

NICK: Ignore my yellow graffiti.

5. Mark the center of the back edge on the bottom side.

6. Measure in 1½" from that edge along that line on the bottom and mark it—this will be the center of the hole for the vertical arm of the lamp.

7. First drill ⅛" deep with a ¹⁵/₁₆" Forstner bit on the drill press.

8. Continue the hole by drilling ¾" deeper with a ⅜" brad point bit.

9. Drill the rest of the way through using a ¹⁷/₆₄" brad point bit—these three diameters will accommodate the rod and the T nut that holds it in place.

10. Flip your slab over. The ¹⁷/₆₄" hole you drilled is now visible on the top of the slab. Mark a line square to the edge, running from the center of the top hole to the back edge. Use your square to continue that centerline down the back side.

11. Along that line, mark two rectangles that are ¼" × ½". These will be the out channel for the cord.

12. Use the drill press with a ⁷/₃₂" brad point bit to clear material from the top-side out channel, drilling two holes side by side within the rectangle. Be sure to stop the bit at the depth of the back-side out channel so you don't drill too far.

13. With a hand drill, use the same ⁷/₃₂" bit to clear material from the back-side out channel, using a piece of tape as a visual stop. Take care to keep your drill plumb so that your channels meet cleanly.

14. Chisel out the rest of the material from the out channel, making a clear L-shaped path through the wood—a flashlight and vacuum are useful for this.

15. From the live edge, remove any excess bark.

16. Sand the flat sides with the orbital sander. Start with 80 grit and move up through 120 to 220 and wet sand at 220.

17. Flap sand the live edge with a sanding star in a drill.

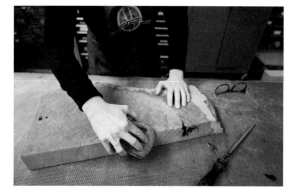

18. Smooth the out channel with a file.

19. Do a final hand sand, easing out the edges and smoothing any rough parts of the live edge. Also ease the edges of the holes.

20. Finish with a wiping oil/varnish mix. Brush it on liberally, wait a few minutes, then wipe off with a clean rag. Let each coat dry thoroughly, doing three coats total. It's amazing how dark and rich the color contrast is once the oil hits the redwood.

METAL ELEMENT

In the steps shown here, I am using an oxygen-acetylene torch to weld, which is technically brazing, a simple form of welding that precedes MIG welding historically, using the heat of the torch and a filler rod. If you are using steel, then the more expedient method of MIG welding is perfectly fine. I use brazing here because I like the technique and the simplicity of the setup. It is also useful for metals that do not conduct electricity well (conductivity is required for MIG welding), such as copper, brass, and aluminum.

Though brazing was used in this case, I will refer to the action as welding to keep it simple.

1. Cut two lengths of ¼" steel rod, one at 17" long and another at 14", using a chop saw with a metal cutting blade.

2. With a hammer, a hard surface, and a torch with a rosebud tip, heat up and hammer both ends of the 14" length and one end of the 17" length to a taper that ends at about ⅛".

3. Drill a ³/₁₆" hole in each flat end using a drill press. For drilling steel, slow down your drill press speed to 700 RPM or so, use an HSS (high-speed steel) bit, a center punch, proper hold-downs, and a little oil to lubricate the bit.

4. Soak the following parts in diluted muriatic acid (ratio 1:10) to strip the zinc off. That way you can weld them or patina to your liking. Careful—use gloves and eye protection!

> 1" of ¼" threaded rod
> One ½" × 10-32 pan-head screw
> One 10-32 wing nut
> One ¼-20 T nut

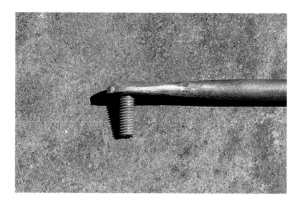

7. Cut the following ⅛" steel rod lengths for the external shape of the "shade."

    Four 7" lengths for sides
    Two 2" lengths for top square
    Two 1¾" lengths for top square
    Two 5" lengths for bottom square
    Two 4¾" lengths for bottom square

5. Insert the pan-head screw into the hole and weld it onto the flattened end of the 17" rod—be careful not to melt the threads.

6. Weld the 1" threaded rod to the other end of the 17" length.

8. Grind ends of those cuts to clean up.

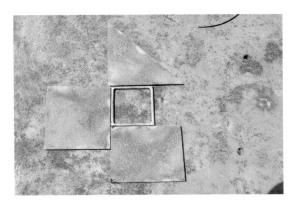

9. Weld the basic shapes of the lamp "shade." Use flat-edged scraps to secure each shape while welding.

10. Cut ornamental pieces for the "shade" and weld into place.

11. Grind, file, and clean up all welds and rough edges.

12. Patina all metal parts with a rust patina mixture of sixteen ounces of hydrogen peroxide, two ounces of vinegar, and ½ tablespoon of salt; apply with a spray bottle for a dappled effect. For more character use a second patina of yellow Dye-Oxide (by Sculpt Nouveau). Set to dry/patina overnight.

13. Gently remove loose patina and dirt with a brush and rag.

14. Lightly spray all parts with a matte clear coat for metal to prevent further rusting.

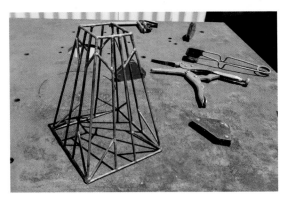

ASSEMBLY

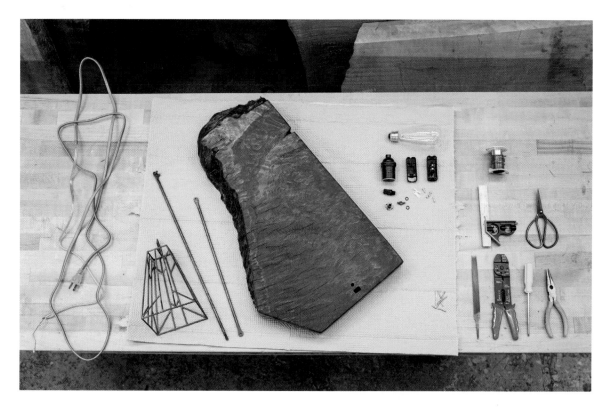

YOU WILL NEED:

- One 18/2 lamp cord with plug
- One switch
- One socket
- One Edison bulb
- Two No. 10/M5 serrated washers
- One 10-32 wing nut (already patinated)
- Four small felt pads
- Copper wire
- Black electrical tape
- Needle-nose pliers
- Ball peen hammer
- Wire strippers
- Ruler
- File
- Tiny screwdriver
- Scissors

1. Feed cord throughout the channel using a string tied to the end of the cord and blowing it through with compressed air.

2. Flip the slab over. Feed the upright metal arm up through the hole in the wood base, screw on the T nut, and hammer it into the bottom of the base.

3. Attach the other arm with washers and a wing nut.

4. Attach the lamp "shade" with copper wire.

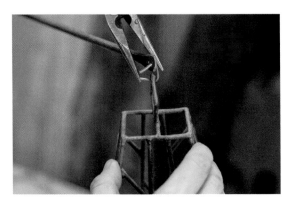

5. Feed the cord along armature and run it through the "shade."

6. Attach a socket to the end of the cord.

7. Pull socket into "shade" with bulb in place. Fix the cord to the armature with bent copper wire cut at 1½" lengths.

8. Attach a switch to the cord length where it looks best for use.

9. Attach felt pads to the bottom, and light her up.

LAURA MAYS

I am moved by the number of woodworking heroes I have met who have been dissatisfied with the direction of their life's path and randomly come upon woodworking by simply meeting one key piece of furniture, seeing the right craftsperson speak, or in the case of this heavyweight, wandering into the right building whilst on a ramble. Laura Mays grew up in Dublin, Ireland, and after high school stayed in Dublin to study architecture for five years, citing it as "a great design education," but something wasn't clicking. "I worked in architecture offices

in the summers, and I disliked the carpeted hush, the murmuring into phones, the high-pitched whine and clicks of photocopiers, so far from the dirt and tangible realities of buildings getting made." So she set off on a bit of a vision quest to Japan (this is all feeling very Nakashima to me—frustrated architect in search of a resolution to his/her yearning for good design, toddles off to Japan . . .), rolled back across Asia and Europe by rail, and ended up on a bicycle in the small Irish town of Letterfrack in the northwest part of Connemara, County Galway. It was here in this crossroads town (the four corners housed pub/pub/pub/decommissioned Catholic boys' reformatory) that young Laura Mays wandered into the old Victorian reformatory, now a woodworking school, and casually took in the exhibit of their impressive summer's work.

Her journey was not over yet, though—far from it. She tried out New York City for a time as a graphic designer; but again, something wasn't clicking. Then, on the spur of the moment she remembered the woodworking school in Letterfrack. She looked it up, discovered the deadline to apply was in three days, and sent off her completed application by midnight via FedEx. She was accepted into the two-year program, and her subsequent introduction to making furniture thrilled her to the core, as she had finally discovered the medium in which she could envision a structural design and then see it built to completion.

The intervening years saw her studying and teaching woodworking and architecture in Ireland, working at a six-month internship at a cabinet shop in England, then setting up shop for

herself making furniture commissions for the folks in County Wicklow, Ireland.

While Laura certainly profited from all this rich real-life experience, she still hungered for more training and continued to read every woodworking volume she could get her hands on. "I remember distinctly being in Waterstones, a bookshop in Dublin, upstairs in their woodworking department (a half shelf), and pulling out *With Wakened Hands*, the book of [James] Krenov and his students' work. I was amazed; I had never seen woodworking as refined, as beautiful. That spurred me to read Krenov's other books. I was struck by his emotional reactions to his work, by his humanity, by his expressions of frailty and failure. This seemed like another whole approach to woodworking, one that encompassed the whole person and all their intellectual and emotional capacities." She immediately applied and was accepted, and suddenly found herself in the redwood trees of Fort Bragg, California, at the College of the Redwoods Fine Furniture program, with no inkling she would one day be running the school.

Founded by art furniture legend James Krenov, the school held its first session in 1981. Despite a certain social awkwardness, Krenov was a wonderfully elfin woodworker who loved wood and "honest" design above all else. His four popular and invaluable books on woodworking extol the virtues of an "unplugged" woodworking experience. That's not to say he eschewed machines, but he preferred hand-planed surfaces; organic, clean, flowing lines; and little to no finish. As a young man he worked for a ship's chandler and always found inspiration in the "fair" lines of boats: "There's hardly a straight line on them, but there's harmony. People think right angles produce harmony, but they don't. They produce sleep."

Thanks to yearly showcases of the school's work in *Fine Woodworking* magazine, I have been an ardent fan of the school since I began my own self-education. Each unique creation has its own personality, seemingly imbued as if by magic with a personal whimsy, superior in charisma to the most painstakingly executed (but less original) museum reproductions. I became less astonished by this wizardry once I saw Krenov's written introduction to new students, which included this: "We hope that in viewing what we are offering here, you will pay attention to the details, notice the results, and come to realize that if one cares enough, if one pays enough attention to the richness of wood, to the tools, to the marvel of one's own hands and eye, all these things come together so that a person's work becomes that person; that person's message."

In its thirty-five years of existence to date, the school has attracted luminaries from around the globe, and produced students who have gone on to win awards galore, astonish the world with their talents, and also become teachers at other very high-end programs. Teachers like Laura Mays, who attended the school in 2002 and 2003, straddling the somewhat acrimonious retirement of the school's founder. Krenov passed away in 2009 and was sadly given to bitterness in his final years. There is a much deeper story here, but his rancor seems understandable insofar as his whole philosophy was founded in humility—that the craftsperson should remain an amateur rather than aspire to competitive professional efforts; this allows one's work to retain a sense of play and enjoyment, and therefore inspiration. He became hard put-upon to inhabit this mind-set when he was treated more and more as a guru, increasingly called upon to bestow benedictory blessings on groups of strangers and would-be disciples.

The school offers a nine-month program, as well as a three-week summer intensive, both durations that I have frequently drooled over. Interestingly enough, I had spent some time in Fort Bragg over the years, as it was the retirement relocation of choice for my teacher (sensei) and theater mentor, Shozo Sato. My favorite thing about Fort Bragg and its sister to the south, Mendocino, is not the gorgeous coastline or the enchanted stands of redwood forest—it's the remoteness. Only a few hours north of San Francisco, often enveloped in mist off the ocean, it somehow feels like a place out of time, which was never more true than when I walked into the bench room of the school for the first time in the spring of 2016.

David Welter, who I believe showed up at the school in 1982, is one of those quiet and gentle souls who you quickly realize is holding the whole place together. He and his hale fellow instructor (well-met) Ejler Hjorth-Westh (a Danish boatbuilder in trademark bright-blue overalls and large beard—my soul mate?) welcomed me warmly, and I had the privilege of chatting with the twenty-three students finishing up their nine-month course. I have to say, the vibe was incredibly mellow and positive, despite the nearness of the final grading.

I found the quality of the work to be terrifically impressive and inspired, and I was delighted by one innovative detail after the next. It did occur to me, however, that it might be hard to make furniture this superb and also make a profitable living in the real world. To this Laura replied, "We don't focus on that. There is enough, in a craft sense, to be learning in nine months, more than enough. So we don't have any formal teaching on running a business or making a living. I think it's valuable for students to make something really well, perhaps finer than they will ever make again. That gives them a bedrock of confidence, and a touchstone of quality, that stand them in good stead no matter what they go on to do." This answer pleased me greatly—it reminded me of Laura Zahn's statement that woodworkers don't go to College of the Redwoods like they would any normal school—it has more the feel of a monastery, where one can ascend to a higher plane. No pun intended.

Speaking of higher planes, I was supremely charmed by the program's Friday-night ritual of gathering around a bonfire for "the Elephants" (referring to the elephant on the label of Carlsberg beer—the suds of choice for the founders of the school). Much mirth ensues, and general socializing, which I thought sounded awfully familiar. Laura, ever the responsible educator, made sure to point out that "the Elephants takes place by stepping over the college property line, which in this case is conveniently close to the program's building, so that alcohol is not consumed on college property."

In a charming turn, elephants have become the symbol of the woodworking program. I saw them everywhere on my visit, especially on really hip printed garments that the students were wearing. I was disappointed to learn that they were one-of-a-kind and not available for this guy to purchase. A couple of graduates even have elephant tattoos. These people are committed, and by crikey, I salute them. They in turn were more than ready to doff their caps in honor of their current leader, Laura Mays.

The students cited Laura's teaching style and its delivery as being one of the most valuable things about the program. They find her playful, still maintaining the demeanor of a student herself, just drifting among them as they work, "suggesting subtle nuggets" like "stay sharp" (keep your tools sharp, especially near the end when your momentum entices you to press on in

dullness). My own suggestion that I subtitle this book "Subtle Nuggets" was met with a reaction that I can only describe as "mixed." Laura can also reputedly examine a student's planned labor, as in "I'm going to do seven dovetails on each corner of this case," and call out with incredible accuracy the amount of time it will take the student to achieve this task.

After speaking with Laura, it occurred to me what an ideal setup she has as a woodworker—she still makes her own pieces on the weekends and in the summers (plus at least twenty minutes a day, even if it's just looking at her tools)—but then she oversees this cultivated woodworking laboratory where twenty-odd woodcraft scientists work together and separately to discover their ideal expressions in wood, time after time. I expressed my envy of this idyllic situation, and she told me that she would go mad without it, without keeping her own work in the center of her life. I had spoken of my work in entertainment as my "waitressing" gig, and she said that's what teaching is for her—an income that allows her to keep making her own superb pieces. The lucky thing is that she's also teaching what she so loves to do as well, which makes for a pretty happy workweek. "Sometimes I feel enormous gratitude for my job at the school. There's a joke that everyone wants to come back for a third year, and I feel like I got that third year, and fourth, and fifth!"

This conversational tack reminded me of some of the other dreamy shop visits I have undertaken for this book, and Laura and I agreed on a notion: The market is shifting in a way, and has been for many years, that is not good for handcrafted works, but the market is increasingly *fruitful* for the burgeoning number of citizens eager to learn *how* to make things by hand. So, gentle reader, perhaps that's how you get to have your cake and eat it too, in this case. First find yourself the best possible education in woodworking, then set up a facility where you are the one teaching a community of the curious about the two sides of a chisel.

Laura said, "The school definitely keeps the Krenov tradition alive; it's in the DNA of the place and I respect that and want to preserve it. But both in the school and in my work, I don't want to get stuck. I try to be reinterpreting, abstracting principles, re-forming them in new ways, whether that is Krenov's legacy or an old chair archetype." I'm not certain where my own career is headed in the field of waitressing, but if time will permit me, I certainly hope to stop by the Redwoods again, if only to see the Elephants.

MATT OFFERMAN

"Oh, brother, I do love this fellow. Growing up as the second and fourth children, with our formidable sisters occupying slots one and three, Matt and I had seven years separating us in age, so we never got to hang out that much until I was finishing college and he was asking me questions about things like beer and how to operate bra snaps. "Matt Mailman," as he dubbed himself in the early years, was always the sharpest of us four siblings, meaning no disrespect to our powerful sisters. Their intelligence was and is magnificent, but Matt was a math-club kid and quickly became the go-to consultant in matters of VCR programming and how to make the answering machine work. He also quickly took to using tools, which was very pleasing to all of us older Offermans, who were always hoping some extra labor would show up—

again meaning no slight to our sisters, whose work with books as teacher and librarian, respectively, will always be revered above our paltry man-cub offerings.

On top of these foundational personality traits, Matt also developed into the funniest person I know. I am very grateful that he has joined me in a lifelong adherence to all things Tolkien, Dungeons & Dragons, and Freemason. He lived in Los Angeles and worked with us at the shop for several years before making the prudent choice of moving his beautiful family back to Minooka and the protection of our sisters. There, he and my dad work together to produce a few items for our shop, from their outpost that I call "OWS Midwest." Whenever the three of us fellas are able to get together, once we have satisfied our sisters' bidding by paying a suitable "tribute" (in cash), we can be found either playing euchre or fishing while

sampling Matt's latest offering from his own waitressing efforts at Solemn Oath Brewery in Naperville, Illinois.

All kidding aside, we hold ourselves the luckiest of males to have the privilege of serving such exalted figures as our sisters. Think about how many guys around the world would swap their very eyeteeth for the opportunity to clean our sisters' dishes or fold their laundry just so, after they have befouled their garments out "on the town," partaking in one of their flagrant, rapacious bacchanals.

Okay, now all kidding aside for real, neither Matt nor I would be living the lucky lives we lead were it not for the exemplary support of our family. Our mom and dad; our sisters, who *are* actually super smart (but also fully decent enough to clean up their own puke-ridden blouses)—not to mention my mom's side of the family, the Robertses, and my dad's folks, particularly his brother, Uncle Mark, an absolute ninja at both the card table and the baking oven. I want to lay out this slight genealogy by way of imparting to you that woodworking works best when connected to everything else—a family or community of loving people who like to cook and laugh and make sure everybody is feeling good. When we all care what the young people are getting up to, and demonstrate our care to them, we stand a better chance of them wanting to produce tables and stools rather than dented bumpers and worse.

NAME: Matt Offerman

SPIRIT ANIMAL: Rick Simon

FAVE TOOL: Knowledge (JK! JK! ROFL!)

FAVORITE HOBBIT: Sharkey

HIRSUTE SCALE: Gimli

CARD GAME: Shoot the Moon

MATH CLUB OR BAND: Both

PETS: One dozen American centaurs, two dogs, two cats, five chickens, and one clone (me)

ILLUMINATI LEVEL/STATURE: Vulcan IV

BURRITO ORDER: Breakfast with steak

FAVORITE WOOD: Barn timber

SLAB CRIBBAGE BOARD

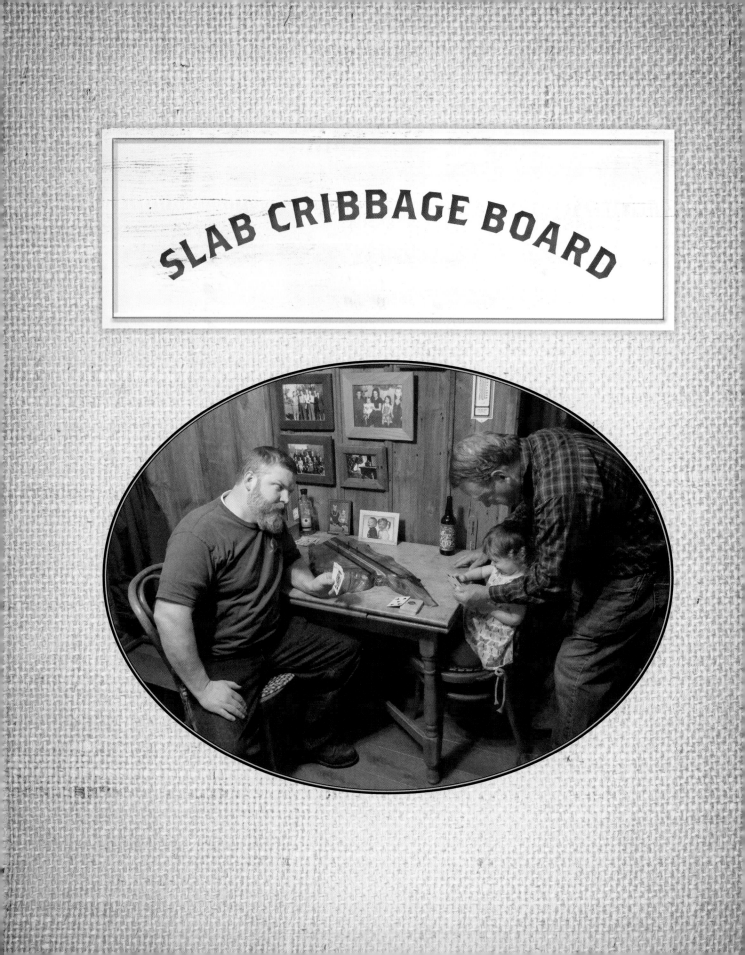

MAKING THE SLAB CRIBBAGE BOARD

Cribbage, the Game of Kings.

The ultimate test of a human's intelligence and stamina, cribbage has decided the outcome of countless wars and royal successions. And, in turn, it is also responsible for cutting short the reigns of some prominent leaders, such as Cleopatra, Richard Nixon, and Napoleon (twice). Most historians will credit Abraham Lincoln's oratory skills for his overtaking of Stephen Douglas during their debates. However, it was their nightly cribbage games that helped shape the path of our sixteenth president.

The liberal media would have you believe that cribbage was created in the seventeenth century, by the poet Sir John Suckling. As if some foppish layabout could create this gauntlet to greatness in between writing love sonnets and "powdering his wig." We know better. Cribbage has been a staple of the Offerman household for thousands of generations. Our current cribbage board was hand carved by Jesus, brought to the new country by the Vikings, and unearthed by Joseph Smith. Its tutelage is what prepared Nick for his chosen career, and it's the reason that I sit here before you today, as THE King of the Hobos.

Originally, when the Illuminated Yeti taught humans how to stand upright, and read and count, the game of cribbage and its scoreboard played an integral part. Designs have changed over the centuries, especially more recently as we have lost the ability to shape wood with our minds. The current design used at Offerman Woodshop was created by a handsome wood elf named Justin. His design was intended to be a gift for humanity: a symbol or a beacon to help bring peace and understanding to us all. Anyway, it garnered all kinds of acclaim on the various social mediums, palantirs and tweets and whatnot, so we decided to share this gift nonvirtually.

Obviously the divine touch of an Offerman was needed to sanctify these boards. Luckily, I was chosen from among the vast number of Nick's siblings who lived in Los Angeles and needed work. I have had the pleasure of laying hands to some fifty-four OWS cribbage boards so far.

Overall, cribbage boards vary in design and size, but as long as you have 120 holes to score with, you're all set. We use a small slab or cutoff with some or all live edges, then apply a simple design that highlights the varying grains, colors, and figuring of our wood. Finally we sow our inlay with the pegging holes in a couple of neat little rows, bookended with varying hardwoods for accent.

For our cribbage boards, we have sourced some beautiful redwood burl slabs from Eureka, California. We've had our holes predrilled into walnut, the most gorgeous of all the hardwoods. Then I line both sides of the holes with something pretty from the scrap bin. Fortunately for me, the scrap bin at Nick's shop has quite an array of species and colors.

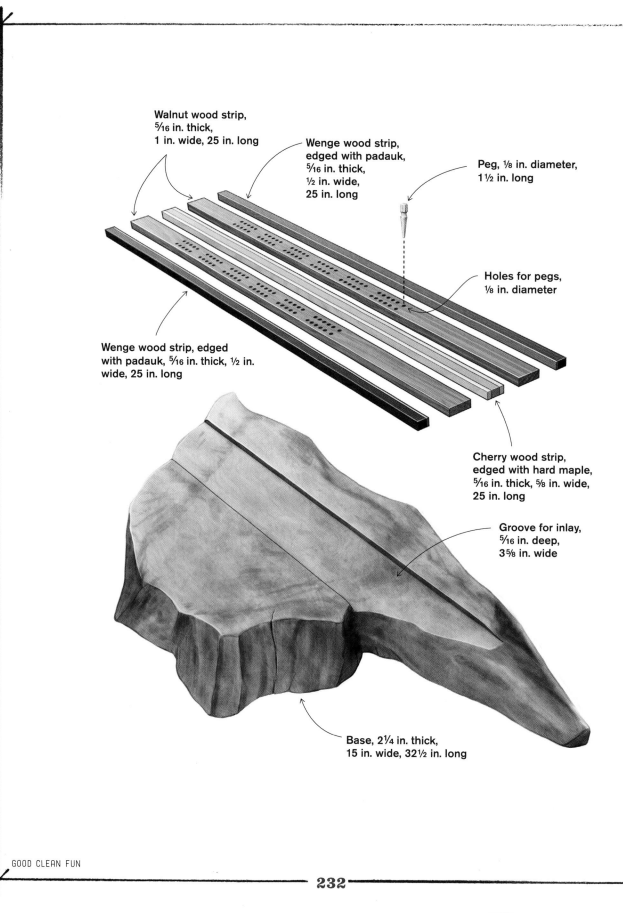

Walnut wood strip,
5/16 in. thick,
1 in. wide, 25 in. long

Wenge wood strip,
edged with padauk,
5/16 in. thick,
1/2 in. wide,
25 in. long

Peg, 1/8 in. diameter,
1 1/2 in. long

Holes for pegs,
1/8 in. diameter

Wenge wood strip, edged
with padauk, 5/16 in. thick, 1/2 in.
wide, 25 in. long

Cherry wood strip,
edged with hard maple,
5/16 in. thick, 5/8 in. wide,
25 in. long

Groove for inlay,
5/16 in. deep,
3 5/8 in. wide

Base, 2 1/4 in. thick,
15 in. wide, 32 1/2 in. long

MATT OFFERMAN: SLAB CRIBBAGE BOARD

1. The first thing I do is level the top and bottom of my slab. Usually my pieces are too wide for our stationary planer, so I utilize a plunge router and a leveling guide (much like the one Nick discusses in *Fine Woodworking*, November/December 2011). If you don't have access to a sturdy plunge router or the time to make this jig, you can flatten your slab with a straight edge, a good handheld planer, and some chalk. This was our previous method during the golden era of Offerman Wood-shop. We would lay the straight edge on its edge and move it back and forth to derive the high points. Then we'd mark the high points with chalk and plane them away. Once the straight edge liked how flat the surface was, we'd belt-sand it smooth. This method takes a lot more time, finesse, and calculation. I abhorred it. Now, I get to let the jig and router do the math and most of the work.

   Generally, I flatten the bottom of the slab first. This way I've used the top's surface as my initial guide for level. Then when I surface the top, my two surfaces should already be almost parallel and I won't have to take as much wood off the top. Now I've revealed the grain and color of the slab. In this case, I've found some gorgeous figuring and a lot of burl in this redwood. This is easily my favorite step in this project. The euphoric sense of discovery as each layer of wood becomes more focused can rarely be duplicated.

2. Since the router will leave some lines, I'll follow next with some rough sanding. Redwood sands easily, so I can jump straight to using an orbital sander and a medium grit like 120. For harder woods, I usually need to start with a belt sander and work my way up (or down) to the orbital. The edges will need some attention also. I like to use sanding stars on my drill to clean up the live edges. Any square edges can be cleaned up easily with the sanders or a plane. **NICK: A card scraper is also great for smoothing tricky grain, but that would qualify as a hand tool—Matt refuses to acknowledge any card that cannot be used as trump.**

3. Now my redwood slab is ready for inlay. I wait to compile and build my inlay until after the slab is ready, because at that point you have a much clearer picture of the slab's coloring. Since I'm building several of these, I have compiled a selection of scraps and milled them all to the same thickness as my walnut strips with the peg holes. However, I have some errant pieces, such as the padauk, that are not uniform thickness. Scraps like these are already so thin that I do not feel comfortable milling them any further. I use them "as is," because I know that the belt sander will make quick work of them.

Once I have my pieces chosen and the design laid out, I'll glue them up. This is a multi-clamp kind of glue-up. I really like using these oversize Bessey clamps because their flat runners are perfect to set all the pieces flush on, and the flat square surface of the clamps keeps the pieces parallel to each other. I get my pieces glued and set, then snug the Besseys enough to hold everything in place, but I make sure to tighten the smaller clamps in the middle and work my way out. Once the glue has set, I will hit the top of the inlay with the belt sander to make sure my playing surface is flat. Then I'll use the orbital up to 180 grit. I complete all this before I glue it in, as I want to make sure I have a flat glue surface on the bottom. More importantly, the hardwood inlay will provide far greater resistance to sanding than the softer redwood slab, so I want to do as little sanding as possible once I have the inlay glued in. **NICK: Another great spot for the card scraper! MATT: I'm told an angel loses its wings every time you use a hand tool.**

4. To cut the wide, shallow dado for my inlay, I will use the same plunge router and jig that I leveled the slab with. The main focus is to make sure that both edges of your mortise are parallel. I try to make sure that my router sits level front to back on the jig. Otherwise, I'll get definitive lines in between routing passes. This will not be an ideal gluing surface. You want to leave no mark at all when you're done routing out this channel, unless you're in a hurry. Let's say hypothetically that you're a month behind writing your chapter for your brother's new book. In that case, rout it as best you can, and then you can clean out the bottom of your trough with a block of wood and some sandpaper.

I usually aim to make the mortise slightly more narrow than the inlay. Then I'll carefully whittle the inlay assembly down to fit on the jointer. **NICK: Use a hand plane.** This allows me to shave off a small amount and keep a square, clean glue surface. Don't tell Nick that, though. He'd probably use a hand plane or a spokeshave; but since we're not Amish I use power tools. Once I have a cozy fit, I'll glue and clamp my inlay in place. After the glue sets, I come to my second favorite part of the job.

5. I now have a rectangular, extra-long inlay seated into a slab with live edges. I carve the ends of our inlay to match the shape and contour of the live edge. Does the verb *carve* apply when you're using a belt sander? This job is a lot of fun for me, and I usually have a surgeon's table of tools set up to complete it: small belt sander to start. Dremel tool for tight spaces or angles. A rasp or file for when I get close to the finished edge and the power tools are too much. **NICK**: Ha! That's a hand tool. **MATT**: Ha! You're an asshole. Then I will usually either hand sand to finish or use a sanding star on the drill. This is one of those jobs that is different every time and I think that the finished product looks great. The squared pieces of the inlay curved to match the live edge.

6. I have my inlay set in place with its ends shaped, so now I just need to finish sanding the top. I want to make sure the inlay is flush with my slab and that it is smooth to touch. I usually sand up to 220 grit for this. I'll definitely need to be careful, as the soft redwood will sand much faster than the hardwood inlay. When my top surface is done and all my edges are smooth, I'll clean the surfaces with mineral spirits. Then it's ready for me to apply my finish. I use Minwax Antique Oil Finish (or simply a mixture of linseed oil, mineral spirits, and polyurethane). This wipe-on finish goes on fairly smoothly. In between coats I give each coat a light sand with 0000 steel wool after it dries.

7. I usually only give these boards four healthy coats of finish, but this redwood burl can really soak it up and look uneven, so I'll apply additional coats as needed. In the end, you end up with a nice satin finish.

I hope you've found these instructions to be enjoyable and they have inspired you to make your own board. Of course if you're reading this secret chapter, then you were granted the special edition entrusted only to our inner circle. If you're indeed among the chosen, then you know that your children need to be cribbage boarded from birth or their futures are already ruined. My daughters play each night to earn their dinner. The winner eats with the family at the table, and the loser then fights the dogs for scraps. In the end, they're both winners. Hail Eris.

PETER GALBERT/
NORTH BENNET STREET SCHOOL

When I first visited with Garry Knox Bennett, whom you'll read about later in the book, I was sitting at his kitchen table with him and his champion of a bride, Sylvia. I was describing my plans for this book, and I mentioned that I wanted to meet Peter Galbert, the chair maker. Garry raised one eyebrow and pointed four feet to my left, where a gorgeous two-person Windsor settee sat. "He made that; I just got it at the furniture show. I don't even know him; I just thought it was such a beautiful piece."

Then, some months later, when I was in Maine interviewing Chris Becksvoort, Chris and I visited Lie-Nielsen Toolworks. There in the showroom (the most charismatic toy store in the nation) sat two black chairs by Peter Galbert in the "fan back" Windsor style. They were exquisite. Apparently great minds think alike, as I've learned from visiting more than a few.

Well. I am tickled pink to launch into telling you about this Galbert fellow; but before I dive into his deal, I'll back up a step to explain how it is that I came to meet him.

As long as I have been reading books and magazines and bathroom graffiti about woodworking, the name of Boston's North Bennet Street School has continued to appear with solid regularity. Woodworker after great woodworker took his or her training there, and the results of that training often look like they should be well on their way to a museum, which is in fact where they're quite often bound.

Founded by Pauline Agassiz Shaw in 1881 to give immigrants the necessary skills to seek gainful employment in their new land, the fledgling institute sought to "train the whole person," not teaching "how to make a living, but how to live." Well, this makes me sit up and say howdy. Who says women can't get into this tool stuff? Here was a woman of wealth and stature, using her influence to promote social service, women's rights, and training in hand skills! This philanthropic hero lady started the first fourteen kindergartens in Boston and put on demonstrations of their usefulness. As for North Bennet Street, Mrs. Shaw hired a fellow named Gustaf Larsson from Sweden's Sloyd school (*slöjd* is Swedish for "craft" or "manual skill") to sail over to the States and establish a similar program at her school in Boston. The original

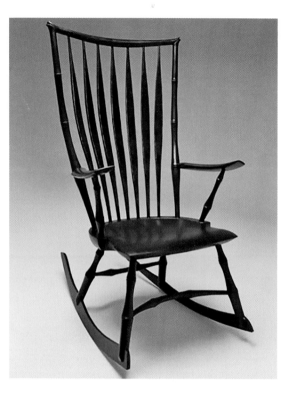

to regain its footing in craft work. Instead of cutting shop programs and trade-skill training, the North Bennet Street School (NBSS) is not only providing its adult students with the means and know-how to make a fulfilling life, but it has also started a pilot program for younger students in Boston's North End. The John Eliot K–8 school has incorporated hand-skills training into its curriculum, and the administrators are citing marked improvement in school attendance and performance. That's what I'm talking about! Some of us like hammers better than grammars!

The school houses eight discrete disciplines within: locksmithing, bookbinding, jewelry making and repair, carpentry, preservation carpentry, violin making and repair, piano technology, and of course, cabinet and furniture making. As I toured it, this venerated institution thrilled me like no school I had visited before. The luthiers polishing the final finish on their immaculately stringed instruments, the bookbinders trimming the pages on their one-of-a-kind art books, and especially the furniture students hurriedly scraping a Chippendale chair or waxing a newly built tool cabinet filled me with an excitement reminiscent of that felt by Laura Ingalls Wilder's sister Mary when she first arrived at the Iowa College for the Blind. Here was a place, I thought, where they could teach me to thrive, despite my being a clumsy white man (a form of blindness). Thankfully, the commencement address came off passably on my part, by which I mean they let me finish my prepared remarks—a gesture that I always take as a compliment.

NBSS has evolved over the years into its current form and curriculum, but it still turns

Swedish school had been developed because it was felt that "the general skill level of the population was declining due to the availability of ready-made objects." Um, this was in the 1880s, gang. I don't know whether to laugh or cry when I consider what those citizens would think of our current level of skills here in America.

I was contacted by the dashing president of the school, Miguel Gómez-Ibáñez, asking me if I would speak at the school's 2015 commencement. As a longtime fan, I was honored to do so, especially when I learned that the ceremony was to occur at Boston's Old North Church of historical fame (*"One if by land, two if by sea"*). Once I began to read of the school's history and mission, I realized that this was just the sort of place that could help every American community out some of the most highly qualified "trade" specialists in their various fields of expertise. North Bennet Street also serves as an artistic hub of one of our nation's most historic neighborhoods. It has the particular feeling of a sort of museum, except in this museum you can enroll in classes to learn how to craft future exhibits for the halls of honor therein. If I had had access to such an august academy in my own youth, it might have saved me from the seductive caresses of showbiz.

The work of their furniture program is of particular interest to the woodworker in me, for obvious reasons, but also to the art lover inside my mortal coil. While I fully applaud the creative "wood-jazz" that artists like Garry Knox Bennett are blowing, there is certainly something to be said as well for those woodworkers who are maintaining the lines and forms of traditional masterworks. Unlike the popular philosophy of the capitalist—"quantity over quality; more is better"—the spirit of this institution inculcates the student body with a rarefied degree of mastery. As President Miguel pointed out to me, if one learns the necessary skills to successfully execute a Queen Anne highboy or a veneered bombe chest, then one stands a solid chance of making any other damn design that one might please.

Depending upon their program of study, full-time students are able to fill one to three years of their lives with some of the richest training available in the country, in an apprentice-like classroom setting. On top of that, the school offers shorter workshops called Continuing Education, which are open to enrollment by the public (jerks like me!). These are golden opportunities for those of us with full schedules to still get a taste of the goodness at such a sweet learning establishment.

It should be easy for you to understand, then, that when I knew I was going to be performing in a play at Boston's Huntington Theatre during the last three months of 2015, I immediately looked up the school's calendar to see if there would be a workshop that I might attend during my stay. Good gracious, there was only but one, but oh, what a one it was! Windsor Chair Workshop with Peter Galbert, said the catalogue. I heard heavenly trumpets in my ears when I read this information and my eyesight went blurry for a minute, but I shook it off and signed up.

There were eight of us in the class, from all walks of life, but every one of us was a woodworker with some experience. I'll just say right now that this was the first class I've ever taken in woodworking. To my classmates, if they're reading this, I would say only that I was lying to you about the "dust in my eyes" and that I was actually just weeping tears of joy. As mentioned earlier, I am self-taught via books and magazines, and so I cannot emphasize this enough: Nothing compares to being in the room with a teacher more experienced than you who is identifying your mistakes and correcting them. Yes, I was crying. I am not ashamed. Let me live, people!

From the get-go, Peter Galbert was enthusiastic and engaged, two qualities far too woefully absent in teachers today. He started us off by demonstrating the use of a froe and the large mallet (or "beetle") used to whap the froe blade into a log. He began to rive small oak logs (8"–12" diameter) into billets of about an inch square, which we then learned to shave with a drawknife, using a shave horse to hold our work. Trust me, unless you're a heartless monster, you would have been crying by this point too. Some consider the drawknife to be archaic or outdated. Apparently no one has informed Mr. Galbert of this information, because he wields a drawknife like John Henry swung a hammer (with aplomb). Our teacher is such a proponent of the drawknife that he invented his own sharpening implement, the Drawsharp, a simple jig that works like gangbusters, and which you can purchase (I did).

This was also my first outing working with "green" wood, and holy cow, it is a gas. "Green" woodworking simply refers to working with freshly cut wood, before it has had a chance to cure, or dry, which is why green wood is also referred to as "wet." The material is much easier for tooling, like eating a fresh slice of pizza or

bread out of the oven versus trying to masticate that stuff after it's been sitting out in the air for a couple of days. . . . Green wood is ideal for the parts of traditional chairs, like the ladder back or the Windsor, because of the organic shapes of the spindles and legs—they are all much more easily shaped with shaving tools than by using shop machines. Parts that require bending also behave much better when green wood is used.

Peter had his pal Tim Manney, another sagacious talent, helping out as we newbies got

the hang of these thrilling new (old) tools. The two craftsmen specialize in chairs and spoons, which I assume means they love nothing more than soup, and they like to eat it sitting down, which makes a lot of sense. The pair coached us through the learning curves of the subsequent processes. Shaving the spindles, shaping the back bow billet before steam-bending it into its extremely curved shape, carving the seats with a couple more new tools: a hand adze and an inshave (a.k.a. "scorp").

Every step of this process was so exciting, and it was such a comfort to be receiving the tutelage of this man who was clearly obsessed with the Windsor chair. His focus was evident in the way he had mastered the drawknife to the point that he knew exactly how best to sharpen and maintain its edge for the best performance, like a race-car driver knows exactly how to calibrate his or her jalopy. I would be remiss if I did not pass along his most oft (by far) repeated admonition: "Skewing and slicing, skewing and slicing." Effectively using a quick sketch on the dry-erase board, he illustrated how a slicing blade, especially if it is skewed (angled to the cut), cuts more cleanly and effectively. Then he threw a thick blank of eastern white pine in a vise and showed us just what he meant. The skill and élan with which he wielded that tool had us all grinning in admiration.

Sure, Peter Galbert is talented. Sure, he's smart as all get-out. However, he didn't come to be such a gifted drawknife-ist by being smart and talented. He did it by practicing (in a smart way, and okay, with talent. You got me); but Windsor chairs weren't always his main squeeze, structurally speaking. After attending the School of the Art Institute of Chicago, he earned his BFA in photography at the University of Illinois at Urbana-Champaign. We believe we may even have vomited on each other at some point during 1993, the year we shared the campus.

After college he moved to Manhattan and started out like many woodworkers—in a high-end shop, building furniture and cabinetry well and quickly, using a lot of sheet goods and machinery. His dream of masterfully working wood with hand tools seemed awfully far away as he spent his days

encased in the restrictive uniform of eye goggles, ear muffs, and a respirator. I agree with Peter that those implements, worn day in and day out, can quickly make employment in a woodshop feel a lot more like a factory job. He looked around him, puzzled at his dissatisfaction, and can today describe his confusion succinctly: "I defined my achievement and skill by my ability to manipulate the wood to fit my will, regardless of its properties."

Reaching outside of his experience, Peter began to examine "the chair" as a possible item of inspiration. After considering different styles from different eras, he settled on the Windsor as a jumping-off point. Not because he was crazy about the look or the period, per se, but because he saw in the Windsor chair just the right framework to allow his creativity to blossom and grow. The nifty thing about any chair is that it has a pretty specific set of requirements to succeed, all based on its function. No matter what it looks like, it must "conform to the needs of the human form," as Peter puts it. As he became accustomed to working with green wood and the traditional hand-tool techniques for shaping chair parts, he realized he had indeed found his wheelhouse.

"After completing my first chair, I realized I had sidestepped all the problems I'd faced when building 'flat' work. . . . I was no longer competing with power tools; they simply didn't meet the requirements of the task. . . . Woodworking was like playing again, and I was sold."

I am so grateful that Amelia Earhart found her airplane; Wynton Marsalis his trumpet; J. K. Rowling her wizard; and Peter Galbert his chair. Once he discovered his intense fascination with this form and its inherent tools and techniques, Mr. Galbert was off to the races. He became obsessed in the best way with making this object by hand as efficiently and beautifully as possible, proceeding to experiment with each stage of the construction until he had developed improvements to almost every step.

In yet another substantial example of the fellowship practiced by the community of all woodworkers, Peter Galbert prototyped and improved centuries-old chair-making tools with his compatriots Tim Manney and Claire Minihan. I've already enumerated Peter's virtuosity on the drawknife, but there's plenty more where that came from. By narrowing their collective focus to the simple actions of the travisher (a sort of chubby spokeshave for "dished" or concave surfaces, like a chair seat), the reamer (twisting-bladed tool for making accurate tapered conical mortises), and the hand adze (mini-adze for the rapid removal of material in carving out the bowl of a chair seat), these woodworkers have damn near reinvented the wheel.

Among his other teaching and building responsibilities, Tim also makes reamers and hand adzes for sale. Claire makes travishers, and I can tell you firsthand that the quality of these implements is top-notch. They are the sort of tools that are annoying not to use. You have to hide them, really, because if you see them they simply command your hands to feel the efficacy coursing through their handsomely crafted hardwoods and brass and steel. All available at PeterGalbertChairmaker.com.

But wait, that's not all! This Peter Galbert guy also invented a super-cool caliper for turning! He calls it the "turner's tape measure": It uses a spring-loaded indicator to give an accurate reading of your spindle's diameter as you turn. This allows you to hold the Galbert Caliper to the far side of your work and simply stop when you have removed the appropriate amount of material to hit your measurement. Ever since he showed it to me, it's been killing me that I can't beat the name "Galbert Caliper": *The Galbiper*; *The Cali-Galper*; *Gal-Cal*; *Calipeter Galbert* is too dirty . . . damn it. I can at least assure you it can be purchased through *PayPaliper*. Blort.

Let me back off for a moment and get some perspective for myself as well as you, my reader. Is Peter Galbert incredibly impressive in the career he has achieved thus far (in his midforties; a kid, like me)? Yes, he does impress. Should I drop everything and start freaking out on Windsor chairs myself? Well . . . hmm . . . I can't really see the downside. Wait, no. I think I am drawing a bead on the takeaway here. I should *not* throw my own hard-earned career away to make only beautiful chairs on my shave horse.

I *should* let Peter inspire me in a more abstract way. I should take his example and apply it to everything I do. Instead of blindly accepting "tried and true" methods of work, I should keep my third eye open to the possibility that I might find a brilliant improvement, even if it's "particular to my own circumstance," as the editors of *Fine Woodworking* have so haughtily repeated every time I have sent in one of my inventions, like the Offerman Scribing Shuriken—"Mark lines accurately whilst defending against attacking ninjas!" *They obviously don't know dick about Los Angeles.*

I apologize, I seem to have gotten off my thread. If you want to warm your own bones by the fire that Peter Galbert has lit beneath my fanny, then you are in luck, my friend. This man has crafted one heck of a book, called *Chairmaker's Notebook*. Check out these numbers: around four hundred pages in length, containing more than five hundred hand-drawn illustrations! They are gorgeous! He can draw like he went to art school and has talent! He is so annoying! Ugh. His book is so good, I told him right to his face that my book was embarrassed to even mention his stupid (and humongous and handsome) book.

He says he stopped counting after three hundred, but he figures that he's made about six hundred chairs so far. I would also ascribe to him the peaceful demeanor of a wise man or woman of the ilk who has discovered the pleasures to be found in simplicity. Starting his journey in the world of plywood and noise pollution, where methods of crafting concerned themselves primarily with speed and profit, he has wandered by a path less traveled to a place that still affords him a life of profit but feeds his heart and soul as much as it does his wallet.

When he was generously teaching me an extra day (I was the only one of eight to fail the workshop) in his own charming old garage shop, we listened to Nina Simone as he demonstrated the virtue of raking a single light source across a surface whilst one scraped it smooth. He likes to leave the surfaces of his chair parts slightly faceted, an effect hard to spot with the eye, but very pleasantly apparent to the touch. This has the combined result of looking like a museum-quality piece, while retaining all the evident charm of being made by hand.

Peter Galbert may be teaching less in the years to come, but here's the good news: He is everywhere. There are women and men in your county, I guarantee, who want to help you learn how to use tools to make whatever it is that floats your boat, including boats. Across this fine nation there remain schools like North Bennet Street,

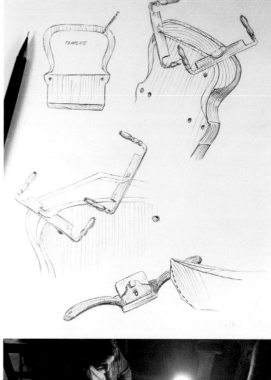

Penland School of Crafts, Arrowmont School of Arts and Crafts, Anderson Ranch Arts Center, Port Townsend School of Woodworking and Preservation Trades, and many more. Just look up schools with words like *craft*, *folk*, *boatbuilding*, or of course, *wood* in the name. Those of us who know the right secrets to chase might have a chance at the contentment Peter Galbert must feel when he sits in one of his rocking chairs and listens to the music.

THOMAS WILHOIT

When Thomas showed up a few summers ago, we were, frankly, circumspect. He seemed a tad too good to be true. His fiancée, Jordan, was studying in a USC master's film program, and so he was visiting LA between his junior and senior years at Harvard University, which he explained to me is a college east of the Mississippi.

"Ah," I replied. "Was that not the alma mater of our twenty-sixth president, Theodore Roosevelt?"

"The very same," came his response.

"Indeed. I thought it rang a bell," I added, with, as my dad would say, the utmost of sargacity. "Kentucky, huh? Might you be familiar with my favorite writer, the magnificent Wendell Berry?" I queried further.

Thomas coolly retorted, "I've seen him speak twice."

I swallowed audibly. How could I seduce this strapping youngster with the perfect pedigree to stick around our humble shop and lend to us his bucolic knowledge and burgeoning hams?

This farm kid from Harvard was in Los Angeles for the summer, and he was bored during the daytimes whilst his beloved attended classes. He had taken it upon himself to seek out a woodshop wherein he might spend his days fruitfully instead of mixing with the hand models and other ne'er-do-wells in West Hollywood. I learned that he sang Gregorian chants, studied medieval history, and had grown up in an excellent family, learning from an early age the ways of forestry and responsibly selective logging, not to mention woodworking and barn-building and all the other skills that come to a curious young fellow on a cattle and tobacco farm. He wanted to volunteer his time to us while in town.

"Can you hang a door?" I asked.

"I can," came his answer.

"All right, hang that new door in the shop kitchen today—you can make it plumb and mortise for the hinges and such—you know these things?"

"I do."

"Okay, I'll look at it tomorrow," I said, before heading up to Burbank to record the voice of a fox in a Disney cartoon, probably.

The next day, I looked at the door Thomas had hung. It had a sharply consistent ⅛" gap all around. I gently opened it and then closed it. Its force was finely and heavily balanced like a massive pendulum. This was a door more befitting a castle on the Isle of Mull than our lowly woodshop. I turned to him with a determined set to my jaw.

"I'd like to pay you wages, sir."

He reddened. "All right."

Thomas of Kentucky, at twenty-two years of age, could hang a door better than I could today, and that's if you gave me a week to do it. He stuck around, and as luck would have it, his winning lady, now his bride, secured some attractively remunerative work in the City of Angels, and so he has stayed under our roof, learning with no minor speed the ins and outs of fine woodworking, while also rehanging most of the other doors I had installed over the years, as well as some assorted others in the neighborhood. I am not ashamed—if someone is willing to do better work than you can, it would be foolhardy to stand in his or her way. He's intrepid and strong, and he can sing like a bird (a deeply baritone-voiced bird). Thomas is also our main operator on the lathe, cranking out baseball bats and shaving implements with equal aplomb, and, boy howdy, can he eat.

NAME: Thomas Wilhoit

NOM DE GUERRE: Tony

BRA SIZE: 42C

FAVE WOOD: Eastern red cedar (*juniperus virginiana*)

FAVE TOOL: Paslode cordless framing nailer

PREFERRED LUNCH: Spicy pork rinds

SHOP BIRD: Anna's hummingbird

FAVORITE POLAR EXPLORER: Vilhjálmur Stefánsson

MUSTARD: Colman's Original English Mustard

CORN PREFERENCE: Silver Queen

 # OF WORK PANTS: 2 pair

FAVE COW BREED: Limousin

RAPPER/DJ NAME: Big Spicy (Pork Rinds)

CARD GAME: Rubber bridge

CLARO WALNUT SLAB TABLE

MAKING THE CLARO WALNUT SLAB TABLE

As far back as I can remember, I've always made things. When I was a child, I made many of my own toys and worked to augment the ones I didn't make. Now, I was no creative prodigy—all my making was very practical and utilitarian, typically an attempt to rectify something that I saw wanting, or to fill a void. Perhaps some set of Fisher-Price pirates needed a hideout, possibly a stuffed bear had insufficient choices in the leather and plate armor department, or maybe eight-year-old me couldn't save up enough money to buy a Ka-Bar. All these problems could be solved in the workshop: Carve a hideout from a driftwood stump, rivet some 22 gauge steel sheeting into a breastplate, cut a combat knife out of a discarded piece of half-inch walnut. These days, I'm constantly making shelves, tables, paper-towel holders, trays—little stuff I need for my apartment. When this book was in the works, there was a lot of talk about what people wanted to make or felt inspired to make, but that wasn't really speaking my language. I'm not someone to get caught up in a fit of creative passion; I just want to make something relevant and useful. So when people worked out their projects of choice, and it became pretty clear that the meat and potatoes of OWS, the slab table, was missing from the selections, that didn't seem right. Don't get me wrong—I wasn't backed into

some corner. I just got the chance to pursue the project that seemed most logical (and most notably absent), and that was just fine with me.

Tables are the kings of the furniture jungle. They're huge, they command a room like no other furniture, and King Arthur had a famous one. Tables even get their own entourage of auxiliary chairs, buffets, credenzas, bar carts, centerpieces, tablecloths, china and silver sets, and so forth. If you think about it, pretty much everything in your kitchen is a servant to your table. The Getty Museum even had a recent exhibit on table monuments and banquet layouts from Renaissance feasts. Sure, there's a lot to be said for beds as well, but nothing has historically dominated our public and private lives like our tables.

In our world, the slab table is an absolute staple, for a number of logical reasons. To begin with, it's easier to rationalize the premium paid for a custom piece of furniture when that piece is eight or nine feet long and the focal point of a room. Plus, pretty much all of us at the shop love slabs, and that sort of excitement is infectious. Talk about visual charisma—you get the chance to see a cross section of history, a look back into the life of an organic being. Maybe you're working with a crotch, and you can see where the years of stress as the two trunks grew apart caused

the wood to continually reinforce itself in layers of beautiful figuring. Maybe you cut through a slab and you dull your saw on what you later discover is a fence post that's now a foot deep in the tree. Or as our shop manager once did, you might cut into a chunk of sycamore and open up a nest of arboreal salamanders. Slabs are so unpredictable and so varied, and that's part of what makes them so beautiful. Finally of course, live-edge tables have become a popular element in modern design. So, we do a lot of slab tables.

Nick and I both love walnut slabs, so that seemed like an obvious choice, and the claro walnut slab that I used for this table was too nice to pass up. The base was a little bit more difficult to decide on, but lately several of the woodworkers at the shop have been playing around with geometric skeletal bases, often ebonized oak or walnut. I find that it appeals to people in the same way that a tubular metal base does, as a contrast to the richly colored organic top and as a less obtrusive structure than a traditional trestle base. Also, to me, the ebonized wood has more warmth and character than a powder-coated metal base, and it subtly retains the grain and color variation of the unebonized wood. The downward taper of this base was something that I was interested in exploring as a way, again, to serve the slab and help the base to disappear into the shadows. It made for some complicated math and joinery, but I think it turned out pretty nice. In the end, a table just needs to stand up, hold your food, and fit your friends (and maybe occasionally hold them too). Thankfully, this one seems more than up to those tasks, and I'd like to think it's halfway attractive as well.

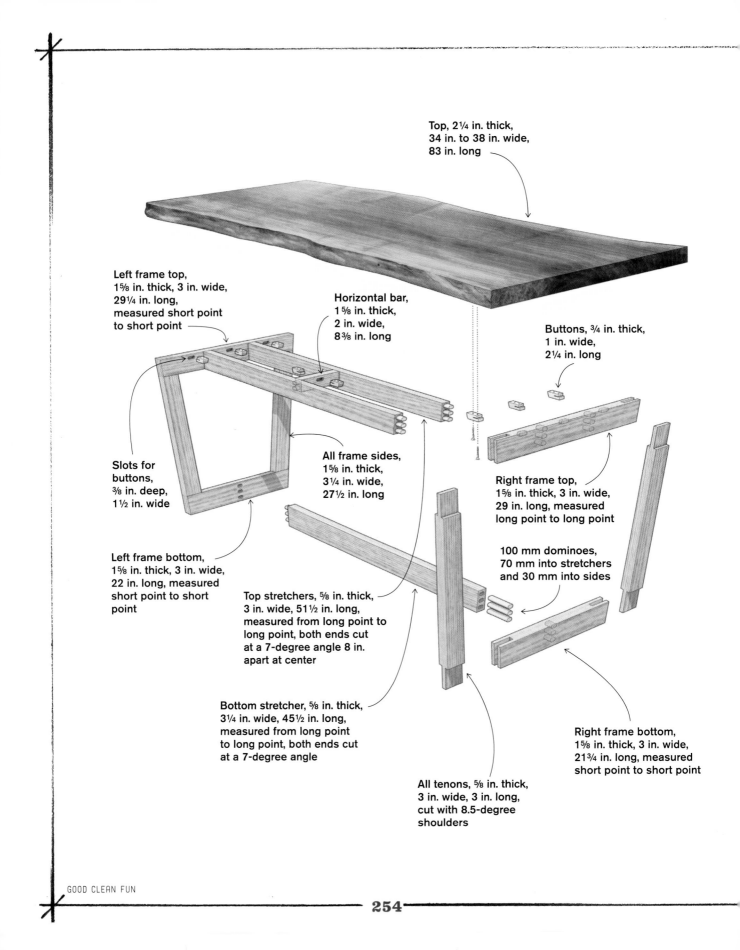

Top, 2¼ in. thick,
34 in. to 38 in. wide,
83 in. long

Left frame top,
1⅝ in. thick, 3 in. wide,
29¼ in. long,
measured short point
to short point

Horizontal bar,
1⅝ in. thick,
2 in. wide,
8⅜ in. long

Buttons, ¾ in. thick,
1 in. wide,
2¼ in. long

Slots for
buttons,
⅜ in. deep,
1½ in. wide

All frame sides,
1⅝ in. thick,
3¼ in. wide,
27½ in. long

Right frame top,
1⅝ in. thick, 3 in. wide,
29 in. long, measured
long point to long point

Left frame bottom,
1⅝ in. thick, 3 in. wide,
22 in. long, measured
short point to short
point

100 mm dominoes,
70 mm into stretchers
and 30 mm into sides

Top stretchers, ⅝ in. thick,
3 in. wide, 51½ in. long,
measured from long point to
long point, both ends cut
at a 7-degree angle 8 in.
apart at center

Bottom stretcher, ⅝ in. thick,
3¼ in. wide, 45½ in. long,
measured from long point
to long point, both ends cut
at a 7-degree angle

Right frame bottom,
1⅝ in. thick, 3 in. wide,
21¾ in. long, measured
short point to short point

All tenons, ⅝ in. thick,
3 in. wide, 3 in. long,
cut with 8.5-degree
shoulders

THOMAS WILHOIT: CLARO WALNUT SLAB TABLE

TOP

1. **SURFACING SLAB**: After selecting my slab, I surfaced it with Nick's surfacing jig and the Infinity 2" mega dado router bit. The key to the surfacing jig is having a level, flat table—then, once you make one side of your slab flat, you can just flip it over and do the other side without having to worry about shims. Our ending thickness was 2⅜". **NICK: A shout-out and tip of the cap to Scot Wineland at Wineland Walnut for this claro slab; he is a true rock-star sawyer in Chico, California.**

2. **DIMENSIONAL SANDING**: A dimensional sander can be an incredible time-saving device, so much so that the dimensional sander I used on this slab was made by a company called Timesavers. The surfacing jig is very effective at creating two flat, parallel faces, but the router bit can leave some tear-out. The sander helps to remove that tear-out while maintaining the perfectly parallel faces. After dimensional sanding, the slab was a hair over 2¼" thick.

3. STABILIZING SPLINES ON UNDERSIDE: These splines were added to stabilize the checking that is visible throughout the middle of the slab. This is a situation where you can use splines or keys of various shapes (the butterfly key being a popular choice), but since they were going to be on the underside, I decided to go with a straight spline. Each spline adds a long and very strong glue seam, which will be more than enough to keep the checks from spreading apart. The six splines are ¾" deep, 1¼" wide, and 10½" long. Each dado was routed to a consistent depth. I then squared up the corners by hand with a chisel and fit each spline. Again, the key here is a good glue seam along the bottom of the spline, so I focused on guaranteeing that the spline would fully seat in the dado, rather than on getting the tightest visible fit possible.

THOMAS WILHOIT: CLARO WALNUT SLAB TABLE

4. EPOXY FILLING CRACKS ON TOP: This is an aesthetic and functional choice, although it can also have some limited utility in stabilizing the checks. In a dining table, it's awfully nice to have a uniform surface, with no cracks, holes, or grooves that are difficult to clean. The epoxy fill takes several applications of a two-part West System marine epoxy. I used a black pigment to match the already oxidized cracks in the slab. It is difficult to prevent bubbles in your epoxy without employing a vacuum system, but I've had some success using a heat gun, which encourages the bubbles to rise to the top and rupture.

5. CUTTING TO LENGTH (GETTING TWO PARALLEL FLATS): With a slab, this is a somewhat subjective choice—since I didn't have a straight side to reference, I chose where to cut one end based on the shape of the slab and then made the other end parallel, at 83", with a table saw.

6. SANDING, INCLUDING EDGE SANDING WITH SANDING STAR: I find that there is little better for cleaning up and making friendly the live edge of a slab than a sanding star. This little invention is composed of many layers of sandpaper, cut into thin strips. You just chuck it into a drill or pneumatic grinder and go to town. The strips separate and spin into all the cracks, grooves, and crevices like a whirling mop head. It was the only tool I needed for handling the live edge on this walnut slab, although sometimes you might need to employ some rifflers and carving tools as well, to clean out tough bark or dirt. I cannot sufficiently emphasize the importance of removing the bark, unless you want a shedding slab table. The bark will eventually delaminate as it dries out fully and stays static while the slab itself moves with changes in temperature and humidity. Finish sanding the top and bottom of the table was a breeze after having it dimensionally sanded to 150. I went back to 80 grit for a quick pass before moving through 120, 180, 220, and 320.

BASE

7. **MILLING**: To mill rough lumber, you have to first joint both a face and an edge so that you have two sides that are flat and perpendicular to each other. Then, you can flatten the third and fourth sides with the planer and table saw, and you should have created a (near) perfect rectangular prism. I used red oak for the base, and I milled it to 1⅝" thickness in the planer.

8. **SELECTING AND CUTTING ELEMENTS**: In order to mill the pieces to their final width and cut them to length, I had to lay everything out to see how the elements would all fit within my lumber. Once I had planned everything out, I was ready to cut the pieces to length and width, ripping the bottom stretcher and the pieces of the side frames to 3¼" and ripping the top stretchers to 3". This difference between the bottom and top stretchers stems from the eventual 7-degree angle to which the side frames will get trimmed. When the bottom of the frame is trimmed, the inside edge of the frame won't have any material removed, and will remain 3¼" wide, so the bottom stretcher needs to match. The top of the frame, though, will lose ¼" on the inside face when it's trimmed, so the top stretcher needs to be 3" wide to fit seamlessly. Due to the variant width of the slab, I made one frame ¼" wider than the other, which

serves to trick the eye—they appear the same, but they also appear to fit the table better than if they were actually identical. The two sets of side pieces for the leg frames are identical, all four elements being 3¼" wide and 27½" long, with the ends cut to parallel 8.5-degree angles (as in a parallelogram). The top and bottom pieces of the left-side frame are, respectively, 29¼" and 22" long, along their bottoms, each cut to opposing 8.5-degree angles (forming a trapezoid), while the top and bottom pieces of the right-side frame are 29" and 21¾" along their bottoms, also cut to opposing 8.5-degree angles. The side frames don't get cut to their 7-degree angle until after they are glued up, but the stretchers are all cut to opposing 7-degree angles at this stage. The top stretchers are 51½" along their bottoms, and the lower stretcher is 45½" along its bottom.

THOMAS WILHOIT: CLARO WALNUT SLAB TABLE

9. CUTTING JOINERY (CORNER BRIDLE JOINTS): Cutting angled joinery always poses a challenge, but luckily bridle joints can be made simple with a few table saw jigs. To cut the male member, the tenon, on the side-frame pieces, I used a miter jig set to the appropriate angle of 8.5 degrees, and ran the angled end of the piece along the fence to establish a uniform shoulder 3¼" in from the end. The tenons are a centered ⅝", which meant each cut had to be exactly ½" deep in the 1⅝" piece. Once each of the four side pieces had the shoulders cut, I hogged out the remainder of the material with a ¾" wide dado stack. Bear in mind,

once I had finished with the angled setup on the first side of my eight tenons, I left the fence alone and reversed the miter jig to 8.5 degrees in the other direction to complete the reverse sides. With the tenons cut, it was time to face the more intimidating task of the mortises—at 3¼", they were too deep to cut fully on the table saw. Using the tenoning jig, I was able to cut the lion's share of each mortise before having to finish by hand, with chisel work. When cutting mortises, it is often helpful to clamp a guide block with the appropriate angle onto your piece so you have a reference to ride on with your chisel.

10. SANDING FOR GLUE-UP: Once the frame joinery was cut, it was almost time for a glue-up. However, I took the opportunity to do a little sanding while the elements were separate and I had easier access with the random orbital sander—once the pieces get glued up, it's much more difficult to sand in the corners.

11. GLUING UP LEG FRAMES: A corner bridle joint makes for a slightly complex glue-up, because each corner needs pressure to be applied across three different axes at once, and only in specific places. You have to clamp across the side pieces applying pressure only on the tenons, across the top and bottom piece applying pressure only on the outsides of the mortises, and you have to clamp the halves of the mortise down onto the tenon. The trapezoidal nature of the frame makes clamping difficult as well, so I made angled blocks to give myself two parallel surfaces on which to clamp. I recommend performing glue-ups with a friend, ideally in the earlier part of the day. I can't count the number of times I've had an evening glue-up go awry because I wasn't mentally or physically sharp enough to do it right and handle the inevitable complications. Even using a glue with a long open time, such as Titebond III, it's a high-stakes race against the clock to get everything covered and clamped before the glue starts to set.

12. TRIMMING LEG FRAMES WITH ANGLE: Once the frames were glued up and the glue had cured, I cut each frame to its 7-degree angle, along the top and the bottom. This is a simple task on a table saw, but be careful, because the blade may want to throw the thin slice, and due to the angles, the slice will be sharp indeed. Additionally, use extreme caution not to rack away from the fence when cutting a piece wider than it is long.

THOMAS WILHOIT: CLARO WALNUT SLAB TABLE

13. CUTTING DOMINOES: The attachment between the stretchers and the side frames was done with the Festool Domino XL, a tool that cuts slots for manufactured beech slip tenons. I'll have to switch to metric for a second since Festool is a German company. Each stretcher joint has three 14 mm × 100 mm dominoes, evenly spaced. They extend 70 mm into the stretchers and 30 mm into the frame. In order to cut the dominoes straight into the angled stretchers and frames, I used a flat MDF table as a reference on which to place the elements and run the domino tool. I added flat spacers under the tool to achieve the correct placement for the additional dominoes. That allowed me to cut the slots for the bottom stretcher all referencing the bottom of stretcher and frame (or "the floor"), and the dominoes for the top stretcher all referencing the underside of the table slab. The single bottom stretcher is centered on the frames, while the top stretchers are spaced 8" apart, on center.

14. GLUING UP STRETCHERS: Dominoes make for easy joints, but they can be difficult to glue up if you haven't worked with them before. It can be difficult to get the domino to seat in the slot unless you sand the domino enough that it slides in and out easily. As with all glue-ups, dry fitting is very important—you never know if your wood has swollen or shrunk since you cut your joinery. The beech dominoes are excellent, but beech is a thirsty wood, so you want to make sure you have plenty of glue in the joint, and that will swell the domino somewhat, making the fit even tighter.

15. **SANDING**: As with the top, the base must be sanded from 120 up to 320 in progression to remove all sanding marks. To keep crisp lines, I broke the edges by hand with a hard sanding block at 220 and 320 before going over them with a softer pad and 400 grit sandpaper.

16. **CUTTING CLEAT SLOTS WITH DOMINO CUTTER**: For attaching the tabletop to the base, I used our standard shop button, an adaptation of Nick's from Peter Wallin's article for *Fine Woodworking* (*FWW* 186) entitled "Improved Tabletop Button Fits Slot Every Time." Our version is 1" wide and 2¼" long, with a 1"-deep kerf spaced up ⅜" from the bottom of the button. The button is ¾" thick and uses two #12 pan-head screws, one spaced ⅝" from the front of the button and one at 1½" from the front. The bottom of the button is cut off ¼" in from the front, producing an overhang that serves as the compressible attachment point to the base. The back screw holds the button in place, while the front screw tightens the button onto the base and takes the tension. The slots are cut with the Domino XL, three per side frame on the base, one centered, and the other two spaced 8½" to the right and left. The slots are cut with the 14 mm cutter, 15 mm deep. Using the "wide" setting on the domino gives you a slot 1½" wide.

17. **FINISH SANDING:** Now that the base and top are ready to begin the finishing process, it's time for a final sanding. I raised the grain on both by wiping them down with water. Then I lightly sanded them, both at 220 and 320. The water causes wood fibers that were flattened rather than sheared off during the sanding process to stand up again, giving the wood a slightly fuzzy or scratchy feel. A quick sanding helps to shear those fibers off without getting down to new material, which would necessitate starting the process again.

18. **EBONIZING BASE:** The process we used to ebonize the oak base is a very old method involving ferrous sulfate (also known as copperas and green vitriol) and logwood extract. Ferrous sulfate stains the wood by reacting with the tannins. Oak is a highly tannic wood, and it reacts well to ebonizing with this method. The steps are fairly simple. I dissolved two ounces each of ferrous sulfate and logwood extract in two eight-ounce cups of hot water. Then I applied the ferrous sulfate to the entire base with a brush and let it dry, after which I did the same with the logwood extract. Two coats of each, in this succession, were sufficient. At that point, the base looked a purplish-gray color. I then brushed on a solution of vinegar and steel wool. This solution is easy enough to make—take a steel wool pad, break it up a little, and submerge it in a sealed container of vinegar with some small air holes overnight. The steel wool rusts and breaks down. You can then strain the solution, and it will have an ebonizing effect on its own, although not as strong as the combination of all three solutions. Once you brush on the rust-and-vinegar solution, the effects are almost immediate, and you suddenly have a jet-black base.

19. FINISHING: For the finish on both the base and the slab, I used Osmo Polyx-Oil, a low-VOC oil-and-wax blend originally designed for floors that has become a great favorite for many woodworkers. It's easy to apply, once you get over the initial purple color, and produces an easily maintained matte finish. I applied three coats over a period of three days, using a 0000 synthetic steel wool pad as an applicator. With Osmo, the main thing to worry about is wiping the excess—the wood should appear completely dry. Install your table buttons and you're ready to feast.

AMENDMENT

If you leave a project sitting around the shop after it's completed, it's hard to avoid making a few late-game tweaks. Nick and I looked at the table a few days after I had finished it and decided it needed an additional structural element in the center of the base that would allow for a couple more buttons. We were concerned that such a span between the buttons at the ends of the base could allow for warpage, and adding two buttons in the center of that span could help to prevent any cupping and keep the table as flat as possible. It was an easy enough fix, but it was time consuming, as it required redoing many of the aforementioned steps.

To add the element, I routed a 2" × 2" slot horizontally into both top stretchers, allowing me to glue in a 2" × 2" horizontal bar, which I had already sanded and cut my button slots into. The added element is invisible from all four sides of the table and can be seen only from underneath. After gluing it in, I had to ebonize the new element and touch up the finish on the base. Thankfully, and damn near miraculously, it went off without a hitch.

THOMAS WILHOIT: CLARO WALNUT SLAB TABLE

GARRY KNOX BENNETT

Most woodworkers first run across Garry Knox Bennett when they read the legendary tale of his *Nail Cabinet*, a six-foot-tall beauty in solid padauk, featuring box-jointed drawers, a curved glass door, custom hardware—oh, and a 16-penny nail hammered into the top cabinet door and bent over, complete with elephant tracks. In 1979, when he presented this work at the Cutting Edge: New Works in Wood show at Contemporary Artisans Gallery in San Francisco, he was simply expressing a desire to knock the stuffing out of the atmosphere of

purity surrounding art and woodworking at that time. By figuratively flipping the bird at the communal reverence being lavished upon neatly compartmentalized gallery works, Mr. Knox Bennett turned the art world on its ear. When his cabinet subsequently appeared on the back cover of *Fine Woodworking*, it was the conservative "fine" woodworkers' turn to get their knickers very much in a twist. The magazine's subscribers reacted with outrage: "Who is this Philistine who did such a horrible thing to that cabinet?!" This pleases me much. When I first read of his act of defiance, I too, like any fledgling woodworker, was feeling the oppression of the "proper" techniques to which I was being told to adhere. I'm all for learning the right way to do things, but part of the apprentice's satisfaction when achieving mastery is found in emphatically

thumbing one's nose at one's teacher and then going one's own way. Here was a fine fellow, thirty-seven years ago, beckoning me to just such a parade.

Born in Alameda, California, in 1934, Garry grew up in a maritime household, the son of a sea captain. He bounced from job to job after high school somewhat without aim until deciding to enroll at the California College of the Arts in 1960. This was also the year he married Sylvia Mangum, whom he had known since high school, and with whom he is still attached at the hip today, the lucky sod. He studied sculpture and painting and produced a number of welded steel sculptures for his first series of works, which is unsurprising, since the stories of his youth are peopled by stevedores, coxswains, and lumberjacks. He and Sylvia moved to the

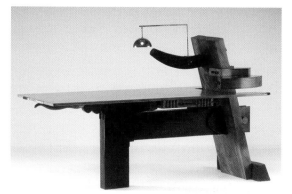

Sacramento Valley to work and live on his ex-stepfather's rice farm, and Garry experienced his first substantial run-in with woodworking when he built an A-frame house in which they could dwell.

Working for a meager $50 per month stipend driving a tractor and running a rice dryer on twelve-hour shifts, Garry and Sylvia found that comforts were few and far between during these years in the early sixties. Garry says they were subsisting on about $800 a year, his stipend being bolstered a bit by the occasional sales of his sculptures. According to a 2001 interview he gave to Abby Wasserman, a neighbor reportedly saved bacon grease for them so that Sylvia could make corn bread from the grease and corn meal. In fact, one year, for Sylvia's birthday Garry bought her eight pounds of butter. "We lived in abject poverty," he said. "Sylvia said you know something's wrong when the fashions in the Sears catalogue start to look good."

In years three and four of their five-year stint in Lincoln, California (thirty miles north of Sacramento), some visiting friends brought an opportunity that would change the course of the couple's butterless existence: Patricia Oberhaus and Peter Neufield of Berkeley, California, basically invented the groovy head shop on the eve of the entire hippie movement. Their store, appropriately called "The Store," sold original paintings, records, antiques, jewelry, and handmade clothing. They wanted Garry to make some jewelry for sale, based on some gifts he had made for Sylvia; so he turned out a collection of huge dangly earrings with a lot of scrollwork and curlicues made from brazing rod. His stuff sold like hotcakes, so he kept making more earrings and also segued into roach clips.

A roach clip, for those of you not familiar, is traditionally a small "alligator clip" with some sort of decorative handle attached. The spring-loaded clip can be used to hold the last little end of a joint of marijuana, when it has burned down to a smoke-blackened nub, or "roach." Garry was into the idea but disliked the aesthetics of the alligator clip, so he devised his own style of pincers with a metal sleeve that would slide down to pinch the joint tightly. An original artist from the get-go. Or was he? We'll get to that.

His roach clips were a huge hit both in the Bay Area and Los Angeles, selling out as fast as he could hammer them out by hand. They moved back off the farm and made a go of it in the city, with Garry working on sculptures while continuing to crank out roach clips and earrings. Dissatisfied with the amount of money they were spending on plating these items, Garry and Sylvia set up their own plating company called Squirkenworks Inc. Meanwhile, Knox Bennett continued to work as an artist, making metal pieces and clocks and light fixtures. He was introduced by a friend to Gump's Gallery in San Francisco, where he was given a show of his unique clocks, which led to further gallery shows and more evolution in Garry's vernacular, until he was experimenting more and more with furniture. Finally, he made the *Nail Cabinet* in 1979, and his growing notoriety suddenly took off like a shot.

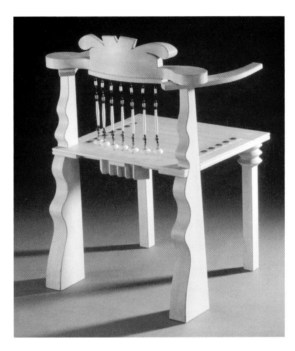

One of the most interesting aspects of discussing this book with Garry Knox Bennett is that he bristles when I refer to him as a woodworker. "I'm a furniture maker," he insists. "When I started showing back east, it was the Tage Frid stuff in walnut and maple and everything, and I've got shows with aluminum, and glass, and paint, and people said, 'What's with this guy?'" Despite his education and early career, Garry also doesn't agree with being called an artist. Over and over again in interviews, he holds up his hands and insists that "no, no, [he's] a furniture maker."

More than any woodworker I've spoken with, *much more*, this noble fellow certainly has an artist's point of view. Partly this seems the result of having come to prominence alongside the great studio furniture artists of last century. You know the ones: Maloof, Wendell Castle, Nakashima, Krenov, Art Carpenter, Esherick . . . But Garry said something that stopped me in my tracks—these luminaries, with whom he was friendly or at least acquainted (his letter of admonishment to a prickly James Krenov is laced with hilarious justice), were trapped. "You're Maloof, and your rocker hits—and I loved Sam, we were very good friends—that rocker hits, and then you're stuck making that goddamn thing for the rest of your life! What kind of artistic journey is that?" What I had never paused to consider as I joined the hordes of acolytes (rightly) worshipping at the altars of Maloof and Nakashima was that popularity and success were wonderful, but they could also encase one's life in a rather gilded cage of sorts,

stifling the artist's need to create original work with a public demand for the greatest hits.

I'll call this man an artist *and* a furniture maker *and* a woodworker, because he is all three, and he's also a sculptor and a welder and a humorist. He said, "I've chosen to work with color because I wanna do something that really . . . that really pushes *me*. I like to use green because it's so hard to work with. I like that challenge." Sounds like an artist to me. Of course, it's all semantics. My mechanic might be so amazing at tuning up the motor on my chainsaw that I call *her* an artist. All depends on your point of view.

When I first arrived at the Oakland studio in which Garry Knox Bennett has been making goodness since 1968, I giggled with delight. Walking down the sidewalk in an otherwise

unremarkable working-class neighborhood underneath a freeway, I came to the shop door: a massive and august edifice, imposing at first, until you focus on the assorted touches of rusted whimsy—which kind of aptly describes the occupant as well. At six foot nine, Mr. Knox Bennett has a physical presence that vacillates between ursine and mountainous. His expansive shop fits him well, what with a 36" Tannewitz band saw from 1927, a 30" Oliver jointer from the '50s, and a 24" Powermatic planer of similar vintage. The workshop seems as though it was outfitted by giants, suited more to the fabrication of ziggurats and foothills than the sometimes delightfully delicate jewelry and clocks that the former curator of the Oakland Museum, Suzanne Baizerman, referred to as "pure play."

Thankfully his demeanor doesn't match his sequoia-like appearance, or I would never have had the nerve to ask him a question. Garry purports to be slowing down a bit in his later years (he is eighty-two), but that claim doesn't seem to hold much water as I watch him assemble his most recent creation—a nearly finished desk for a friend's jewelry store. With his trademark collage of materials—plywood, color core, Formica, aluminum—the piece was simultaneously classy and irreverent; it spoke to me as we sat and analyzed it together. Or, I should say he analyzed it and I soaked in the tutelage.

He said, "What is the one thing that's driving me crazy about this, can you spot it?"

"Um . . ." (I wanted so badly to spot the indiscretion and impress my mentor) "is it . . . ?"

"Yeah, you're lookin' in the right area! [I had no idea.] It's that curved element. It should be tapered from top to bottom, not a consistent thickness. Damn it," referring to a single leg element with an extreme curve that I learned he had steam-bent in one piece, without slicing it into laminations, certainly a badass way to go about it. Expecting me to pick out this leg as the one indiscretion on his work of art would be like asking me to tell him which horse in a herd of dozens had any talent. There is a quality to his furniture that leads me to opine that Garry would have made a splendid cartoonist.

Not only do his designs evoke a sense of sharply drawn mirth, but he loves a one-liner as well. "'Experience is what you get when you didn't get what you wanted.' . . . Isn't that great? I can't remember whose that is" (looked it up: Randy Pausch, *The Last Lecture*, 2007). Garry carries a little black calendar book in his vest pocket that has

"1996" embossed upon it in faded gold—brought to mind of his cache, he pulls it out and flips into it: "'. . . A crushing certainty that eliminates doubt'— that's Larry Wright on religion—f-ing great, isn't that?" (It's from the doc *Going Clear* by Alex Gibney.) Then Garry says, still flipping through his little black book, "Here's one I won't repeat about a barrel, a jar of Vaseline, and the Hells Angels." One of his clocks from 1972 bears this inscription on the back: "A little rough but who gives a shit? C+" To me, that is the sentiment of an artist who is in the batter's box taking swings. He won't hit it out of the park on every pitch, but his passion makes even his foul balls works of genius.

In a recent David Savage video, Garry offered this advice to aspiring artists: "Don't use a computer. The computer cannot make art or craft, it can't do it . . ." He goes on to say that a world run by technology is what Ruskin and William Morris feared, and that we may be on the verge of such a takeover even now. The interviewer asks him, "What is it you feel we'll lose?" Garry holds up two prodigious, calloused and crooked hands, crowned by nine and a half fingers, and says simply, "These."

His 1979 *Nail Cabinet* was only the beginning of an immense furniture career for Garry Knox Bennett. His series of exploring (and exploding) the accepted forms of chairs and tables has continued to delight and anger the public audience for decades. His slab tables practically sit up on their meaty haunches and tell you a story—one that you've never heard before but is strangely as comforting as it is novel. I highly encourage you to explore his work deeply and find within it a tacit permission—to fly your own freak flag as high as you dare.

MICHELE DIENER

"In the summer of 2011, I had been skipping about in the environs of Santa Rosa, California, collecting slabs of fallen redwood, walnut, and maple trees from some of my "dealers," when my Ford F-250 and I arrived at a parking lot in the Cotati region. This was the prearranged drop zone for one RH Lee, without whom I could hardly be expected to lift the heavier of my new stump purchases. Her deliverance was masterfully executed by a couple of attractive but slightly underfed nature-lovers, on their way south from the fantasy camp known as the College of the Redwoods woodworking program in Mendocino, California. I was as relieved to be reacquainted with Lee, my team captain, as I was charmed to meet Michele and her estimable fellow, Ronnie, laden down with backpacks, camping gear, and a thermos of tea. We hit it off rather readily, but the cards were certainly stacked in our favor. Anytime you can make new friends by admiring the figure and growth ring count in what anyone else would see as a pile of firewood in the back of a pickup truck, you know you are meeting the right people.

Little did I then know just *how* right, as Michele would go on to become an absolute star at Offerman Woodshop, one to whom I often refer as our Han Solo. For those of you youngsters who may be reading this, to refer

to a person as the pilot of the *Millennium Falcon* is the highest of compliments, though perhaps somewhat archaic. Not only was Michele the woodworker in our fold with the most actual training, she also was the most dependable wellspring of explosive mirth. Her not-quiet laugh could be heard for a radius of three city blocks, and it was always an unexpected source of delight. She would pause in the middle of chopping the most delicate dovetails to cackle at some hijinks that Matty was getting up to with one of his puppets or "dance moves." And if those attributes weren't enough, her trusty sidekick, Ronnie the Aussie, was ever about, designing our website, revamping our sound system, or sanding meat paddles until the cows came home. The pair were deeply intrinsic to the lifeblood of the shop, and an important source of both mirth and productivity, not to mention sauerkraut and lentils. That is why we were heartbroken when they moved to Tasmania in 2015, to pursue further woodworking opportunities, and also to start up a concern of pickling products and education in the art of fermentation. Thanks to modern communications, we are still very much together, despite being at opposite ends of the globe. You can see more of Michele's work at MicheleDiener.com and get a load of their kimchi at SouthernWild.com.au.

I also suppose it would be untoward of me if I didn't mention that Michele was very pregnant during this photo shoot and build, which just goes to show you all the more what an unstoppable steamroller she is in the shop.

NAME: Michele Diener

HOMETOWN: Santa Fe, New Mexico

FAVORITE TOOTH: Left canine (Sharky)

FAVE OFFERMAN: Ric Offerman (very wise in the ways of Tasmanian history)

SPIRIT ANIMAL: Zozobra

NEW FAVE WOOD: Tasmanian myrtle

FAVE TOOL: Lie-Nielsen No. 102 low angle block plane

PREFERRED LUNCH: Anything green or fermented!

FAVORITE MONOTREME: Platypus

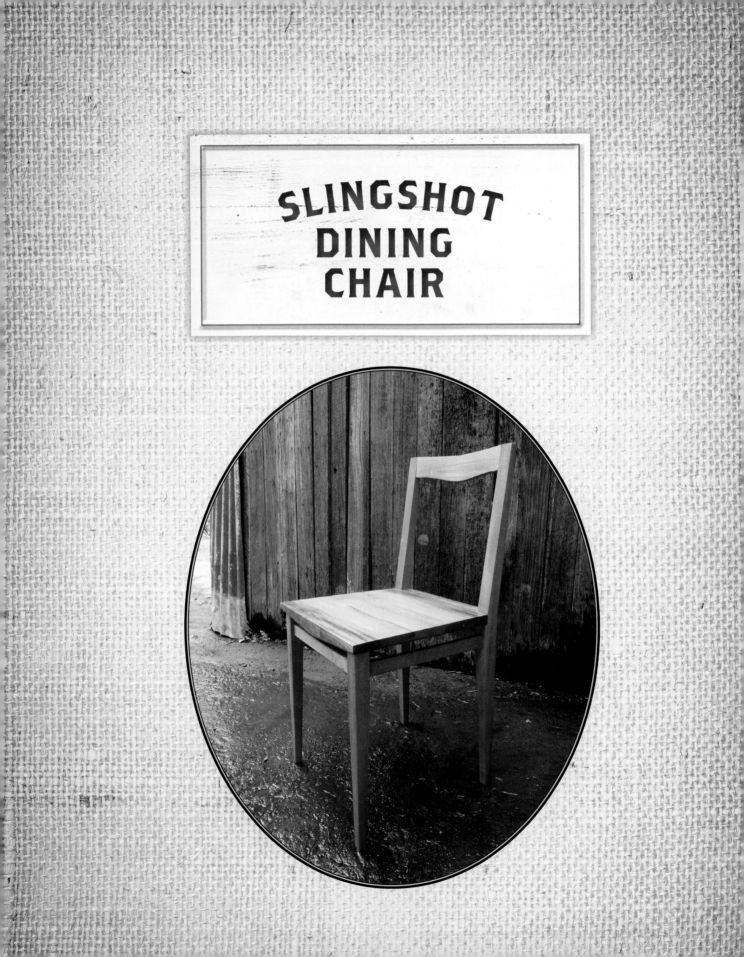

SLINGSHOT DINING CHAIR

MAKING THE SLINGSHOT DINING CHAIR

I am Michele Diener: maker, woodworker, designer, teacher, woman in wood, sculptor, artist. Simply said, I am someone who is passionate about craft. Making beautiful objects and spreading the knowledge of craft to the younger generations is something I will continue to be a part of until the end of my days.

Originally from New Mexico, I spent my first twenty-two years growing up in Santa Fe and Albuquerque. I moved to California in September of 1999 and spent the next sixteen years in both the northern and southern ends of the state. California is as much my home as New Mexico, as both places informed my life path and led me to where I am today.

My earliest memory of woodworking is making a pinhole camera in my senior high school photography class. I was dedicated to building a large-format camera to capture the world around me, and it had to be well constructed to do just that. At the time I had some building influence from my stepfather, who is a talented metalworker, and it's safe to say his knowledge of fabrication had started to rub off on me. The camera ended up being a success, and its sound design made me confident I could move on to bigger projects. Studying photography and sculpture in college allowed me the time to experiment that I was looking for.

Working with wood resonates with me the most, but I am not exclusive to any one material in my designs. In art school I had the luxury of using a variety of different materials to design and build sculptures, art installations, and furniture. It was during this time I started to lean toward wood as my desired medium. I appreciated learning about all the varieties of hardwoods I was using in projects; properties such as the color, texture, and grain structure of each species. However, it didn't stop there. Once I finished my undergraduate degree, I spent six years building interactive science exhibits for the Exploratorium in San Francisco, California, where I learned how to work with synthetic materials, plastics, and metal on a very intimate level. I learned where and when a given material was the appropriate choice to use for a specific job, whether it was a table for the dining room or an art installation in a gallery.

I've decided to design and build a chair as my contribution to this book for many reasons. Seating is the first furniture consideration people have in most social and solitary environments. Whether you are in a jail cell or your mother-in-law's living room, you will always want a place to sit. Chairs give the maker the opportunity to create a beautifully considered object and the user the opportunity to appreciate it. They can be very idiosyncratic and personal, portraying an identity of their very own. As a craftsperson, I think it is important to face the challenges a chair poses and add it to my repertoire of experiences. Not to mention I need a couple of new dining chairs for my kitchen table!

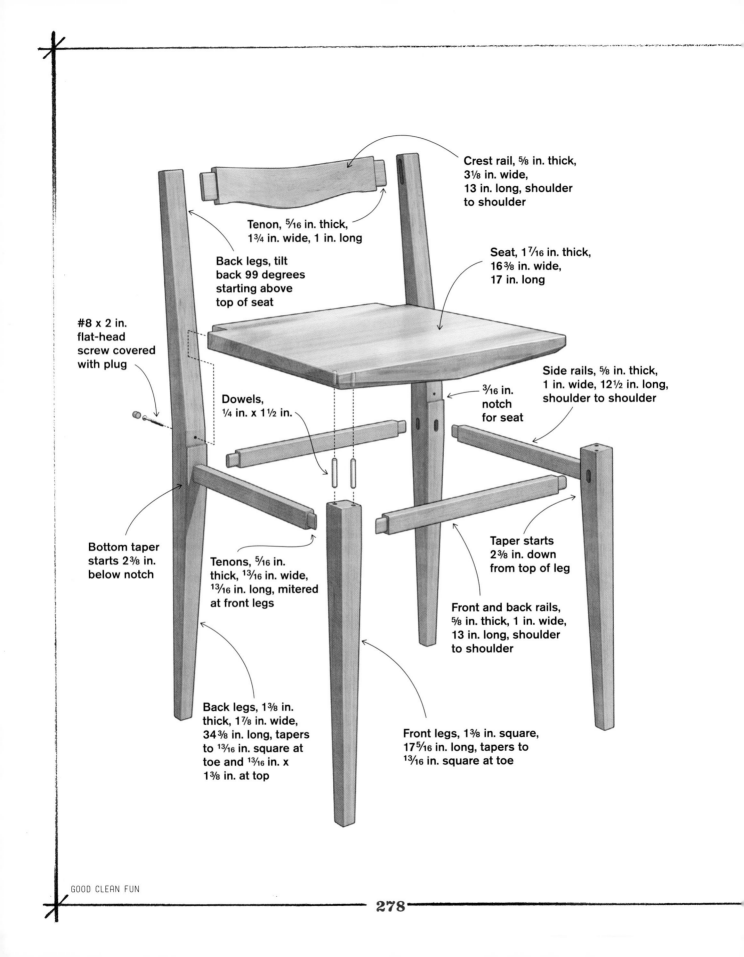

Crest rail, ⅝ in. thick, 3⅛ in. wide, 13 in. long, shoulder to shoulder

Tenon, 5/16 in. thick, 1¾ in. wide, 1 in. long

Back legs, tilt back 99 degrees starting above top of seat

Seat, 1 7/16 in. thick, 16⅜ in. wide, 17 in. long

#8 x 2 in. flat-head screw covered with plug

Dowels, ¼ in. x 1½ in.

3/16 in. notch for seat

Side rails, ⅝ in. thick, 1 in. wide, 12½ in. long, shoulder to shoulder

Bottom taper starts 2⅜ in. below notch

Tenons, 5/16 in. thick, 13/16 in. wide, 13/16 in. long, mitered at front legs

Taper starts 2⅜ in. down from top of leg

Front and back rails, ⅝ in. thick, 1 in. wide, 13 in. long, shoulder to shoulder

Back legs, 1⅜ in. thick, 1⅞ in. wide, 34⅜ in. long, tapers to 13/16 in. square at toe and 13/16 in. x 1⅜ in. at top

Front legs, 1⅜ in. square, 17 5/16 in. long, tapers to 13/16 in. square at toe

MICHELE DIENER: SLINGSHOT DINING CHAIR

1. In order to fully visualize the project before you build it, you need to take your sketch from SketchUp or any other isometric drawing you've made and translate it to a 1:1 scale or full-scale drawing; front and side views are best. Having this drawing as a reference will help you make your templates. I like to use a large piece of craft paper, T squares, and other drafting aids to sketch a front and side view of the chair. What's more, I usually build a full-size mock-up or prototype out of scrap lumber so that I can fully visualize all the chair's aspects.

2. Make templates for the back legs, front legs, crest rail, and seat; ¼" MDF or plywood will do for these templates—you just need enough of an edge to be able to retrace the shape several times. To make the templates I reference the drawing as well as my prototype for exact measurements, translate them onto the substrate, then cut the templates out on the band saw. A quick pass with a spokeshave or a plane takes the band saw marks away, fairs the curves, and gives your pieces a nice square edge for accurate tracing. It's nice to use the prototype in addition to the drawing when working out structural and aesthetic choices—for example, it helped me decide to make the chair back using no spindles, only the curved crest rail. Be thorough. What seems wise in the drawing doesn't always translate well to three-dimensional space.

3. Picking out wood is usually a fun beginning to any project. Not only are you deciding on the species (color, workability, finishing qualities, price), but you're also deciding on the grain structure to ensure stability and a visually stunning graphic quality. For the chair I'm using Tasmanian myrtle, a tree that grows natively on the island of Tasmania, Australia. The wood color varies from soft pink to reddish brown, and it is very agreeable to work with. Tasmanian myrtle is often figured, so I'll look for a piece that has some character to show off in the seat. **NICK: Not a euphemism.** Once I bring my lumber to the shop, I let it sit for a few days to acclimate to the climate so any movement I may encounter premilling is worked out.

4. Use your templates to mark the lines on your material (choosing proper grain direction) for back legs, front legs, curved crest rail, and seat. When I'm at the lumberyard, I have an idea of grain direction and a cut list with dimensions for all the parts of the project. In this case I know I want rift-sawn pieces for the legs and stretchers and either rift- or quarter-sawn for the seat and curved crest rail. This has mostly to do with stability and movement, but I also like to consider the graphic quality of each piece, as I would like to see nice straight grain on all four sides of the legs and stretchers. The curved crest rail and seat you have a bit more flexibility with, just as long as they tie the project together. As I'm tracing my templates onto the wood I have all these things in mind.

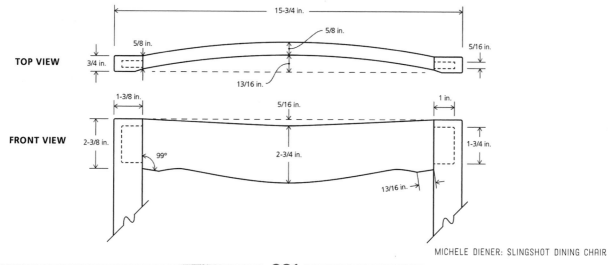

MICHELE DIENER: SLINGSHOT DINING CHAIR

passes and finish shaping the curve with hand tools. Once you're finished with the planer, shape the underside of the seat into a subtle curve with a low-angled hand plane and sanding blocks. The edge details exaggerate the curve as well.

5. Find the most attractive pieces of timber for your seat, since that will be the place where you really showcase the graphics and character of the wood. Mill up some chunks so you can glue up your seat into a piece wide enough to fit the base of the chair. Using your seat template, transfer the lines onto the blank, then draw out where the curve will be so you can remove enough material to make the shape. I built a jig to use with the planer where I braced the seat at the desired angle, 92 degrees, to remove the excess wood. You sneak up on your line with light

6. Next, cut out the back legs. You've already used your template to mark the layout. Take the scribed material to the band saw and cut close to the lines. Make sure to leave enough material so you can rout the excess off.

7. Once you've cut the legs out on the band saw, attach the template, using double-stick tape and a clamp, to the leg stock right along the lines you previously scribed. I used the router table and a 1½" double bearing inverted flush trim bit to avoid tear-out, so the template was above or below the material, depending on the direction I was cutting. This is called pattern routing.

8. At this point you're ready to mill and square up the rest of the parts for the chair. Prepare the wood for the front legs, the curved crest rail, and the stretchers.

9. Mark out where all the mortises are located on the front and back legs/back supports. I like to use my marking gauge to scribe all the lines since they need to be extra fine, and a pencil line tends to be a bit too fat. When scribing both the mortises and the tenons, I make sure to split the difference of the placement so I'm cutting the shoulders at an equal depth on all sides of the joint. The legs have mortises, and the stretchers and curved crest rail will have tenons.

10. There are many ways you can go about cutting the mortises, and for this project the best way was to use the 8 mm cutter in the Festool Domino. I marked where all the mortises needed to be cut on the leg stock, made sure I had enough flat surface area on which to rest the Domino, and cut away! If there are any mortises that needed to be longer than the setting would allow, move the Domino over slightly to cut out the excess.

11. Once you've used the marking gauge to lay out all your tenons, set up a stop on the crosscut sled and then adjust the height of your blade on the table saw to cut all the shoulders of your tenons. You will have two different setups for the chair parts with tenons—one for the stretchers and one for the curved crest rail. Once you've cut the shoulders, you'll need to cut the cheeks to reveal the entire tenon. I like using the band saw with a fence setup to cut the cheeks a hair oversize, then use a chisel to pare to the exact thickness. It's a good practice to pretest the cuts on an extra piece as you go along so you're not making the wrong cut on the final pieces. It's also good to test the fit of the practice tenon in the mortise it's paired up with.

12. The blank for the crest rail is cut exactly to size with the tenons cut in advance, so now it's time to trace the curves using the templates and cut the excess material off the blank on the band saw. The first cut will be from the underside of the blank—it's important to have at least two points of contact (three is better) that support the blank when you cut the opposing side, so make sure to leave enough material. The second and third cuts are to create the primary curves of the crest rail. The blank is big enough that you have plenty of material to hold on to for the first pass. On the second pass make sure you are stabilizing the curved section, so once the blade exits the cut, the curved piece is still firmly squared up to the blade. Remember your cuts don't have to be exact because you finish the shaping of the curves with a spokeshave, curved sanding blocks, and/or a cooper's hand plane. You should get it close before you glue it up and then finish matching the curve once it's glued together with the back supports.

13. I haven't finished tapering the front and back legs, so now is the time to do it. I like using my hand plane to make the final passes; it leaves the surface so nice and clean, especially if your blade is freshly sharpened. The jointer will also work for the front faces of the back legs/supports, still using a hand plane and/or spokeshave to get into the tight corner of the back side. **NICK: Folks, I apologize for the prurient language— this is just how they talk in Tasmania.**

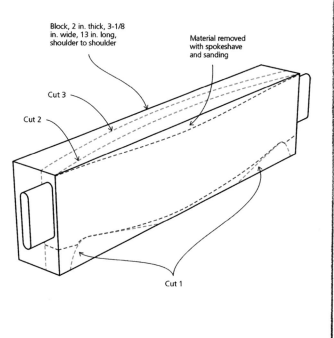

Block, 2 in. thick, 3-1/8 in. wide, 13 in. long, shoulder to shoulder

Material removed with spokeshave and sanding

Cut 3

Cut 2

Cut 1

14. When cutting and fitting joinery, it's best to consistently use your square as a reference and to make sure your tools are sharp and accurately set up for making perfectly square cuts. Using a paring chisel and a shoulder plane for fine-tuning, fit all the mortises and tenons of the chair. You should be able to clamp the base together and test that everything is in its place.

15. Now it's time to fit the seat. First take a bevel gauge to your plans and find the angle of the underside of the seat to the front and back legs. Scribe a line on both the front and back legs from the underside of the seat. Take the front legs to the chop saw and cut the desired angle off the top. On the back legs an angled ¼"-deep ledge is cut out with chisels and a block so it supports the underside of the seat. Make sure the top of the front legs and top edge of the back-leg ledge are the same height. Next mark the inside edge of the back supports onto the seat, scribe some lines indicating the thickness of the back legs at that point, and take the seat to the band saw to cut out the scribed sections. Once notched, the seat should end up sitting nearly flush to the back side of the legs.

16. Glue up the back legs, front legs, and lastly the entire chair base in three separate glue-ups to make the process easier on yourself. So that you won't have to sweat clamps overlapping, bruising the wood, and glue setup times, glue up the chair in three separate steps, in the following sequence:

    a. Back legs/supports, curved crest rail, and back stretcher

    b. Front legs and front stretcher

    c. Two previous glue-ups with side stretchers

17. Once you know exactly where the seat will be placed, dowels can be installed on the tops of the front legs. Drill the holes; then, using dowel centers, match the holes to the underside of the seat. Don't glue it together just yet; you want to apply finish to the seat before installing it. You can see here the tapered chamfer I placed on the lower edges of the seat for visual interest.

MICHELE DIENER: SLINGSHOT DINING CHAIR

18. Now that all the parts have been glued up, they all need their final shaping, detailing, and sanding. The curved crest rail needs to be shaped further to be flush with the back supports. Once the chair back is locked together, fairing the curves with a spokeshave will make it all come together. The legs will be lightly shaped with a file and spokeshave, and the seat will have its final once-over.

19. Time for finish. The chair is being finished with Organoil Hard Burnishing Oil, a tung-oil-based wipe-on-/-off finish. All surfaces have been sanded to 220, so the first coat will be applied with 320 grit wet sandpaper. The second coat will be applied with steel wool, and any subsequent coats will be wiped on and off with only a soft cloth. Once the finish has fully cured, burnish the surface with a soft cloth (I prefer distressed denim) for the final sheen.

20. Now it's time to glue the seat to the chair base. Glue two ¼" dowels into the holes previously drilled into the front legs and underside of the seat, then clamp the seat into place. Secure the back side of the seat to the back legs by screwing a #8 × 2" screw through each of the back legs into the seat. Plug the hole with a ⅜" myrtle plug. I used a ⅜" plug cutter and cut a series of plugs into a scrap piece of myrtle, popped them out with a chisel, and glued them into a bored hole after I drove the screw through the back leg and into the seat. Chisel the plug flush to the back legs, sand it, and add a bit of finish. You're done!

COOKOUT

ONE OF OUR FAVORITE THINGS to do at the shop, we manufacturers of sawdust, is stop working and cook some foodstuffs. Then, often seated around a small fire, we consume those comestibles with the appropriate pleasing beverages.

Everybody at Offerman Woodshop is a pretty good cook, and some (not me) are actually great. To me, sharing meals with the people in my life is not only fun—it's a great way to curate our collective health. We're making delicious grub from locally sourced ingredients, with a little butter and a lot of love, and, okay, maybe a little more butter.

We regularly take our lunches together as well, which I think adds greatly to the well-being of our hearts and our brains, not to mention our pocketbooks. We're choosing to share our recipes and our mealtimes together, which has the distinct advantage of saving us any travel time at lunch, especially to a fast-food drive-thru. Our lunchtimes and cookouts also provide us with invaluable social interactions; it's when we can check in with one another and hear about the goings-on in everybody's personal lives, which then has the added advantage of keeping the chatter to a minimum during shop hours. We also clamor to claim a front-row seat from which we marvel daily at the spectacle of Thomas eating

his lunch, the accumulated mass of which is usually the rough equivalent of a bushel of potatoes, a pail of milk, and a horse. You gotta see this guy eat.

Here then, please enjoy a representation of an OWS cookout, complete with neighbors and a rousing game of Corn Hole, followed by some tried-and-true recipes from our talented participants. It just goes to show that if you make things with the right people, including the making of a good time, you might suddenly find yourself with no need to go to the mall ever again.

OFFERMAN WOODSHOP PLEDGE

By Matty Micucci

I promise to do my best

To keep my tools sharp and honed

To work safe

And to clean up my sawdust at all times

To make things by hand with respect and honor to the spirit of the tree

Maintain our loving shop

Support my fellow woodworkers

And to respect the traditions of the craft

To work hard and dirty

Play John Prine

Eat lunch as a family

Honk my horn when leaving

And if I sprinkle when I tinkle

I'll be a sweetie and wipe the seatie

BURGERS

Thomas

The burger is the undisputed king of the grill, just like Elvis Presley is the king of people who may not actually be dead. And there are as many ways to construct your burger as there are Elvis impersonators. You can get fancy and grind up a dry-aged New York strip and mix it with pancetta, but we're going simple here: 80/20 ground chuck. The perfect fat ratio that doesn't shrink too much or end up dry. That's your burger right there. Here's how I do it:

1. Take that ground chuck and gently separate it into 8 oz. portions.
2. Try to avoid kneading—don't kill the meat!
3. With as little pressure and agitation as possible, form patties. Use your thumb to put a small dimple in the middle of each patty and liberally salt and pepper both sides (I recommend freshly ground pepper, if possible). If you salt the meat before you form the patties, it can affect the texture.
4. Now, you can fly by sight here, or you can use science. I use an instant-read meat thermometer, and I love it. However you want your burger cooked, always keep in mind that the meat will continue to cook after it's removed from the grill, so you may want to take it off a little shy of temp. We're going for medium, so I'm gonna take them off at 150–155°F and

let them rest for a few minutes to reach about 160°F.

5. Top that sucker with whatever you want, and eat it on a soft bun, perhaps a brioche.

GRILLED PORK CHOPS

Thomas

Pork chops are another iconic grill option, but they're tough to get right. We've all had charred, tough, or dry pork at a cookout, but it doesn't have to be that way! The secret to flavorful, juicy pork chops is brining and, again, using a meat thermometer. Also, getting good, thick (at least 1") chops is imperative.

THE BRINE

2 cups beer—use whatever you like, but we're using Solemn Oath's Nourri au Fourrage

2 cups water

¼ cup salt

This step is simple. Mix the above ingredients until the salt is dissolved, then stick the chops in there and refrigerate for a few hours.

While those are chilling, have a beer yourself, and prep your rub. I'm doing a basic rub with the following ingredients—use measuring devices if you want, or just eyeball it:

THE RUB

3 tablespoons paprika

1 tablespoon fresh ground black pepper

1 tablespoon coarse salt

1 teaspoon brown sugar

1 teaspoon chipotle powder

1 teaspoon garlic powder

1 teaspoon onion powder

1 teaspoon cayenne pepper

I also use sage, cloves, coriander, oregano, etc., when the mood takes me.

Once the chops are solidly brined, take them out and pat them dry before rubbing them down. Let them come to room temperature before grilling them so they cook evenly. Scrape and oil your grill and go to town; it should take about 20 minutes, but use that meat thermometer as your guide! It's important to note that you may have outdated info on safe internal temperatures for pork. The current USDA guidelines call for 145°F for intact pork cuts (nothing ground; that's still 160°F), and lemme tell you, a nice medium-rare pork chop is a delight worth experiencing.

GRILLED STEAK AND SALMON

Nick

Something I find both puzzling and amusing is the public misconception that both my character from *Parks and Recreation,* Ron Swanson, and by association myself, are somehow experts in the field of any sort of meat preparation. We are both certainly great *fans* of meat preparation, and have both on occasion consumed impressive quantities of meatstuffs, but I don't believe that qualifies us as chefs in any way. That said, I do greatly enjoy cooking meats on a charcoal grill, which is a skill I have learned from my dad, who I *would* call an expert in the field. I am lucky to study under him yet, as his class sessions are delicious.

Can I cook a steak that would make Ron sit up and giggle into his bib? You bet your sweet ass. Would Ron enjoy my salmon? Hell no, son, where do you think you are, Paris, France? Ron's distaste notwithstanding, salmon is damn delicious and quite good for you, so maybe we can all begin to comprehend that Ron is a well-wrought comedy character, whilst I am a human animal living in reality.

The recipe for my steak and salmon is the same. It's simple and delicious.

6 rib eyes
6 king salmon fillets
2–4 cups olive oil
Coarse sea salt
Fresh ground black pepper
Fresh rosemary
Fresh thyme

1. Purchase the nicest salmon fillets (or steaks) you can afford. If I just got in a residual check from *Miss Congeniality 2: Armed and Fabulous,* for example, I'll get the king salmon. I also try to buy the wild stuff, if I can, for the most flavor, not to mention its sustainability. Same goes for your rib eyes—definitely hunt your own wild cattle if you're able. If not, try to find the best beef you can. For our cookout I got the Wagyu grass-fed wonder-steaks. Marble-icious!

2. The night before your bacchanal, make a marinade in a couple of gallon-size Ziplocs. I pour in a cup of olive oil, some coarse sea salt, and fresh ground black pepper, then I glean the stems of rosemary and thyme, say six stems per bag—rub some of that goodness between your palms and inhale deeply; it will further improve your already celebratory disposition.

3. Mix the marinade well by simply squishing it around in the bag so that the oil is infused with the flavors of the herbs and spices.

4. Add your meat to the bags, obviously fish in one bag and beef in the other. Use more bags if necessary, with commensurate increases of marinade.

5. Squish the marinade around so that all the meat surfaces are inundated with goodness. Distribute the herbs as evenly as you can. Put the bags in the fridge to marinate overnight. If you're running late and you can marinate for only an hour, it'll still do you a world of good. Either way, let your meat sit out of the chiller box for an hour before grilling to bring it to room temperature.

6. Time to fire up the grill! I light my coals 20–30 minutes before I plan to start cooking, as I want the flames to be subdued and the coals to be red with a little ash starting to show white for the ideal cooking heat.

7. I pull the steaks out of the marinade and let a lot of the oil run off onto a dish before it can flare up on fire and cause the meat to be immolated. I throw the steaks on the grill and then I start with my salmon fillets, skinless side down.

8. Thomas uses a little meat robot thermometer drone pen, which looks pretty nifty, but I just

grill by feel and sight. I like my steaks medium rare, so after about 4–5 minutes I flip the steaks, then after another 4–5 minutes I slice one with my knife to check the pinkness.

9. Meanwhile, I keep an eye on the salmon and usually flip it after 3–4 minutes, depending on taste. I like to leave it a little uncooked in the middle. Sue me.

10. Thomas's robot probe says that the steaks should come off at 130°F, and we remind each other (through a series of beeps) that the meat will continue to cook after it comes off the grill. The salmon is ready at 135–140°F. I like the ease of the gadget, but I'm stubborn, so I have not come around to it yet. Perhaps one day in my dotage, the meat robot will aid my failing peepers. Until then, I'll eyeball it.

SPANAKOPITA

Sally

A favorite recipe from my and Lee's dear Yia Yia and my dear mother, both wonderful cooks and teachers:

3 packages (approx. 1 pound) frozen greens, like collards or spinach, thawed, with water thoroughly squeezed out
¼ cup fresh mint or dill (or both), chopped
4 eggs
10 ounces feta
2 leeks, chopped, or 1 bunch scallions, finely chopped, lightly cooked in oil
Salt and pepper to taste (light on salt, because feta is salty)
1 pound phyllo dough, thawed in refrigerator overnight
½ pound butter, melted

1. Grease a large cookie sheet with butter or olive oil.

2. In a large bowl, mix collards/spinach, mint/dill, eggs, feta, leeks/scallions, salt, and pepper. Make sure the mixture is as dry as possible.

3. Use half the phyllo to make a bottom layer. Brush each layer with butter after you put it down (keeping the butter hot so it spreads thinly), and press gently to keep it flat.

4. When you have used approximately half the sheets, spread the mix evenly over the base.
5. Continue layering and buttering phyllo until used up.
6. Score the top into whatever size squares you prefer by barely cutting through the top layers of the phyllo, being careful not to allow any of the filling to escape.
7. Bake at 375–400°F, 30–45 minutes, until nicely browned on top.

MASHED POTATOES

Krys

When I was a young child growing up with my grandmother, I loved to cook—and still do. One of my favorite things to cook was mashed potatoes with cream cheese, chives, butter, some seasoning salt, and pepper. It was definitely a family favorite, and if there were leftovers the next morning, we would put a little oil in the skillet for the potatoes to fry. Oh my god, amazing! Potato medley.

> **Russet red, white, and regular potatoes**
> **Cream cheese**
> **Chives**
> **Rock salt**
> **Coarse ground black pepper**
> **Granulated garlic**

Cook potatoes until soft. Mix with the rest of the ingredients to taste.

CORN . . . MY WAY

Nick

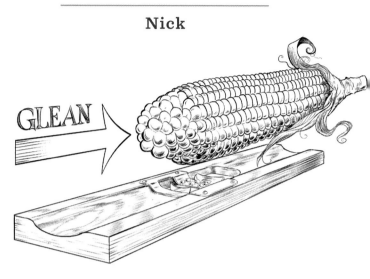

GLEAN

When we were married (I still feel lucky just typing these words thirteen years later), my wife and I received a very generous gift card from her agents at the time to the fancy spatula store Williams-Sonoma. As I stood in the checkout line with an embarrassment of pots, pans, and of course, spatulas (spatulai?), the cashier pointed out that I had some $37.00 or so left on the card. Drunk with the delight of a lottery winner, I quickly skipped about amongst the doodads and sundry items near the register, until my eyes fell upon the Corn Creamer. Talk about love at first sight. I wrapped it brusquely in my hands and whispered softly, "I know you. I know your meaning." Armed with this simple but mighty weapon, I developed my signature dish, which has been dubbed "Corn . . . My Way" (by my discerning and patient friend Tom). It takes a little bit of labor, but isn't that true of the best things in life? This dish is so yummy you could serve it for dessert.

1. The Corn. Find the freshest, local-est sweet corn you can. I prefer yellow corn, but it tastes just as good with white. Prepare two ears per guest. I'm often cooking for ten, so I just do an even two dozen ears, because the surplus never seems to hurt anybody's feelings.

2. Now you get to husk the corn, which is one of my favorite nostalgic activities, as I spent so much time doing this as a kid with my folks and their folks. If you can get your corn from my mom's family, the Roberts Brothers farm in Minooka, Illinois, do. There is not a finer dozen to be had from the vast, resplendent gardens of earth.

3. Time for the magic. I do this outside if possible, as the corn kernels tend to spatter a bit of juice as they are processed, and the grass minds it less than the kitchen floor. Take your largest pot and lay the flat trough of the creamer across it. Holding the creamer in place with one hand, use the other to drag an ear of corn from fanny to tip across the hardware. As the corn slides over the business area, the first blade and teeth tear open the kernels, then the curved scraper gleans all the pulp and juice from each kernel. Gravity then dictates that the goods fall through the middle hole into the pot. The width of the hardware covers about 1/5 of the ear's circumference, and I like to drag each segment across two or three times to get every drop of goodness. Then you spin the ear to the next 1/5 and repeat. It's pretty easy to get the hang of this.

4. Now, once you've cleaned up your magic corn stick and wiped the juice spatters into your jeans, take your pot of glory juice to the stove (or if in the shop, to a hot plate). The next step is to simply simmer the mixture on low heat to remove as much water as possible. This whole process can be done with just a medium saucepan, but I have learned that the greater the surface area of the corn, the quicker the water evaporates. Science. Not to brag. You must remain vigilant and stir often so that your precious pudding doesn't get scalded on the bottom of the pan. I usually get to this point with my corn and then begin prepping the rest of my dishes, so that I can stop and stir every few minutes.

5. Once your corn reaches the consistency of moist mashed potatoes, you are pretty much ready to delight some eaters. I add some salt to taste and 1/4 stick of butter (or maybe 1/2 stick if it's Friday night), and then right before the dish is served I stir in some fresh chopped chives. I keep a tablespoon of chives in reserve to sprinkle over the top once the corn is in the bowl, purely for the pleasing color, because I'm sensitive like that.

6. That's it! Couldn't be simpler. Upon serving, get limbered up and prepare to break up some fights when your dinner guests get near the bottom of the bowl. It happens regularly, and you should absolutely take every bloody nose as the highest of compliments.

SOUTHERN WILD'S APPLE & JUNIPER SAUERKRAUT

Ronny and Michele

Members of the vegetable kingdom are generally not welcome at the woodshop, but a handful of notable exceptions are bestowed upon a fortunate few, those being the noble potato, the corn (of course), and anything that falls into the category of "meat-enhancing accoutrement." In regard to the latter, we like to bestow a wreath of living sauerkraut atop our glistening brats wherever possible. True to the Germanic roots of the mighty *bratwurst*, this traditional European recipe for apple and juniper sauerkraut serves as the perfect companion.

MAKES ABOUT 4½ POUNDS

2 heads white cabbage (approx. 4–5 pounds)
4½ tablespoons unrefined, non-iodized salt (such as sea salt or Celtic salt)
½ tablespoon juniper berries
2–3 medium-size apples (approx. ⅓ pound)

Cutting board
Sharp knife
Large mixing bowl
Peeler
Fermenting crock, or several large glass jars with airlocks and plastic lids
A glass or ceramic plate that fits within the internal diameter of your vessel (if it does not come with your crock)
Brine weights (if they don't come with the crock)

1. Remove a few layers of outer leaves (approx. 2–5 layers) from the cabbage until you reach the clean and dense inner leaves. Keep 2–3 pieces of your cabbage leaves whole, and set aside for use later on.

2. Cut each head into quarters and trim the core out of each quarter.

3. Slice the remaining cabbage into ¼-inch-wide ribbons. If you slice too thickly, it will be difficult to extract sufficient water from the cabbage later on. If you slice too thinly, too much water will come out of the ferment and the kraut may get mushy.

4. Add all the sliced cabbage to the mixing bowl and add the salt.

5. Massage the salt into the cabbage with your gnarled and calloused hands for at least 7 minutes. This is an opportunity to excise any embedded frustrations or stress that you are currently holding within. It is important to "bruise" the cabbage a little with your brute strength, as this helps the cabbage to release its juices. The salt helps to pull the liquid from the watery cabbage and creates a safe, briny environment in which to ferment your other ingredients.

6. When the cabbage has released its juices, you should have a small pool in the bottom of your bowl. At this time you can add the juniper and let it rest while you do other things.

7. Peel and core your apples, then dice into pieces about ½-inch thick.

8. Add the apples to the bowl and lightly mix through all the ingredients.

9. Begin packing your ingredients into your fermenter and compress the ingredients as much as you can as you pack the fermenter. This ensures that the brine rises above all the vegetable matter and protects it from contamination.

10. Add the whole cabbage leaves that you set aside earlier. Place them on top of the vegetables in a thin layer and press down so that the brine floats above the whole leaves. This helps keep the top of your ferment from spoiling.

11. Add your plate on top of the whole leaves and push down.

12. Add the weights on top of the plate. You should still see brine covering the ingredients, and perhaps submerging the plate too. If you have a fermenting crock, it should have come with some ceramic weights. If you don't have that, you can use either sanitized river stones from a place that has no lime in the rock substrate (granite is a good example) or glass weights such as jars containing water with plastic lids. Do not use metallic weights (or jar lids), as the high salinity of the brine will rust them and spoil your ferment.

13. Close the lid of your fermenter and add water to the moat. If you used a glass jar, you can insert an airlock into the plastic lid by drilling a hole and using a rubber grommet. These items are all commonly available from a home-brew store.

14. Ferment your recipe in a dark place (no direct sunlight, please) that is cool and has minimal temperature fluctuation until you are satisfied with the results.

As a general rule, we like to ferment our products for between 7 and 21 days at around 65°F. If your location is hotter, the ferment will go faster; conversely, if the storage place is cooler, then you will need to ferment for a longer time frame.

Younger ferments are typically crunchier, but the flavors lack infusion. Older ferments (two weeks or more at 65°F) tend to have an improved flavor that is greater than the sum of its parts. It should taste a little "sour," but in a good way, and will be ready for adorning your noble brats!

GUACAMOLE MONTERREY (FIESTA SIZE)

Josh

Before I was a woodworker, I was a professional trombonist. After college, I played principal trombone with the Orquesta Sinfónica de la Universidad Autónoma de Nuevo León in Monterrey, Mexico. While I was living there, my landlady taught me how to prepare Mexican cuisine, including this simple guacamole. I've since realized that a career in music wasn't the right path for me, but I still eat guacamole at least once a week.

4 large, ripe avocados, halved, pitted, and peeled

½ cup diced yellow onion

¾ cup diced tomato

4 cloves minced garlic

1 serrano pepper, finely minced (leave seeds in if you prefer spicy, like me)

¼ cup chopped cilantro (de-stemmed)

1½ limes, juiced

Salt and pepper

Mash avocados slightly in a bowl. Mix in remaining ingredients. Add salt and pepper to taste.

POTATOES & ONIONS

Ric

1. Count your number of guests. Use one medium-size potato per person, slice thinly, and spread on aluminum foil.

2. Use one onion per two guests. Slice thinly, and spread into rings and place on top of the potatoes.

3. Pour olive oil on top of the pile. How much? I don't know; I never measured. If you put too much, they won't burn on the bottom. If not enough, the bottoms will be black. A lot of my family like the burned ones. You have to get there early to scrape those off.

4. Add sea salt and pepper to taste.

5. Cover with another sheet of foil and throw 'er on the grill. The time will depend on the heat of your grill. If you do not like burned potatoes, throw them on a cool spot on the grill and

leave them 35–45 minutes with the top on and you should be all right. You can always test them through the foil with your pocketknife, you know. Don't have a pocketknife? Hmm . . .

PICKLED CUCUMBER SALAD

Jane

I learned this recipe from a roommate of mine who made the best Korean food. I'm not sure how true I've kept it to the original recipe, but it still tastes great.

5 large cucumbers

A lot of salt

Sesame oil

Rice vinegar

Sesame seeds

1 clove garlic

1. Slice the cucumbers as thinly and evenly as possible. The ceramic slicers work best, or just sharpen your knife and get Zen with it. As you slice the cukes, throw them into a large bowl and periodically cover them with a decent amount of salt. Keep adding cukes and salt until the cukes run out.

2. Gingerly toss the cukes around by hand, making sure they are all smothered in salt.

3. After about 15 minutes they will start to pickle. When they are a little flexible, squeeze them in handfuls until the majority of the water comes out (carefully so they curl up but don't break),

transferring each handful to a new bowl. Once they've all been squeezed you can rinse them thoroughly with water and squeeze them all out again, transferring them back to your original bowl, which has since been rinsed.

4. Add sesame oil, rice vinegar, salt, and sesame seeds to taste. If you like a little zest, stir in a clove of crushed garlic.

DRINKS

By Matt Offerman

SOLEMN OATH BREWERY SELECTS

Let me start by asking, Are you interested in pairing your beer with your meal? Yes? That sounds like fun? Then continue below. No? Sounds like something they do in Butthole City? Okay, no problem, just skip this section entirely.

All right, are the rest of you still with me? Good. Those weaklings were dragging us down. This will be a lot easier now. Although they do get to skip ahead and see Nick's high school pictures . . .

Still here? Great. Glad to be rid of those weirdos too. Let's talk about beer, shall we?

OWS had one of their really nice potluck cookouts, and I was lucky enough to pair some of the courses with beer. I've totally lost touch with Los Angeles's craft-brewing production, so I'll admit that I paired beers from the greater California area (also Oregon). For those playing at home, I used a pairing chart that I found on CraftBeer.com, via the Google. It generously offers two beer styles per food group, so I was able to lean toward the style I favored.

CORN . . . MY WAY: Deschutes Black Butte Porter. Nick's dish is nine parts butter and one part buttered corn, so I wanted an equally rich porter to match.

POTATOES & ONIONS: Murphy's Irish Stout. I love this pairing of the roasty, smoky potatoes with the same notes of the stout. Also, we went with Murphy's because Guinness tastes like the liquid they found in King Tut's Canopic bedpan.

GRILLED PORK CHOPS: Green Flash Le Freak. CraftBeer.com suggests an Imperial IPA or a Belgian dubbel. How about we just have a Belgian-style IPA and call it a day. In this case, Green Flash's Le Freak was an easy choice.

GRILLED STEAK: Bruery Terreux Saison Rue. I really like drinking saisons in general, but I love having it with a steak, as the two different pepper notes play off each other. Bonus: Josh brought a homemade saison that I wish I could have been around to try.

MOM O'S BLUEBERRY PIE: Firestone Walker Pivo Hoppy Pils. Finally, I paired a flavorful and clean pilsner with my mom's blueberry pie. The crust and the malt match well, and the fruit flavor balances right on top of the hops.

My mouth is watering right now as I type this, and I just finished eating dinner. (Cheddar Wurst with Solemn Oath's Whisper Kisses.) I have to admit that I didn't spend a lot of time worrying about this menu. I chose styles that I enjoy and beers that I know I enjoy. Worst case scenario:

The pairing isn't 1,000 percent perfect, and we're stuck drinking beer we love with food that's delicious. Penthouse problems, I says.

I did worry about the fact that we didn't have enough time to cater a very local beer list. You should really do your best to drink locally. We are currently drinking in an unprecedented time for beer production. There are so many fantastic small breweries making beers right now that are interesting and flavorful. Find the ones near you and support them. If you live near Chicago, I can personally vouch for one or two places: 3 Floyds, BrickStone, BuckleDown, Corridor, DryHop, Forbidden Root, Goose Island, Half Acre, Haymarket, Metropolitan, Moody Tongue, Off Color, Penrose, Pipeworks, Spiteful, Temperance, Tighthead, Tribes, and Werk Force. Oh yeah, and Solemn Oath. These breweries make great beer, and some even offer pairing ideas on their websites and menus. Go visit them and try their beer. If they have food, see what they would pair together.

Or if this all sounds like too much work, there are a lot of places offering pairing dinners now. Even most craft-forward restaurants will offer beer options for your meals. If you're in Chicago, I can highly recommend going to Hopleaf or Farmhouse. They are two of the best examples of how beer pairing is done. So, your homework, now that we're concluding: (1) Go out and drink delicious, local beer; (2) Pair it with food (optional); (3) Enjoy it (not optional).

Sláinte!

MOM O'S BLUEBERRY PIE

Cathy

Pastry for 2-crust pie (My mom liked to use lard in hers; Ric's mom also used 7Up instead of water. Both made great pies!)
¾–1 cup sugar
¼ teaspoon nutmeg
¼ cup all-purpose flour
½ teaspoon cinnamon
1–2 teaspoons lemon juice
⅛ teaspoon salt
½ teaspoon lemon zest
4 cups blueberries (If you're sending Nick to pick them, tell him you need 8 cups, because he'll eat at least half!)
1 tablespoon butter
Heavy cream and sugar for glaze

1. Preheat oven to 425°F. Roll out half of the pastry and line a 9-inch pie plate with it.
2. In a bowl, combine all ingredients except blueberries and butter.
3. Arrange half the berries in the pie plate, sprinkle with half the sugar mixture, repeat.
4. Dot filling with butter.
5. Roll out the other half of the pastry. Moisten the edge of the bottom pastry with water and

lower the top pastry in place. Trim overhanging edges* and crimp as desired.

6. Brush cream over pastry and sprinkle with sugar. Cut some vents into the pastry (or if you want to be fancy, cut out shapes with a sharp knife or cookie cutter after rolling it out).

7. Bake 40–50 minutes, until filling begins to bubble and crust is golden brown. Enjoy.

*Boy Pies (named by Mike Roberts, my dad, but the girls liked them too!): Gather remaining pastry scraps and form into a ball. Roll out into a rectangle, sprinkle with sugar and cinnamon. Roll up lengthwise. Cut into ½-inch slices, and bake until brown and crisp. Remove from the oven and get out of the way of hungry kids!

CORN HOLE

Lee

No cookout is complete without a sport with which to both work up an appetite and practice the hand-eye coordination necessary to efficiently stuff your face. In the past, we have been known to play parking-lot badminton, baseball, football, and soccer. However, Corn Hole, because of the game's titular food item, always seemed to me the quintessential OWS game. Perhaps due to the game's historic roots in the hills of Kentucky, Thomas easily beat us all, and Gus made off with most of the bags before we could play a second round. Regardless of our generally poor performance, it did the trick—the food made it into our face holes with professional aim.

1 sheet ½" plywood cut into 2 parts at 2' × 4"

1 × 3 pine cut into 4 parts at 22½" and 4 parts at 48"

2 × 4 legs cut into 4 parts at 11½", with one end (the feet) at 10 degrees

Compass and pencil—draw a 6"-diameter circle centered and 9" from top

Drill pilot hole for jigsaw blade

Jigsaw and steady hand to cut out the circle

Sandpaper to round the hole edges

Handful of flathead screws

8 cloth (canvas or duck) sacks filled with dry beans or corn

Season with plenty of beer

Can a tree feel pain?
Can you touch your eye?
Is saw good...

RH LEE

" Aw, Jeez. Now it's time to tell you about Lee. I am welling up like a sap just at the prospect of it.

When I knew it was time to add some hands to the shop, 'round about 2008, I put the word out in my small community of pals and malcontents in the handcrafting studios of Los Angeles. Almost immediately, my compatriot (the swell and devilishly handsome woodworker) Sam Moyer told me he'd just countenanced the ideal prospect:

> *I was installing a kitchen in Eagle Rock; I needed some help, and somebody recommended this woman, Lee, who's fresh in from San Francisco. Friend, she completely outworked the other three guys on the site—who were all twice her size, by the by.*

Well, hell. I was able to secure Lee for an interview, and it quickly became apparent that Fortuna had sent me a tiny and powerful superhero. She grew up woodworking in a charismatic and creative family in Berkeley, California, before heading east to study art and philosophy at Brown. While attending that noble institution, she became involved in building scenery for the theater (okay, I have a scenic carpenter problem), which she continued to do after graduating in 2000 and moving back home to the San Francisco Bay Area. These skills subsequently landed her a particularly sweet gig thriving in the shop at San Francisco's Exploratorium, building exhibits and interactive displays for this venerable science/art museum. She then studied for a summer at the Krenov

School for Woodworking up in Fort Bragg, California, at the College of the Redwoods Fine Furniture, and here she now sat in my shop—an obsessively skilled woodworker, with the organizational skills and knowledge of materials and hardware, developed in her time at the museum. She is powerfully athletic, brightly enthusiastic, and blessed with inspired artistic talent as well. It was all I could do to keep my voice steady as I inquired whether she might like to take the helm of my woodshop while I was to be frequently away portraying a guy with a moustache.

Obviously, and gloriously, she agreed. Reliving this moment of inception is quite warming, and I do believe I will send Sam Moyer a fine bottle of Scotch as soon as I finish writing this introduction, for he has done me right, and then some.

The shop? The website? The collective of winning characters? The elfin mirth? None of this happens without Lee. She makes this whole thing tick, and she keeps it ticking, even while suggesting further improvements to our ticking mechanisms. Folks like to ascribe most of the achievements of Offerman Woodshop to me alone, I suppose because they want to think that it's the guy they like from film and TV (and *People* magazine's Sexiest Man Alive 2010 issue, of course) who made their cutting board, but this couldn't be further from the truth. That is why a book about my shop must necessarily include the actual producers of the shop's goods, for without this merry band of sawyers, there is no OWS. If you would like to throw some accolades our way, I will say thank you, and then I will tell you that it is Lee who deserves a parade above all.

NAME: Lee

POSITION: Center Midfield

HOMETOWN: Berkeley, CA

HIRSUTE SCALE: Mediterranean

CRAFT HERO: Aunt Mary

BENCH PRESS 1 REP MAX: 3 Offermans

PREFERRED TRUCK MAKE/ MODEL: All-City Space Horse bicycle with Surly rear and front racks and redwood extended cab for Gus

BOOTS: Blundstone

MORE GOODNESS: LeeBuild.com

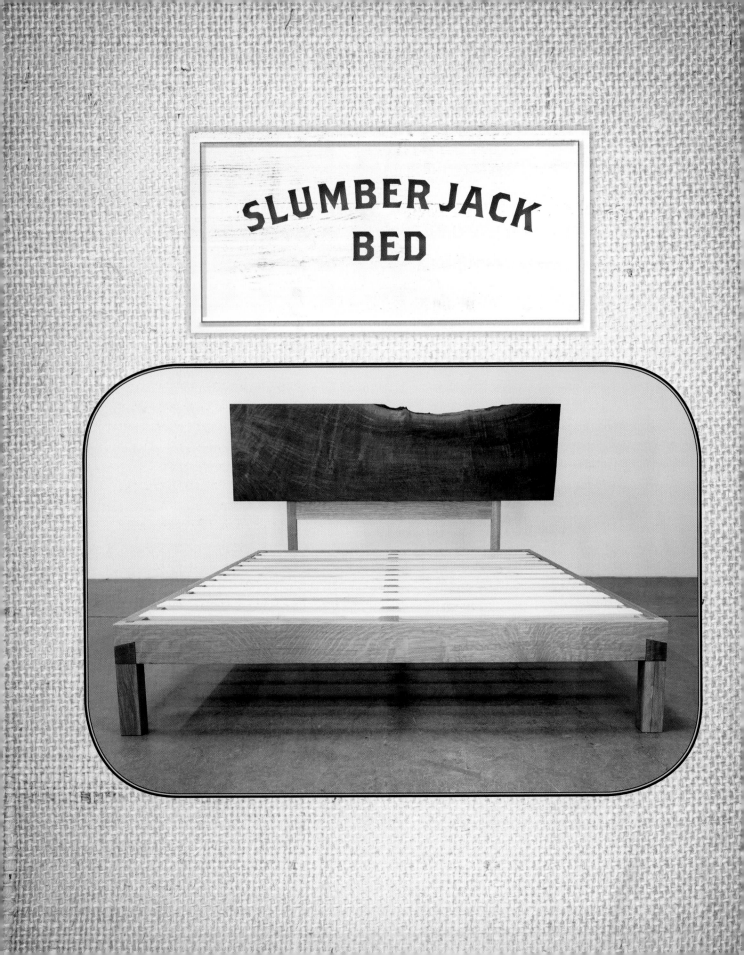

SLUMBER JACK
BED

MAKING THE SLUMBER JACK BED

My parents tell me as a young kid I could entertain myself for hours playing alone with a pile of pebbles or, as evidenced in one photograph from a beach picnic, an enormous washed-up sponge of unknown origin. Thankfully, nothing has changed, except that I now have access to finer materials and more complex tools of manipulation.

I owe this development to an after-school program called "Kids Carpentry" at our local Berkeley public school, where I enrolled at the tender age of seven. There, I not only learned how to create more advanced props for my imaginary worlds—like the 6″ mechanized towboat I built for my colony of pebbles—I also learned the fundamental principles of entrepreneurship and craftsmanship that have guided my career ever since. Out of this humble after-school program I launched my first business as a professional woodworker: building, painting, and selling plywood skateboards to my parents' friends. (This enterprise was much more lauded by my poor parents than was my second official woodworking business ten years later: making and selling weed pipes to my friends at Berkeley High School.)

From these ventures I learned that you better love woodworking, because making money from it is hard, even for a talented eight-year-old. More invaluable than this first lesson is what I learned about the standards of good craftsmanship. I can still hear our teacher, Al Mayberry, holding my brutishly cut, crookedly drilled, and poorly measured board of maple in his hands and exclaiming to my elation his signature phrase, "Perfection at its highest pinnacle!" Was he ever right; because now, thirty years later, when I visit my parents' home, it is that perfectly terrible cutting board that has withstood the test of time under my mom's unforgiving bread knife while all the other store-bought and conventionally geometrical chopping boards have since been discarded. In other words, perfection in my work has always had more to do with utility and individuality than it has had with straight lines and infallible surfaces.

That said, I've also spent some time in the church of Krenov and the masters of fine detail—a summer at the College of the Redwoods in Fort Bragg and five years working in a museum cabinet shop at the Exploratorium in San Francisco—where the tolerances were tiny and the surfaces impeccable. Even in my own furniture practice these days I've been known to sand to 400 grit on occasion. However, I have also worked many years as a scenic carpenter for theaters, and alongside my dad—master of duct tape—on absurd and grand Halloween installations that need only look "pretty good" from a hundred feet away in the dark.

As a designer and builder, I now like

to keep a foot in both schools. From the Krenovians I've learned to pay close attention even to the hidden details of a piece and to value focused and disciplined workmanship. From theater and from my parents, I've learned to value creative individuality and spontaneity—to produce freely and to find joy and fun in the process, whether it's building a twelve-foot Medusa head out of papier-mâché and irrigation pipe in an evening with my dad or spending ten months tirelessly fine-tuning a Dutch pullout dining table for a client.

I designed this bed to engage both aspects of my creativity. The complexity of the joint gave me plenty of problem solving to keep my precision math-mind busy. While the large scale of the joinery (inspired by traditional Japanese and Western timber framing) gave me flexibility with the fit. The dovetails and mortise and tenons are all cut on machines

and fit by hand—broad strokes on the band saw, followed by slow, careful work with my shoulder plane and paring chisels.

Since building out a series of mobile cargo tricycles and carts for the Exploratorium a few years ago, I've had a growing fascination with nomadic or "knock-down" furniture: furniture that is designed to move, come apart, pack flat, and reassemble with ease. The most compelling designs rely completely on only wood joinery, such as a removable wedge or peg, a sliding dovetail, slotted joints, or a simple dowel hinge. Finding an appealing bed design that did not include metal fasteners proved difficult, so I decided to design my own.

Because fully assembled bed frames don't fit through most doors or around tight corners, most beds come apart for transport. But a bed also needs to be stable and strong if it's going to support a woodworker, a dog,

and a girlfriend with restless leg syndrome. And investing in a well-made, aesthetically pleasing bed is important—as this is the piece of furniture on which we spend the most time (if, like me, you need your eight to ten hours a night to sleep off the soreness of building enormous beds all day).

The challenge with designing furniture that can pack up and move is striking the perfect balance between portability and strength. If you are not using any metal fasteners, but rather relying completely on wooden mechanical joints, as I am with this bed, this relationship of strength to portability becomes crucial in your tolerances. In order for your joints to hold strong mechanically, they have to be tight; but in order for them to come apart relatively easily, they can't be *too* tight. Discovering this small window in tolerance was the biggest takeaway from this project, a lesson I had to learn on occasion

the hard way—with vise grips, a mallet, and/or expletives. Krenovians be warned: There will be gaps.

Exhausted from a month of hand fitting complex joints, I decided to give in and employ the machine screw for attaching the slab headboard. I am no purist, after all—remember, I come from a scenic carpentry background. The screw is a wonderfully strong and fast solution to many design dilemmas; and if you want to actually make a living in this field, you had better familiarize yourself with the entire McMaster-Carr catalog of fasteners. Fully satisfied by conquering the all-wood knock-down challenge with the frame, I believe it's now high time to get on to other jobs (and of course delicious naps in my new bed). So please, pass me my cordless drill, a fistful of screws, and let the melodic whine of flatheads driving deep into oak be my bedtime lullaby tonight. ZZZZZzzzzzz . . .

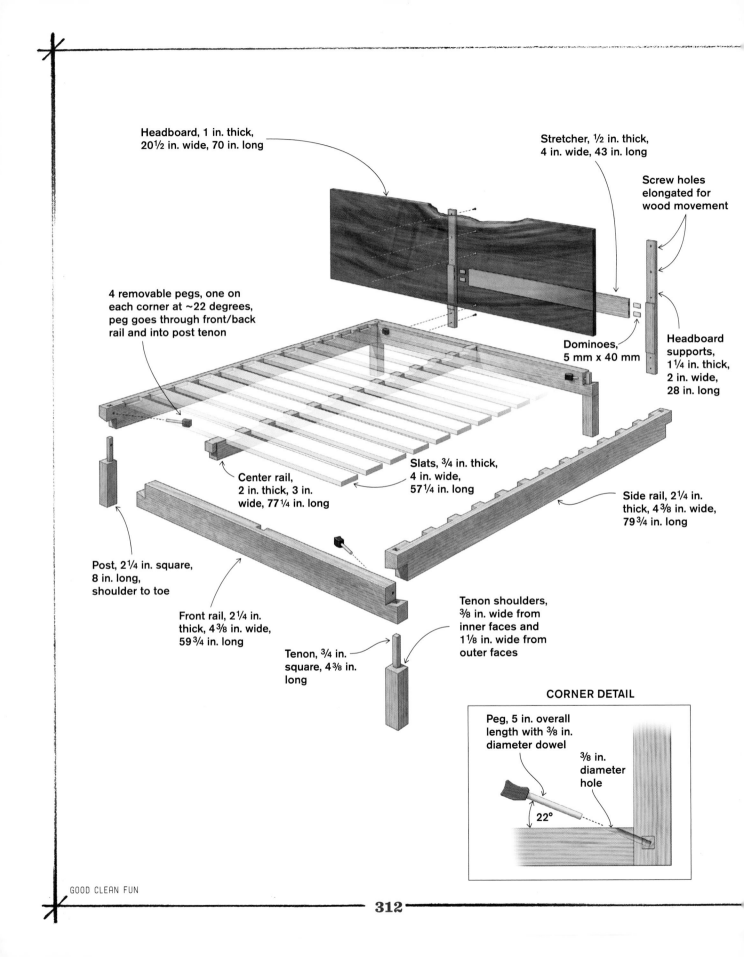

Headboard, 1 in. thick,
20½ in. wide, 70 in. long

Stretcher, ½ in. thick,
4 in. wide, 43 in. long

Screw holes
elongated for
wood movement

4 removable pegs, one on
each corner at ~22 degrees,
peg goes through front/back
rail and into post tenon

Dominoes,
5 mm x 40 mm

Headboard
supports,
1¼ in. thick,
2 in. wide,
28 in. long

Center rail,
2 in. thick, 3 in.
wide, 77¼ in. long

Slats, ¾ in. thick,
4 in. wide,
57¼ in. long

Side rail, 2¼ in.
thick, 4⅜ in. wide,
79¾ in. long

Post, 2¼ in. square,
8 in. long,
shoulder to toe

Front rail, 2¼ in.
thick, 4⅜ in. wide,
59¾ in. long

Tenon, ¾ in.
square, 4⅜ in.
long

Tenon shoulders,
⅜ in. wide from
inner faces and
1⅛ in. wide from
outer faces

CORNER DETAIL

Peg, 5 in. overall
length with ⅜ in.
diameter dowel

⅜ in.
diameter
hole

22°

LAY OUT PARTS

1. My first step is to lay out all the different parts of the bed onto my lumber. I make sure to leave plenty of extra length (1"–12"), some extra width (~½"), and up to ¼" in thickness to allow for the material lost in the milling process. I'm also paying attention to grain direction of the different parts—for example, I will make the posts out of the rift-sawn edges of the board so that the grain is straight on all four sides. I mark off any checks, knots, sapwood, or other defects that I will try to cut around. If I can, I always buy enough lumber so that I can make a couple of extras of each part, which I can use for joinery tests or mess-ups.

ROUGH CUTS

2. I use the chop saw to crosscut my parts down to my *rough* lengths (+1"–12").

3. I use the band saw to rip my parts to rough width (+~½").

ROUGH MILL

4. Some boards have to be brought down to rough thickness. While I could do this on the planer, I prefer to resaw on the band saw—that way I waste less material and can get two boards out of one. To prepare for resawing, I must first flatten a face and edge-joint an edge on the jointer.

5. Once my boards have two square, flat surfaces, I can accurately resaw my board in half. Notice how the two resawn boards are severely cupped after being cut in half. The rough milling process often releases hidden tensions in the wood, which is why we give ourselves so much extra material to work with.

6. I sticker all my rough-cut parts and leave them overnight to acclimate and adjust to their new shapes. The stickers allow for equal air flow around all four newly cut surfaces of the board.

MILL RAILS FOR GLUE-UP

7. Because my lumberyard did not carry quarter-sawn white oak in the full thickness I needed, I have to glue two boards together for my bed rails. To achieve a good, flat glue surface, I flatten the adjoining faces on the jointer. Because of the severe cupping that occurred during the rough mill, I end up losing too much material in this process and my bed rails become 1/16" thinner than I had initially designed.

8. I plane the other surfaces parallel so that all my material has a consistent thickness.

LAMINATE RAILS

9. In preparation for glue-up, I lay out all the boards just how I want them to go together—matching grain direction and tone when possible. I draw the "cabinet maker's triangle" on the top edges. The cabinet maker's triangle is my favorite marking system to keep track of the orientation of and relationship between all the various parts of a project: top and bottom, left and right, and the direction of outward-facing surfaces. This simple marking trick helps ensure my boards go together in the intended order during the sweaty panic of a glue-up.

10. I always do a full dry-fit with clamps to make sure that I have everything I need and that my seams are coming together nicely.

11. I apply glue in a squiggle pattern and then roll it out with a rubber veneer roller for full and even coverage. I use plywood-clamping cauls that are the same length and width as my boards. The cauls both protect the oak from being marred by the clamps and help distribute the clamping pressure. I finish one side of the cauls with paste wax to keep them from sticking to the oak in the glue-ups. I mark these sides with "IN." Again, simple, bold notes help guide me against human error during the stress of glue-ups.

12. Using plenty of clamps, I work from one end of the glue seam to the other, tightening as I go. Vertical clamps help align the edges of the boards, which want to slide around once the slippery glue goes on. I stagger the clamps along the bottom and top to get even pressure across the height of the boards. As I tighten, I'm looking for a nice, even bead of glue squeeze-out along the seam.

MILL POSTS AND RAILS TO FINAL THICKNESS

13. After the glue dries and I remove it with a card scraper, I can mill my posts and laminated rails to final thickness—first re-flattening on the jointer, then running the other surface through the planer. Because my posts and rails are the same thickness, it saves time to mill them all at the same time. I also mill my extra parts and test pieces at this point.

14. With a pencil, I draw hatch marks along the surfaces to show me which areas of the board have been flattened or planed. Once all the marks are gone, I know my surfaces are perfectly flat and parallel.

15. To mill to final width, I first edge-joint on the jointer to achieve one flat edge that is 90 degrees to my milled surfaces. Then, I rip the other edge parallel and to final width on the table saw. I clean up any roughness or burn marks left by the rip blade with a very shallow pass on the jointer.

16. I cut the ends square on the Kapex (chop saw), removing any checking or snipe, but otherwise leaving all my parts long for now. That way if something goes wrong with the joinery on one end, I can lop it off and try again.

LAY OUT JOINERY ON FRONT AND BACK RAILS

17. I set my marking gauge to the thickness of the rail plus an extra ¹⁄₃₂" and scribe a line all the way around one end. The ¹⁄₃₂" extra ensures that the end grain of the joint protrudes slightly from the face grain of the joining member. It is much easier to trim the end grain flush than the other way around if things don't line up perfectly.

18. I set my combo square to half the width of the rail and scribe a horizontal center line across to my marking gauge line. I then scribe a vertical mark at the center point of this new line, halfway between the rail end and the marking gauge line.

MAKE JOINERY JIG: FRONT AND BACK RAILS

19. With my protractor set to 12 degrees—the most common angle for dovetail joints—I position it so that it hits the center point where my two lines intersect. This sets the angle and precise position of my joint.

20. Jig design could be a chapter unto itself, and like most things we do in the shop, there are multiple ways to skin a cat. I designed this first jig—for the front and back rails—based on jigs I've made for cutting tapered legs or bigger wedges. On the chop saw I cut a 12-degree angle on a scrap of plywood to create an angled fence. I then screw it down to a square piece of ply, being careful to keep the 90-degree edges flush. A toggle clamp helps to hold the rail down and tight to the fence, and the stop block at the top ensures that every rail will hit the blade at the exact same point once I set the band saw fence.

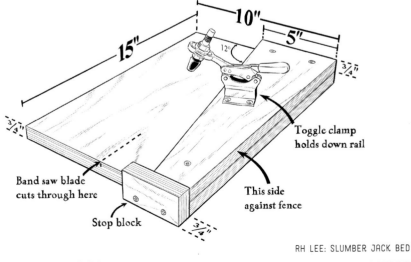

10"

15"

5"

12°

¾"

Toggle clamp holds down rail

Band saw blade cuts through here

This side against fence

¾"

Stop block

¾"

CUT JOINERY:
FRONT AND BACK RAILS

21. I set the band saw fence so that I am cutting on the correct side of my angled line (I always draw a big × on the offcut side). With one hand guiding the jig along the band saw fence and one hand supporting the rail, I cut carefully up to my marking gauge line.

22. On the Kapex, I set the depth stop so I'm cutting down to just shy of my angled kerf, to account for the square ⅛" at the bottom of the Kapex kerf. Then I pare away the tiny angled remainder with a chisel. This creates accurate 90-degree shoulders on my front and back rails. Satisfied with the joints I've cut, I can now safely cut the front and back rails to final length and complete the same joinery on the other ends.

LAY OUT JOINERY ON SIDE RAILS

23. At this point, I must determine the orientation of all the rails—front, back, right side, and left side—so that I can lay out each *particular* joint. Rather than returning to the squares and protractors, I use *relative* measurement to lay out the corresponding joints on the side rails. This way, if any of my cuts missed their mark slightly, I still have a nice tight joint. **NICK: Not a euphemism.** I align the shoulder of the front rail with the inside edge of the corresponding side rail and transfer the 12-degree edge with a marking knife.

MAKE JOINERY JIG: SIDE RAILS

24. This jig is a bit more complicated, as the side rails involve compound angles. I set the table saw blade to 12 degrees and rip a long, wide strip of maple. I screw this strip down to a square piece of plywood and add a solid wood fence that is tall and wide enough to keep the toggle clamps from interfering with the band saw fence. The toggle clamps hold the rail securely against the angled strip and the fence.

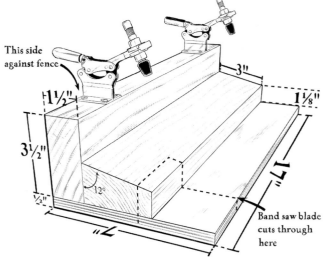

This side against fence

3½"

1½"

½"

12°

3"

1⅛"

17"

Band saw blade cuts through here

CUT JOINERY: SIDE RAILS

25. I set the band saw fence so that my jig rides against it and the saw blade cuts on the offcut, or waste side, of my marking knife line. Guiding the jig along the fence with one hand and driving with the other, I cut just to the marking gauge line drawn at the thickness of the rail +1/32".

FIT JOINERY

27. Luckily, any slop that occurred in that last step is easily fixed by my hand tools. I pare the corners, cleaning up any crumbs or high spots where the two cuts meet. This is an easy first step that eliminates one of the most common obstructions to a well-seated joint.

26. Now things get a little messy. I turn my jig 90 degrees and rest it against the saw's miter gauge to make the next cut. With my short test pieces, this jig worked perfectly to crosscut to my angled kerf. However, now that I have the weight of an ungainly long rail fighting me, I find that I need clamps to hold the jig against my miter gauge, and one Josh to support the flailing far end of the rail. If I was to do this again, I would build a more substantial base to this jig—more of a band saw bed extender—to better support the length of the rail.

28. I clamp the corresponding joints together and mark any high spots that are creating gaps along the seam.

29. I give myself some hatch marks with a pencil along the surface to be removed so I can track my progress and carefully pare away at the high spots with a shoulder plane, being sure to check my fit often and adjust my markings accordingly.

LAY OUT MORTISES

30. Now that my dovetails are fit, it's time to lay out the mortises that will connect vertically through both halves of the joint. This is where the tenon of my leg post will come through, holding the joint together. I offset the mortise toward the inside corner of the joint so that there is enough meat remaining on the ends of the rails, where the weaker short grain will be under stress. I use a marking gauge set to 1⅛" and scribe the location of the two far corners of my mortise.

CUT MORTISES IN RAILS

31. At these lengths, clamping the joint together on the bench mortiser requires some ingenuity. I use big engineer squares to check that the rails come together at a square corner, and a level to check that they are both level. This ensures that when the tenon gets driven in, the rail joints will seat nicely and my bed corners will be square. I use adjustable roller stands to support the long ends hanging off the mortiser. I line up my guides so that the corner of my ¾" hollow chisel hits right at the intersection of my marks. I plunge all the way through the joint, which guarantees that my joint will come back together just as I have it clamped. This same process could be achieved on a drill press with a ¾" Forstner bit, followed by a chisel to square up the mortise corners. **NICK: If your drill press or mortiser lacks the stroke length to drill all the way through this thickness, just go a little ways into the lower piece to mark your location, then remove the top piece and finish the job.**

TRANSFER TO POST

32. Using an angled waste block, I now clamp the leg post into position flush to the outer corner of the rail joints. The margin of human error on mortise placement makes each joint unique, so at this point I mark each post (*front left, front right*, etc.) and again use *relative* measurement to lay out the tenon.

33. I use a Japanese corner chisel to carefully transfer the placement of the mortise corners onto the top of the corresponding post.

CUT TENON ON POST

34. On the table saw, I set the blade height to my mark and cut my first shoulder. I like to cut my shoulders just a hair deeper than the tenon cheek—this reduces the need for cleaning up the corners later and doesn't compromise the strength of the tenon.

RH LEE: SLUMBER JACK BED

35. Because the tenon is off-center, I'm in the unusual position of having to cut each shoulder separately at a different depth. However, the tenon placement is close enough to the same location on all the posts that I can cut the same shoulder on all four posts with each adjustment of the blade height. I cut the shoulders with a crosscut sled and a stop. I add a piece of painter's tape to the stop when cutting the two opposing short shoulders. This gives me a slightly higher shoulder that I can then easily pare down to the others in case my consecutive cuts get slightly out of square in the rotation of the post. As I mentioned in the dovetail section, I like to leave a little extra length in my joinery to trim down after fitting.

36. I'm most concerned with establishing a square shoulder all the way around the post so any slight inconsistencies in shoulder depth/tenon alignment can be fixed later with hand tools.

37. I cut the cheeks on the band saw with a stop so I don't cut into the shoulder. I adjust the fence for each cut, lining up the blade with the outside of the chisel lines on the end grain.

38. I save the offcuts and tape them back in place to support the bottom of the cut as I rotate the post around, cutting all four cheeks.

39. I hear Nick's voice in my head saying, "Not bad, kid."

40. Each tenon requires a little bit of cleanup with my block plane, small shoulder plane, and paring chisel until I achieve a smooth friction-fit in the mortise.

CLAMP UP JOINTS AND DRILL HOLE FOR PEG

41. Because this is a "knock-down joint"—no glue or permanent fasteners—I will use a removable wooden peg to lock the joint together. While the dovetail angle limits any side-to-side movement in the joint, it is the peg (aided by gravity and friction) that will hold the rails down onto the post. I use the versatile Kreg jig—designed for drilling pocket screws—to drill a ⅜"-diameter hole at the acute angle necessary to hit the tenon on center. **NICK: That is indeed a very cute angle.**

42. I glue ⅜" oak dowels into a block of walnut—giving me a handle for easy tool-free peg removal. I carve the walnut block into a friendly shape for pulling and chamfer the leading end of the dowel rod.

43. With the peg fully seated, my corner joint is locked and complete!

TRIM JOINTS FLUSH

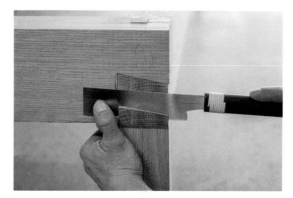

44. Now it is safe to trim and flush up the ends of my corner joints. I use a Japanese pull saw to trim the bulk of the excess, then follow with a block plane to get rid of any rough saw marks.

CENTER RAIL JOINERY

45. With the outer frame of the bed all assembled, I can now determine the final length of my center stretcher. I lay out the front dovetail first with a bevel gauge set to 12 degrees.

46. I cut the shoulders of the dovetail on the Kapex with a depth stop. Again, I cut these slightly shallow and then clean them up with a paring chisel.

47. I can use the same band saw jig I used on the front rails to cut the cheeks of the dovetail on my center rail.

49. Once my joint is cut, I lay it out on the center of the front rail with a marking knife.

48. It's a haunched dovetail, so I rip off the bottom using the band saw fence for parallel. I crosscut the lower dovetail waste with the Kapex, using a depth stop like the other cuts.

50. On the drill press, I hog out the majority of the mortise first with a Forstner bit and then with a smaller brad point bit in the corners.

51. I clean up the edges and corners of my mortise with a set of sharp chisels.

52. Because the center rail will need to be removed without too much stress to the joint, I carefully pare down the tenon to reduce friction. Since this is a knock-down joint, a little bit of slop is okay, as it is the taper of the dovetail that keeps the center rail locked into place.

SLATS

53. I make a simple plywood jig for routing out pockets for the slats at the right spacing. Because I'm using a bushing guide, the jig must accommodate a ⅛" offset all around.

1/8" offset for bushings

54. I clamp the side rails and the center rail together, making sure that the shoulders line up and that the orientation front-to-back is the same on all three. Routing all three members at once ensures that the slats will line up perfectly across the width of the bed.

55. Nick's spring-loaded corner chisel makes it a snap to square off the rounded corners left by the router bit. I can't believe it took me seven years in this shop to discover this genius tool!

56. Ready to test the fit.

57. The poplar slats seat perfectly. I have a bed.

HEADBOARD SLAB

58. No bed is complete without a slab headboard. This claro walnut slab came from Northwest Timber already flattened and dimensionally sanded, so they have made my work easy.

59. I remove the bark from the live edge with a drawknife and then smooth it out with a flexible hand-sanding pad. All that's left to do is finish-sand the surface.

HEADBOARD FRAME

60. I pocket out the vertical frame members so that the weight of the headboard is supported by a ¾" shoulder. This helps take some of the stress off the fasteners. I also create a slight pocket at the bottom of the frame members, creating a shoulder upon which the headboard frame rests as the lower length is fastened against the back rail. Similarly, these shoulders take some of the weight and stress off the screws connecting the headboard frame to the back rail. A center rail supports the length of the slab between the two verticals.

61. The headboard frame comes together easily with dominos.

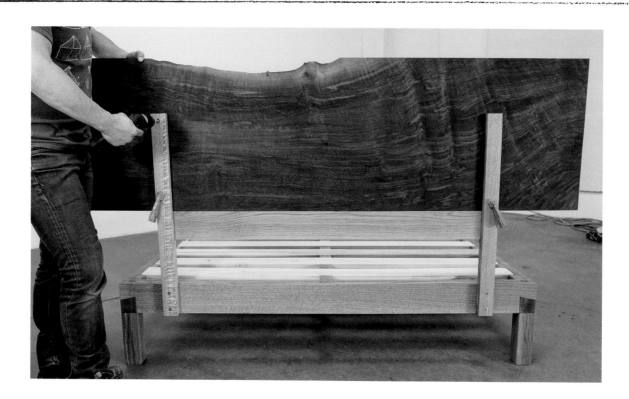

62. When the headboard frame is all glued up, I clamp it to the slab and the back rail and pre-drill the screw holes. I drill a larger clearance hole through the tops of the frame, thus allowing the top screws to "float" in the oversize holes. If the slab expands and contracts with humidity changes, the floating screws will not restrict or bind that movement.

SANDING

63. I sand all surfaces with an orbital sander, moving progressively up through the grits to 220. With a sanding block, I chamfer all the joint edges to protect them from breaking or tearing during assembly and breakdown. This also creates a consistent shadow line, which will mask any unsightly gaps in the fit.

FINISHING

64. Because I plan to spend at least one third of my remaining respiratory years in this bed, I choose to use a natural vegetable oil–based finish with no VOCs, made by a Danish company called WOCA. Like any oil, it's easy to apply—I brush it on and wipe it off with a clean rag.

FINAL ASSEMBLY

65. The bed frame breaks down into nine flat parts, plus twelve slats and four pegs. One person can assemble the frame without any tools. The headboard frame attaches with screws and it is helpful to have two clamps and extra hands to support the slab in place during attachment.

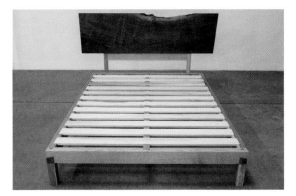

ESSAY

ON WOOD

By James Richardson

At dawn when rowboats drum on the dock

and every door in the breathing house bumps softly

as if someone were leaving quietly, I wonder

if something in us is made of wood,

maybe not quite the heart, knocking softly,

or maybe not made of it, but made for its call.

Of all the elements, it is happiest in our houses.

It will sit with us, eat with us, lie down

and hold our books (themselves a rustling woods),

bearing our floors and roofs without weariness,

for unlike us it does not resent its faithfulness

or question *why, for what, how long?*

Its branchings have slowed the invisible feelings of light

into vortices smooth for our hands,

so that every fine-grained handle and page and beam

is a wood-word, a standing wave:

years that never pass, vastness never empty,

speed so great it cannot be told from peace.

ACKNOWLEDGMENTS

First and foremost, I must offer gratitude on all our parts here at Offerman Woodshop to wives, husbands, and partners, who took care of so many of the other chores so that we could stay in the shop for the application of "one more coat." These include my own intelligent, luscious bride, Megan; my mom, Cathy Offerman; Corrin Buchanan; Kristen Kang; Lise Offerman; Jordan Reddout Wilhoit; Ronald "the Walnut" Aveling; Jayreisha Rasberry; and Maya Ferrara.

Good Clean Fun contains "shop visits," or profiles, of eight different woodworkers and/or entities who all gave to me generously of their time and creativity. For this largesse I would like to sincerely thank:

Garry Knox Bennett and Sylvia

Mira Nakashima/Nakashima Woodworker
Studio

Joan Barrett and Ted Moores/Bear
Mountain Boats

Laura Mays/College of the Redwoods Fine
Furniture

Peter Galbert/North Bennet Street School

Christian Becksvoort

Jimmy DiResta

Laura Zahn/Off the Saw/Allied Woodshop

My book agents, Monika Verma and Daniel Greenberg, take exceptionally good care of me, and I continue to be pleasantly surprised at their ability to stomach my company for the duration of entire meals.

If you are still reading this, it's only because for the third journey now, my editor, Jill Something, has safely piloted me through even more vast and rough, uncharted waters. Not only do I find her support unflagging and her navigation without flaw, but she is extremely chipper about the whole mishegoss to boot. Downright ebullient.

Her assistant, Adam O'Brien, turned in a generous display of knot-tying and even took a few turns in the crow's nest. Without his keen eye, we would surely have foundered upon the shoals before we even began to tell you about pith.

Maddy Newquist and Marya Pasciuto kept us all dry in their turns around the capstan, pumping like madwomen all the way to Halifax.

I am also very grateful to Jamie Knapp and Emily Brock for their gentle treatment of me in the art of semaphore—signaling by flag.

Our vessel has been magically blessed under the influential pull of sirens LeeAnn Pemberton, Susan Schwartz, and Dora Mak, who treat my crew, my sails, and my words with patience and acuity.

This, my first official picture book, could not have been realized without the top-drawer design work of Shubhani Sarkar and the ladies manning her respective oars, Amy Hill and Cassie Garruzzo.

Jane Parrott and Josh Salsbury were our in-house photography team, and Jane also corralled all the photos for our later retrieval, a successfully realized chore of organization that I still find astonishing.

I would also like to acknowledge the work of Ian Phillips and Christine Fuqua for their additional design work and photography. They will both receive beer.

Stephen Gass of SawStop and his marketing VP Matt Howard both took the time to fill me in on their side of the story, for which I am deeply grateful.

Emily Shur exhibited such a neighborly attitude when she came to shoot the book's cover that she and I had to come to blows to see her properly paid. I did not win the tussle, as she has a tenacious left jab, but I did see her recompensed.

For years of guidance and free access to the encyclopedic knowledge of woodworking housed in his charismatic melon, for his particular and invaluable consultation on the pages you now hold, and despite his love for the game of soccer, I thank Asa Christiana.

For favors of all sorts that added to the richness herein, such as it is, I thank Ed Pirnik, Miguel Gómez-Ibáñez, Paul LeBourgeois, Will Bogdan, Mike Pekovich, Festool, Trevor Groth, Bill Holderman, Lie-Nielsen Toolworks, Laura McCusker and Peter Howard, Justin Goldwater, Rhonda Hefton, Soomi Amagasu, David Welter, Ejler Hjorth-Westh, John Lutz, Jonathan Yarnall, Bohnhoff Lumber, Harold Seward, Scot Wineland, Cam Bender, Corey Rodell, David Waelder, and Taylor Forrest.

If you have enjoyed your time with us but don't see yourself firing up a table saw, you can always find our goods and services at www.OffermanWoodshop.com.